Visualizing the City

This book presents a range of interdisciplinary explorations into the urban environment through film, photography, digital imagery, pictorial art and signage. Collating a panorama of urban contexts, *Visualizing the City*'s diverse essays investigate visual representations of urbanism and modernity reflected through the prism of global cultures using a cogent array of methods and texts.

Visualizing the City brings together a compelling trove of visual imagery which represents and engages with twentieth-century architecture, in order to foster new ways of seeing, revealing and revisiting the urban. These essays unpick interwoven city fabrics, whether in Beirut or Paris, Berlin or Rio de Janeiro, London or New York, in an effort to discover how they equate with one another in their intertextual configurations.

This collection is grouped into four clusters that build upon one another, the first providing a foundation for *Reflecting*, exploring visualizations of the urban past. *Remembering and Reinventing* focuses on the way perceptions of cities are affected by the legacy of their past, while *Reframing and Reshaping* considers representations of the contemporary city. The final section, *Revisualizing*, exposes the city remixed, posing questions for a redefinition of the city in the twenty-first century.

Visualizing the City will be of strong interest to scholars and students in the different areas that contribute to the visualization of the urban environment – from architectural and art history to urban studies, film and visual culture.

Alan Marcus is a Reader in Film and Visual Culture and Head of the Film Programme at the University of Aberdeen. He is a cultural historian and filmmaker and as former Director of the Centre for Screen Studies at the University of Manchester he chaired the international conference 'Visualizing the City' in 2005.

Dietrich Neumann is Professor for the History of Modern Architecture and Urban Studies at Brown University in Providence, Rhode Island, and the Vincent Scully Visiting Professor for the History of Architecture at Yale University.

THE ARCHITEXT SERIES
Edited by Thomas A. Markus and Anthony D. King

Architectural discourse has traditionally represented buildings as art objects or technical objects. Yet buildings are also social objects in that they are invested with social meaning and shape social relations. Recognising these assumptions, the Archi*text* series aims to bring together recent debates in social and cultural theory and the study and practice of architecture and urban design. Critical, comparative and interdisciplinary, the books in the series, by theorising architecture, bring the space of the built environment centrally into the social sciences and humanities, as well as bringing the theoretical insights of the latter into the discourses of architecture and urban design. Particular attention is paid to issues of gender, race, sexuality and the body, to questions of identity and place, to the cultural politics of representation and language, and to the global and postcolonial contexts in which these are addressed.

**Edited by Alan Marcus and
Dietrich Neumann**

Visualizing
the City

Routledge
Taylor & Francis Group

LONDON AND NEW YORK

First published 2007
by Routledge
2 Park Square, Milton Park, Abingdon, OX14 4RN

Simultaneously published in the USA and Canada
by Routledge
270 Madison Avenue, New York, NY 10016

Routledge is an imprint of the Taylor & Francis Group, an informa business

Typeset in Frutiger by
Florence Production Ltd, Stoodleigh, Devon
Printed and bound in Great Britain by
The Cromwell Press, Trowbridge, Wiltshire

British Library Cataloguing in Publication Data
A catalogue record for this book is available from the British Library

Library of Congress Cataloging in Publication Data
Visualizing the city / edited by Alan Marcus & Dietrich Neumann.
       p. cm. – (The architext series)
     Includes bibliographical references and index.
   1. Cities and towns – Case studies.   2. Urban violence – Case
studies.   3. Sociology, Urban – Case studies.   I. Marcus, Alan
R.   II. Neumann, Dietrich.
   HT119.V57 2008
   307.76—dc22   2007028444

ISBN10: 0–415–41970–0 (hbk)
ISBN10: 0–415–41971–9 (pbk)

ISBN13: 978–0–415–41970–3 (hbk)
ISBN13: 978–0–415–41971–0 (pbk)

Contents

Illustration Credits

The authors and publishers would like to thank the following individuals and institutions for giving permission to reproduced illustrations. We have made every effort to contact copyright holders, but if any errors have been made we would be happy to correct them at a later printing.

Some of the images have a patina of age, but the publisher has reproduced them to the best quality possible.

2.1, 2.3	Biblioteca Nacional/Acervo da Fundaçaõ Biblioteca Nacional, Brasil
2.2, 2.4	Acervo Arquivo da Cidade do Rio de Janeiro, Brasil
2.5	British Library (Maps 27.b.32)
3.1, 3.3–3.5	Sabine Hake
3.2	Agentur für Bilder zur Zeitgeschichte, Berlin
3.6	Nicolaische Verlagsbuchhandlung
3.7, 3.8	Gebr. Mann Verlag
4.3	Dachau Concentration Camp Memorial Site
4.4, 4.6, 4.7	Alan Marcus
4.5	www.dachau.info
6.1	Julian LaVerdiere
6.3	Private collection
7.1, 7.3	British Film Institute
7.2	Rosemary Laing and Tolarno Galleries, Melbourne
9.1	Guildhall Library (Collage No. 28028)
9.2, 9.3, 9.5, 9.6	Cityscape
9.4	GLA/MillerHare/Ordnance Survey
10.1–10.4	Scott Burnham
10.5	Darius Jones
10.6	Ed Zipco
11.1–11.8	David Michalski
12.3	J. Stoner

Contributors

Co-editor, **Alan Marcus** is Reader in Film and Visual Culture at the University of Aberdeen, Scotland. Following studies in industrial design and film theory at the University of Illinois, he received a Ph.D. in cultural history from Cambridge University. His publications include books on indigenous peoples' interactions with the physical and built environment, *Out in the Cold* (1992) and *Relocating Eden* (1995), articles on film and visual culture, and guest edited journals on the theme of visualizing the city in *History of Photography*, *The Journal of Architecture*, and *Film Studies*. His experimental documentary, *Beautiful Dachau*, was released in 2006. He chaired the international conference, 'Visualizing the City', at the University of Manchester (2005).

Co-editor, **Dietrich Neumann** is Professor of the History of Modern Architecture at Brown University in Providence, Rhode Island and Vincent Scully Visiting Professor at Yale University. He was trained as an architect in Munich and London (AA) and received his Ph.D. from the Technical University in Munich. He has published frequently on American and European architecture of the nineteenth and twentieth centuries, as well as the history of film set design. Among his publications are *Film Architecture: Set Design from Metropolis to Blade Runner* (1997), Richard Neutra's *Windshield House* (2002), *Architecture of the Night* (2002) and *Luminous Buildings* (2006).

Giuliana Bruno is Professor of Visual and Environmental Studies at Harvard University. Her seminal book *Atlas of Emotion: Journeys in Art, Architecture and Film* (Verso, 2002) won the Kraszna-Krausz Book Award, a prize awarded to 'the world's best book on the moving images'. Her previous book, *Streetwalking on a Ruined Map* (Princeton University Press, 1993), was the winner of the Katherine Singer Kovács prize for best book in film studies and of Italy's national book award for moving-image studies. Her most recent book, *Public Intimacy: Architecture and the Visual Arts*, was published by MIT Press in 2007.

Scott Burnham is an independent creative director and researcher, writer and lecturer specializing in cultural innovation and developments in urbanity, design and visual culture that occur at the edges of contemporary creativity. He is Creative Director of the 2009 Biennale de Montréal and creator and curator of the Urban Play guerrilla design project with Droog Design, Amsterdam. Formerly Creative Director of the Urbis Centre for Urban Culture in Manchester UK, in 2005 he was ranked as one of the UK's 100 most influential people for his work in cultural innovation. His work, writings, lectures and media commentary have appeared throughout Europe, North America and China.

Maite Conde is Assistant Professor of Spanish and Portuguese at Columbia University, where she teaches courses related to Latin American culture. She has published articles on Brazilian cinema and literature and is currently completing a study of the intersection between literature and visual culture in turn-of-the-century Rio de Janeiro.

Stephanie Hemelryk Donald is Professor of International Studies and Director of the Institute for International Studies at UTS, Sydney. Her books include *Tourism and the Branded City: Film and Identity on the Pacific Rim* (2007), *The State of China Atlas* (University of California Press, new edition 2005), *Little Friends: Children's Film and Media Culture in the PRC* (2005); *Picturing Power in the People's Republic of China* (1999) and *Public Secrets, Public Spaces: Cinema and Civility in China* (1999).

Sabine Hake is the Texas Chair of German Literature and Culture in the Department of Germanic Studies at the University of Texas at Austin. She has published several monographs on Weimar culture and German film including, most recently, the expanded and revised edition of *German National Cinema* (Routledge, 2007) and *Popular Cinema of the Third Reich* (UT Press, 2001). Her new book *Topographies of Class: Modern Architecture and Mass Society in Weimar Berlin* will be published in 2008 by University of Michigan Press.

Lina Khatib is a Lecturer in the Department of Media Arts at Royal Holloway, University of London, where she teaches media theory, international cinema and television. Her research interests include the link between politics and media representations of the Middle East. She is the author of *Filming the Modern Middle East: Politics in the Cinemas of Hollywood and the Arab World* (I.B. Tauris, 2006) and is a founding co-editor of the *Middle East Journal of Culture and Communication*.

David Michalski is in the Cultural Studies programme at the University of California, Davis, where he is also the Social and Behavioral Sciences Librarian. He studies and writes on urban culture and information environments. He is the editor of the online publication *Xcp: Streetnotes*, and the author of *Cosmos and Damian: A World Trade Center Collage* (Bootstrap Press, 2005).

François Penz is Reader in Architecture and the Moving Image at the Department of Architecture, University of Cambridge. He co-founded Cambridge University Moving Image Studio (CUMIS) in 1998, and more recently the Digital Studio (incorporating CUMIS research), where he runs the Ph.D. programme. François is a fellow of Darwin College and teaches on the M.Phil. in Screen Media and Cultures. His research focuses on the narrative organization of space and the expressive use of digital media for design and communication in architectural and city-related issues. He has published widely on the history of the relationship between cinema and architecture, and how it informs current debate and practice in the use of digital media.

Jill Stoner is an Associate Professor in the Department of Architecture at the University of California at Berkeley. She was winner of the international visionary competition 'San Francisco Embarcadero Freeway' (1993) and the US competition 'Dead Malls' (2003). She received a Graham Foundation grant to study the architectural implications of the literature of solitary confinement, which resulted in a solo exhibition, *Rubashov's House*, at the Berkeley Art Museum. She is author (essays) and editor (poems) of the book *Poems for Architects* (William Stout, 2001), and is currently working on a new book, titled *Fictional Space*.

Robert Tavernor studied architecture in London, Rome and Cambridge. He is currently Professor of Urban Design and Director of the Cities Programme at the London School of Economics (LSE). He was the Forbes Professor of Architecture at the University of Edinburgh (1992–95), and Professor and Head of Architecture at the University of Bath (1995–2005). He has been Visiting Professor at UCLA (1998), Texas A&M University (2002) and São Paulo University, Brazil (2004).

Acknowledgements

It can be difficult to trace the origins of the gestation of a book, but in this case I have to thank an undergraduate student, whose final year dissertation I supervised on the theme of cinematic representations of the urban. At that time relatively few publications were available in what was clearly an exciting and growing area of scholarship. His questions sparked my interest, and some years later an international conference, 'Visualizing the City', came to fruition in June 2005 at the University of Manchester. The overwhelming interest of the 180 speakers and delegates underscored an interdisciplinary interest in further exploring a field that was now growing in leaps and bounds, as exemplified by the many fine texts on film and the urban which had emerged by then. The University of Manchester was generous in its support, as was the palpable enthusiasm of our participants. It is to them that this book is dedicated.

A number of people have been most helpful in bringing this book to fruition, including Caroline Mallinder and Georgina Johnson at Routledge, and our series editors, Anthony King and Tom Markus, who approached us with the suggestion of writing the book, and provided astute criticism on individual chapters and structure. Alan Marcus would particularly like to thank Penny Woolcock for her support and good humour throughout this project.

Introduction: Visualizing the City

Alan Marcus and Dietrich Neumann

We are all unreliable witnesses, caught forever in space and time, our perceptions prescribed, our flight frozen, wings as set as those of an insect in amber in an Egyptian sarcophagus. *Visualizing the City* navigates a number of historical, theoretical and imaginative encounters with urban space as written about at the beginning of the twenty-first century.[1] The essays in this volume reflect interwoven themes on the city, shared preoccupations about the politics of visual representation – as strong an interest in what is absent from the frame as in what it reveals, in the city as a living text, an imaginative construct, a name which glitters seductively on the departure board of an airport lounge, conjuring up images, desires and experiences, advertising its charms in travel brochures. But the city is also a place where most of us live, with streets we travel through and buildings in which we eat, play, work, rest and reproduce. Is the city a character in our narratives or are we characters in the story of the city?

Beyond a common interest in narrative, an unsettled quality can be detected across these essays. The city is more of a process than a product and a process with multiple identities at that, providing no respite, no fixed place of reference, nervously defending iconic landmarks and familiar skylines to remind us of where we live and who we might be. Walls are built to barricade in the rich and keep out impoverished migrants, but however high and robust the barriers are, they prove porous, permeable; the poor, as well as our anxieties about them, are always with us.

The opening chapter, which establishes an historical underpinning for the study, and the final chapter, which gazes into the near future, cogently frame the book. The middle ten essays are situated in the twentieth and twenty-first centuries. Despite their diversity, one can discern an undercurrent of fear seeping out from that most bloody time. In the last hundred years, humankind has achieved previously unimagined heights of destruction, with the development of new weapons, both more sophisticated and more barbaric than anything seen before, capable of wiping out vast numbers of people and reducing cities to rubble. Hatred has found new languages with which to speak out and these languages have left deep scars on the texture of cities. Across the world there follows a Sisyphian struggle to erase the signs of yesterday's violence – whether it be the legacy of slavery in Rio (Chapter 2, Conde), the death camps of Dachau (Chapter 4, Marcus) or the civil war in Beirut (Chapter 6, Khatib), denial of guilt appears as the one constant in an ongoing project to obliterate uncomfortable memory. In the case of the planes crashing into the Twin Towers (Chapter 5, Neumann) one could argue that the wound is left open to justify other projects. That event offered a spectacle of violence and invited a spectacular response.

While war has accounted for much of the smashing of the old and building of the new, this was also a century with periods of calm and prosperity – at least for those in the developed world – and modernity made firm strides, slums were swept away, tower blocks came and went, replaced by a magpie postmodernist aesthetic which bent back on itself in ever more convoluted and inventive ways. In these essays, we make journeys through the backstreets of specific cities, through time and space, but there are few linear narratives here. The story is slipping out of our control. Few things are as they seem.

For well over a century, cinema has been portraying the city in all shapes and forms, providing us with screen renditions of 'real cities' (shot on location), 'reconstructed cities' (shot in the studio) and now, of course, virtual cities. Undeniably, films have contributed to the image, legibility and branding of our cities. In a world that is increasingly media and screen orientated, it is crucial for architects, designers, planners and policy makers to understand the mechanisms by which one can read and portray a city on screen. These controlled narratives with their three-act structures, primarily male authored and metropolitan, have shaped the way we see ourselves in relation to the spaces we inhabit. Carefully written, directed and edited pieces, intended for a global ticket-buying audience, are now acquiring a somewhat Jurassic quality, as we enter a digital age where almost everyone is a film director and archivist, and we are all actors featured in multiple narratives, watched 24/7 by shopkeepers, security men, police and night watchmen.

As we have become more fearful, public space has come under intense scrutiny. Every journey we take, every move we make, the money we withdraw and how and where we spend it, are watched and recorded in blurred black and white moving images. The resolution can only get better. Private space does not escape this ongoing inspection, as we frantically document our experience of being in the world with digital cameras, taking snapshots, making our own little movies and flying them into cyberspace as attachments, or posting them on web sites for others to see too. It is as if an experience and the representation of it have become almost indistinguishable. These undigested, unedited narratives fuel a queasy sense of ourselves as liminal creatures with no boundaries, while conversely promoting privatized anxieties about increased isolation and personal insignificance in the urban spaces we inhabit. Our well-reported journeys are replete with both meaning and feeling. What we need are translators and interpreters to help us make sense of them.

The 12 essays in this volume are grouped into four clusters that build upon one another, blurring boundaries in the process and revealing many inter-connections as they interrogate different means of visualizing the city. The first section provides a foundation for *Reflecting on the City*, as three authors consider visualizations of the urban past (Bruno, Conde and Hake). The second cluster, *Remembering and Reinventing the City* (Marcus, Khatib and Neumann) focuses on the way perceptions of cities are affected by the legacy of their past and the way traumatic events are incorporated into their reinvention. In *Reframing and Reshaping the City*, three essays (Donald, Penz and Tavernor), explore visual repre-sentations of the contemporary city, experiencing its own growth-associated conflicts. The final cluster, *Revisualizing the City* (Burnham, Michalski and Stoner), investigates the city remixed, finding its hidden orifices and postmodern inter-ventions, posing questions for a redefinition of the city in the twenty-first century.

REFLECTING ON THE CITY

In the first chapter, Giuliana Bruno addresses the relationship of the moving image to urban mapping, the culture of travel and the mobilization of narrative space in the visual arts. She traverses a varied cinematic landscape, making forays into the fields of architecture, design, cultural geography, cartography and art. Insisting on the inseparability of seeing and travelling in modern culture, her essay offers a panorama of urban visualization, retracing the origin of mobilized space back to early modernity. Bruno reflects on painted landscapes, city views and carto-graphic representations as important precursors in the genealogy of film. She lingers in the eighteenth century's tactile and mobile modes of representation, claiming them as navigational routes, leading to pre-cinematic, haptic space. In a montage of words and pictures, Bruno offers a cultural journey that turns the *voyeur* into the *voyageur*, emphasizing not only that 'sight' and 'site' but also 'motion' and 'emotion' are irrevocably connected. Transporting us through the landscape of moving images, this outlook on topophilia opens up the world of emotion pictures.

Discussions concerning the homologous relationship between early cinema and urban space are the subject of Maite Conde's essay. It focuses on the ways in which the introduction and development of film in Brazil was part of a project of urban transformation at the start of the twentieth century in the country's then capital, Rio de Janeiro. Implemented by a newly installed Republican regime, the centre of Rio was radically reconstructed. Its colonial Portuguese structures were destroyed and replaced with a modern and universal topography, modelled on Baron Haussmanns Paris. She traces the segregation of contemporary Rio back to this time. Former slaves and impoverished migrants were chased out of the city centre and into the hills – where they still live in the notorious *favelas*, coming down to work as maids, dance in the carnival or to engage in criminality. Employing a range of cultural intertexts from films, music, photographs, newspapers and magazines, Conde explores the complex relationship between the reception and production of early film in Rio and the construction of this new urban topography and its emergent identities. This chapter suggests that cinema helped to document and chart new and alternative spatial practices in which Brazilian spectators negotiated their own local experiences within the contours of Rio's modern spaces.

Sabine Hake explores the photographic representation of an iconic early twentieth-century building, Berlin's Mossehaus of 1922, and charts its transformation into a symbol of Weimar modernism in architectural publications, photo-books and the illustrated press. The dynamic central section of this hybrid building was designed by Erich Mendelsohn. It gained drama and urgency from the immediate contrast with the existing sandstone façade of 1903. Mendelsohn's repair and addition was both a necessary response to the damage wrought by revolutionary forces in the war's aftermath, and a largely skin deep dressing up of an existing structure. The highly evocative new façade thus served as advertising (for the liberal orientation of the magazine as much as for the power of modern architecture), and its photographic image not only became a trademark for the newspaper's advertising division, but was frequently reproduced. It thematized mediations between the social and the spatial, and the politicized nature of corporate photography. Weimar photography, Hake points out, was deeply implicated in the ideologies of the modern and the urban – in particular when it presented projects associated with *Neues Bauen*. The new architecture was perceived as an expression of modern society, and modern, mass-produced images introduced new definitions of urban culture, alternative notions of social class and a visual vocabulary and perceptual matrix for the New Berlin.

REMEMBERING AND REINVENTING THE CITY

In 1933, 11 years after the opening of the new Mossehaus, the Nazis assumed power in Germany, immediately took control of the news industry and all artistic production, and tightly regulated the publication and distribution of images. The concentration camp in the town of Dachau, outside of Munich, was set up in the same year. In Chapter 4, using an observational film as an integral component of his analysis, Alan Marcus sets out to explore the fraught relationship between the beautiful, old city of Dachau and its infamous concentration camp. Close to a million visitors a year reach the camp by taking a short train ride from Munich and a five-minute bus ride from the station. Most are unaware that they are only a few minutes away from the centre of a well-preserved medieval town with 40,000 inhabitants. After years of studiously seeking to ignore the concentration camp and erase memories of the town's close involvement with its legacy, city fathers have woken up to the commercial appeal of attracting the legions of camp visitors to also visit the town. The city is re-branding itself as 'A Place of Learning and Remembrance', with the camp as just one of the sites worth visiting, along with the local palace, art galleries and museums. Marcus observes that many visitors seem to treat the trip now like any other tourist experience and, in spite of its inherited weight of history, the nature of their interaction with the site is transforming its meaning. This essay evaluates the visitors' engagement, as they stroll around the grounds, ending up at the former crematoria which ring with the sound of cameras clicking and whirring as visitors pose themselves and their children in front of the ovens. With local traffic thundering past its watchtowers, apartment buildings and a golf course redefining its space, the camp, now awkwardly embedded within the city, presents an icon of contested and reinvented urban space.

At the end of the Nazi dictatorship, German cities lay in ruins. A whole genre of so-called *Trümmerfilme* emerged after 1945 that exploited the devastated cityscape of Berlin as backdrop and metaphor in filmic narratives about the traumatized German psyche. One cannot help but think of such 'rubble films' when reading Lina Khatib's account of the representation of the city of Beirut in post-war Lebanese cinema. Beirut had been celebrated as the romantic, affluent playground of the Middle East in pre-war cinema before it became a byword for chaos and anarchy. The city was at the heart of the conflict in Lebanon, a place Khatib refers to as having 'multiple exclusions' during 20 years of a brutal Civil War that ravaged its historic centre. When the war finally ended, its residents reacted as trauma victims often do, by ignoring the violence and damage of the recent past. The ruins were cleared to make way for new buildings, a project of reconstruction, with few attempts at acknowledging the past by repairing and restoring its former glory. The old souks have become the stuff of myth, things one's grandmother remembers. In a curious reversal, after the conflict ended the reality of war has been denied in the quotidian reality of today's Beirutis, whereas in Lebanese cinema it is as if the war never ended. Memories of repressed pain and violence slip onto the screen in fictional form, the scarred body of the disfigured city symbolizing the inherent contradictions of 'being Lebanese' – a state and a space of both exile and return, marginalization and resistance.

The trauma of the experience of violent destruction in an urban environment and the desire to commemorate the dead are explored by Dietrich Neumann in his essay on the public debate over a light installation consisting of two strong beams. The *Tribute in Light* serves as a memorial to those who died in the attacks on the Twin Towers of New York's World Trade Center in 2001. Although the installation was popular, some onlookers complained about the environmental cost while others found it offensively reminiscent of Albert Speer's *Cathedral of Light*, designed for Nazi Party Rallies. Neumann asks whether it matters on what previous occasions these materials have been used and investigates what these might be. He illuminates the controversy by tracing the history of light memorials commemorating a range of events. He finds a complex tapestry of references, although he notes that they seldom stray too far from militarist connections. Light shows began in the World's Fairs of the late nineteenth century, rejoicing in the new electric power and the dramatic changes it was ushering in. But it soon found employment as searchlight beams in warfare, a use that continues to this day. Triumphalist displays to celebrate victory in battle range from the US navy rout of the Spanish fleet near the Philippines in 1899, to Speer's megalomaniac stagings, and the celebratory blue V above

Buckingham Palace in London 1946. Light mourned those who died after the sinking of the Titanic and now, once a year, stands in for solid chunks of concrete and iron obliterated on a fateful day in 2001.

REFRAMING AND RESHAPING THE CITY

The imagery of the attacks on the World Trade Center reminds us of the widespread destruction of an urban fabric which has been endemic in films such as *The Day after Tomorrow* (2004), *War of the Worlds* (2005) and many others. In Chapter 7, Stephanie Hemelryk Donald re-examines themes of disaster and race neuroses in American popular film. Donald suggests that the central assumption in these movies is that anything that happens in America signifies that it is happening 'everywhere'. The barbarians who used to come over and threaten us from other countries or outer space are now emerging and breaking out ever closer to home, but they are less and less like *us*. Donald critiques the city writer, Mike Davies, taking issue with his relentlessly apocalyptic visions of Los Angeles. She reflects that for him, too, Los Angeles has become a metonym for the entire world, the focus of all that is evil and the site for its biggest disasters. Whereas on the other side of the Pacific, the cinematic imaginaries and architectural trajectories of films set in Sydney and Shanghai, cities that share histories of colonial intervention and hybridity, also explore catastrophes of colonialism and genocide, but 'the streets remain clean and the buildings pretty much intact'.

Violence, race relations and economic inequality in the suburbs of Paris are at the centre of the essay by François Penz. He looks at iconic Parisian films from *A Bout de Souffle* (1960) to *La Haine* (1995) and examines the impact the *reel city* may have on our reframing the *real city*. Godard talked about shooting fiction in a documentary style in order to create a compelling portrait of the city, filming on location and using real people. This approach has become a staple of the French post-war cinematic tradition, even in such highly romanticized fables as *Le Fabuleux Destin d'Amélie Poulain* (2001). Penz notes that with *A Bout de Souffle* and *La Haine*, directors Godard and Kassovitz were interested in the notion of casting *the city as itself*, while also paying overt homage to American cinema. The films are shot in black and white with protagonists who are small-time criminals motivated by greed and boredom, and both have violent denouements. *A Bout de Souffle* takes place in central Paris, jump cutting the famous stroll around familiar landmarks. Although part of *La Haine* is played out there too, the main characters are clearly ill at ease in that section of the city. Feared and suspected by most of those they meet, the rest of the film takes place in their Paris, one unfamiliar to most of us, in the outlying suburban *banlieue*, Chanteloup-des-Vignes. In a reworking of *cinema vérité* methodology, cast and crew lived on the housing project for six weeks and cast all extras locally. Penz recounts that ten years later, when the dystopian vision of *La Haine* was fulfilled in the burning riots of autumn 2005, the director Kassovitz was treated as a spokesperson who might offer explanations for the destruction of the real Paris.

On the other end of the spectrum, the image of the city of London is increasingly composed and crafted by the staff of 'The London Plan', a municipal agency that uses film and multiple photography to control the impact of new buildings for a number of privileged views. Robert Tavernor considers the city's town planning initiatives in order to reveal the reshaped and constructed nature of the London skyline. He explains that planning decisions about the positions, heights and clustering of tall, new buildings are regulated by expert assessments according to their visual impact from fixed viewing positions. Ten principal 'strategic views' were established across London in 1991, intended to safeguard the settings and silhouettes of St Paul's Cathedral and the Palace of Westminster. In 2004, The London Plan refined these in a 'view protection framework'. Whenever a major building is now proposed, its visual impact on the cityscape is assessed through photographs taken from between 20 and 130 different viewing positions. These form the basis for an accurate montaged computer-generated model of the proposed development. Buildings are consequently assessed 'in the round' – as if they were sculptural objects in the urban landscape. London is a city that reflects its history, national identity, language and culture. While it needs to reinvent itself to be livable and progressive, it must also retain visual links with the past that are recognized internationally as being truly 'London'. To paraphrase Lampedusa, London must change in order to stay the same. In order to be packaged and sold, London must bear some resemblance to the city of novels, chocolate boxes and jigsaw puzzles – the London of the tourist imagination.

REVISUALIZING THE CITY

For a city's inhabitants to inhabit an urban space and feel in control of it, unusual measures might prove necessary. As urban environments become denser and their influence on our mental and physical selves grows greater, new relationships are emerging between the individual and the visual environment of the shared spaces and surfaces of the city. Urban dwellers are constantly bombarded by advertising suggesting we consume more, and by governmental hoardings and notices admonishing us to slow down, speed up, turn this way or that and generally stop doing what we want. Small groups of artists have decided that this one-way communication is deeply unsatisfying and have started altering and remixing symbolic signs in potent and innovative ways, inviting others to join in and reclaim their cities. In Chapter 10, Scott Burnham features recent witty street art and urban interventions in London, New York, Stockholm, Chicago and Amsterdam. He provides a multimedia street-level overview of the visual rewriting and remixing that is taking place in urban public spaces, and discusses the influence this has on our relationship with the city. This essay concentrates on skilful projects by erstwhile art school graduates such as Banksy – creative artists who have chosen to use the fabric of the city as their canvas in order to challenge the status quo, while enhancing the environment in inventive and often amusing ways. Corporations are now appropriating these interventions and copying techniques they see on the street to give their own sales campaigns street-cred. The art market follows suit by putting a high value on the best work, ironically transforming it back into the commodity it set out to reject. Meanwhile, less attractive forms of vandalism, which just as clearly spell out dissatisfaction with the establishment, remain a different kind of visual challenge, one that is far less open to co-option.

There is a hidden, but powerful visual language in the contemporary city, one that operates just beyond the phantasmagoria of consumption. Through photographs we look behind the scenes to focus on the visual signs of mundane infrastructure and workspaces, which also constitute consumer society. By applying a critical aesthetic to technical and administrative markers, such as those framing employee entrances and emergency exits, David Michalski argues in his essay that municipal and corporate networks have constructed a public visual language that is effectively used to distinguish between different social spaces. He examines how this aesthetic system informs the performance of work and leisure, private and public life, ideas about safety and authority, and current conceptions of geography. Michalski reveals how this visual language is crucial to the propagation of the consumer spectacle which obscures it, and why the spaces where this system is deployed most robustly often become heightened contested sites. Standardized signs work globally in shopping malls as transformative mechanisms for changing identities, shifting individuals from consumers to employees and back again. Exit beacons glow ubiquitously, signalling to all of us a constant state of emergency at a time of heightened fear of terrorism – transforming shopping itself into a 'dangerous and even heroic activity'.

'Fantasy is a place where it rains', observed Italo Calvino. In the final chapter, Jill Stoner presents some of her own architectural fantasies conceived over the past dozen years in a revisualization of the city. These imagine both additions and subtractions to the urban landscape that bear little resemblance to almost all of what now passes for both architecture and urban design. She proposes to deconstruct buildings with the force of nature and makes an odyssey upstream against the currents of technology, progress, capitalism, professionalism, and most aggressively new urbanism. Stoner takes us on an abbreviated tour of Detroit, Houston and São Paulo, glancing at J. G. Ballard and Ray Bradbury, Diana O'Hehir and Wendell Berry along the way. She imagines their urbanism compromised and enriched by birds, farms, wilderness and wetlands. We learn that the recovery of the peregrine falcon from the brink of extinction depended upon us seeing the city not as a metaphorical 'urban jungle', but as a literal landscape of height, distance, airspace and foothold. We stand on the twentieth floor of San Francisco and imagine this entire layer of the city returned to natural forces, swept by wind, colonized by alpine plants, traversed by birds, penetrated by torrential rains, and even visited, though respectfully, by humans.

In *Visualizing the City*, the urban is visited, revisited, projected and reprojected for our inspection and introspection. Collectively, these essays unpick inter-woven city fabrics, whether in Rio or Paris, Berlin or Beirut, London or New York, in an effort to discover how they equate with one another in their intertextual rearrangements. From celebrated citadel to the destruction of iconic monuments, the promise of urban power, coupled with efforts to fill the void – be it ground zero with twin beams marking the spot where 2,800 people lost their lives, or the vacuous space of KZ Dachau, where over 30,000 people were systematically destroyed, the city's constructs and visual representations remind us of our mortality. As these essays explore, urban life pursues a looped struggle for sustainability and advancement, charting the exit of its inhabitants and the entrance of new structures with which to punctuate the skyline and our need and fascination for the built environment.

Alan Marcus
Dietrich Neumann
Aberdeen and Providence, 2007

NOTE

1   The impetus for this book grew out of discussions following the 'Visualizing the City' conference held at the University of Manchester in June 2005.

Part I

Reflecting on the City

Chapter 1: Haptic Space

Film and the Geography of Modernity

Giuliana Bruno

As an art of viewing the city, film was born out of the geography of modernity and its visual culture. The invention of cinema is set at a transformative moment in the cultural panorama of modern life. A new spatiovisuality was being produced as film emerged. The city was the center of this transformation. Alongside the urban aesthetics of panorama paintings and dioramas, architectural venues such as arcades, department stores, the pavilions of exhibition halls, glass houses and winter gardens, along with the railway, incarnated the new geography of modernity.[1] These were all sites of transit. Mobility – a form of cinematics – was the essence of these new architectures. By changing the relation between spatial perception and motion, the new architectures of transit and travel culture prepared the ground for the invention of the moving image, the very epitome of modernity.

Film emerged out of a visual field in transition. It implanted in a shifting terrain marked by changes in the history of art, visual representation and the design of the city. In charting the movement of this visual geography, in this essay, we will look at the encounter between film and the architecture of modernity focusing on the agency of haptic motion in the making of modern space. As the notion of the haptic will play a feature role in this cultural panorama, let us first consider its genealogy.

HAPTIC SPACE

Haptic refers to the sense of touch. As Greek etymology tells us, *haptic* means 'able to come into contact with'. As a function of the skin, then, the haptic – the sense of touch – constitutes the reciprocal con*tact* between the environment and us. It is by way of touch that we apprehend space, turning contact into communicative interface. As a sensory interaction, the haptic is also related to kinesthesis, or the ability of our bodies to sense their own movement in space. In this sense, then, I take the haptic to be the main agent in the mobilization of space – both geographic and architectural – and, by extension, in the articulation of the spatial arts themselves, which include motion pictures.

Architecture and cinema, usually confined to optical readings, are thus remapped in the realm of the haptic. Moving from optic to haptic, we will pursue a tangible sense of space, and address the movement of habitable sites, including their actual 'moving' quality.[2] In fact, as we embark on a cultural journey between the urban map, the architectural wall and the film screen, we aim to express the emotion of our motion through space. Motion, we claim, produces emotion, and, correlatively, emotion contains a movement. Even the Latin root of the word *emotion* speaks clearly about a 'moving' force: it stems from *emovere*, an active verb composed of *movere*, 'to move', preceded by the suffix *e*, 'out'. The meaning of emotion, then, is historically associated with mobile space, with 'a moving out, migration, transference from one place to another' (OED 1989: 183). Emotion is, literally, a moving map.

It is there, in this very emotion, that the moving image was implanted, with its own psychogeographic version of transport and lived space. Cinema was named after the ancient Greek word *kinema*. Interestingly, *kinema* means both motion and emotion. Proceeding from this kinematic premise, then, we will see that the emotion of cinema extends beyond the walls of the movie house. It is genealogically implanted in the movement of modernity. Filmic emotion is part of a vast mobilization that includes metropolitan itineraries, landscape design, and the design of memory as housed in the urban museum. Keeping this haptic frame of mind in visualizing the cine-city, let us now take a few architectural walks through modernity and its cultural memory. We will set the city in the broader context of a history of 'moving' images.

FILM AND MNEMONIC ARCHITECTURE

As we approach the geography of modernity, we can take a cue from the urban historian Lewis Mumford. Mumford's work can enlighten the movement of modernity across film, art and architecture, and guide us in mapping spaces in this time. It was Mumford who, in 1937, articulated an interaction between cinema, the city and the museum as products of the modern era. He spoke of modernity as a site of cultural memory:

> Starting itself as a chance accumulation of relics, with no more rhyme or reason than the city itself, the museum . . . presents itself to use as a means of selectively preserving the memorials of culture . . . . What cannot be kept in existence in material form we may now measure, photograph in still and moving pictures.
>
> (Mumford 1937: 267)

The urban historian recognized that cinema has an active place in the 'memorials of culture'. Interestingly, this view of modern memory passes through a joined image of the city and film, and invokes urban motion. It offers us a moving picture. The urban rhythm and the geographic narrative of cinema are joined in cumulative assemblage. Mumford identifies cinema as a moving imprint and an active mnemonic 'measure': that is, as a *mapping* of an archive of images. Rhyme and rhythm accrue to the collection of relics mobilized in urban forms of exhibition. On Mumford's moving map the celluloid archive can thus join the city and the museum.

FILM GENEALOGY AND THE INTIMACY OF PUBLIC VIEWING

Indeed, cinema emerged from a mobile 'architecture' of vision: the interactive geovisual culture of modernity. The museographic spectacles and practices of curiosity of early modernity gave rise to the very architecture of 'interior' design that became the cinema.[3] This composite genealogy was characterized by diverse georhythms of site-seeing. It was a spectacular theatrics of image collection that activated recollection. The spaces for viewing that became filmic architecture included cosmorama rooms, cabinets of curiosity, wax and anatomical museums, performative *tableaux vivants*, georamic exhibition, panoramic and dioramic stages, maps and surveys, fluid and automated spectacular motions, vitrine and window display, view painting, and other techniques of urban viewing.

Film exhibition developed in and around these *intimate* sites of public viewing, within the history of a mobilized architectonics of scenic space in an

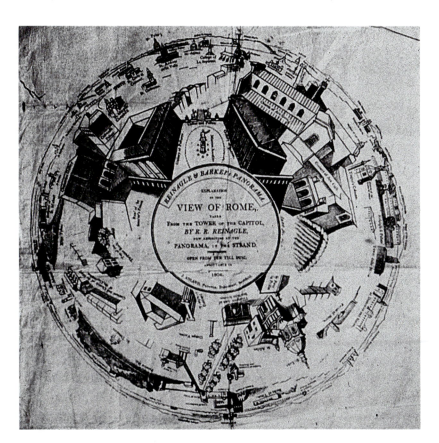

Figure 1.1
Explanation of the View of Rome, R. R. Reinagle and R. Barker, 1804 etching.

aesthetics of fractured, sequential and shifting views. Fragments were crystallized, serialized and automated in the cabinet of curiosity, the precursor of the museum; objects that were cultural souvenirs offered themselves to spectatorial musing; views developed into *vedutismo*, an actual art of viewing, becoming a gallery of *vedute*. This absorption in viewing space then became the georamic architecture of the interior that represented a form of art 'installation' *avant la lettre*. Panorama paintings literally turned into 'light installations'. Cinema descends from this travel of the room – a waxed, fluid geography of exhibition that came of age in the nineteenth century and moulded the following one.

What turned into cinema was an imaginative trajectory that required physical habitation and liminal traversal of the sites of display. As wandering was incorporated in the cinema, film viewing became an imaginary form of *flânerie*. By way of the cinema, new horizons of urban 'street-walking' opened to women. Cinema, an intimate geography born with the emergence of a public penchant for *flânerie*, is architecturally attached to this notion. The movie house signals the mobilization of public space with its architectonics of display and architectural promenade, experientially implanted in the binding of imaging to spectatorial life.

SITE-SEEING: FILMIC AND URBAN PROMENADES

To further explain the journey of the imagination that links cinematic to urban space, it is helpful to revisit Sergei Eisenstein's (1989 [1938]) essay on 'Montage and Architecture'. Here, Eisenstein envisioned a genealogical relation between the architectural ensemble and film. He designed a moving spectator for both, while taking the reader, quite literally, for a walk:

> The word *path* is not used by chance. Nowadays it is the imaginary path followed by the eye and . . . the mind across a multiplicity of phenomena, far apart in time and space, gathered in a certain sequence . . . ; and these diverse impressions pass in front of an immobile spectator.
>
> In the past, however, the opposite was the case: the spectator moved between [a series of] carefully disposed phenomena that he observed sequentially with his visual sense.
>
> (Eisenstein 1989: 116)

The film spectator moves across an imaginary path, traversing multiple sites and times. Her fictional navigation connects distant moments and far-apart places. Film inherits the possibility of such a spectatorial voyage from the architectural field:

> An architectural ensemble . . . is a montage from the point of view of a moving spectator . . . . Cinematographic montage is, too, a means to 'link' in one point – the screen – various fragments of a phenomenon filmed in diverse dimensions, from diverse points of view and sides.
>
> (Eisenstein 1980: 16–17)

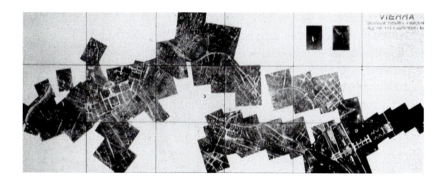

The filmic path is the modern version of the architectural itinerary, with its own montage of cultural space. Film follows a historical course – that is, a museographic way to collect together various fragments of cultural phenomena from diverse geohistorical moments that are open for spectatorial recollection in space. In this sense, film descends not only historically but also formally from a specific architectural promenade: the geovisual exploration of the architectures of display. The consumer of this architectural viewing space is the prototype of the film spectator.

THE ARCHITECTURAL PATHS OF THE ART OF MEMORY

Eisenstein's 'imaginistic' vision of the filmic-architectural promenade follows a mnemonic path. It bears the mark of the art of memory and, in particular, its way of linking collection and recollection in a spatial fashion. Let us recall that the art of memory was, itself, a matter of mapping space and was traditionally an architectural affair.[4] In the first century AD, Quintilian formulated his landmark understanding of the way memory works architecturally.[5] To create a memory, one would imagine a building, and, peripatetically, populate each room and part of the space with an image; then, to recall the memory, one would mentally retraverse the building, moving around and through the space, revisiting in turn all the rooms that had been 'decorated' with imaging. Mobilized in this way, memories are motion pictures. As Quintilian (1922: 221–3) has it, memory stems from a narrative, mobile, architectural experience of site.

The art of memory is an architecture of inner writing in which *places* are constantly reconfigured as if drawn on wax.[6] It bears the peculiar celluloid texture of a filmic 'set' – a site of constant redrawing, a place where many stories 'take place' and take the place of memory. Before motion pictures spatialized and mobilized discourse – substituting for memory, in the end – the art of memory made room for a montage of images. By means of an architectural promenade, it enabled this process of image collection to generate recollection.

To pass through the doors of the memory archive, memories must be affectively charged. Emotionally striking images are able to 'move' us as they chart the movement of the living world. As its own 'art of memory', film itself draws these moving memory maps. In its memory theatre, the spectator-passenger, sent on an architectural journey, endlessly retraces the itineraries of a geographical discourse which, reading memories as places, 'sets' memory in place and in motion. As this architectural art of memory, filmic site-seeing, like the museum's own version, embodies a particularly mobile art of mapping: an *emotion*al mapping.

TENDER GEOGRAPHY

The notion that memory, imagination and affect are linked to movement was advanced in yet more geographic ways in seventeenth-century emotional cartography. In 1654 Madeleine de Scudéry designed the Carte du Pays de Tendre, a map of the land of tenderness.[7] The Carte de Tendre was a geopsychic architecture. This map visualized, in the form of a landscape, an itinerary of emotions.

The haptic map was 'designed' as a place that evoked emotion in the shape of motion as one travelled through it. Scudéry's map designed a landscape of emotions to be experienced as a series of sensational movements. In a 'moving' way, it made 'sense' of the place of affects, as it traced their movement in space. The emotional map produced an emotion, and the motion inscribed therein was not only kinetic or kinesthetic. As in garden design, there was a liminal passage. It made it possible for the exterior world of the landscape to be transformed into an interior landscape, and vice versa. Emotion materialized as a moving topography.

To traverse this land is to visit the ebb and flow of a social psychogeography. The borderless map creates this itinerary for anyone who navigates its tender landscape. There are no rigid directives for this map tour, based on an interplay between natural and architectural setting. Villages and even cities are designed on the map to *house* sentiments. Just as cinema, architecture creates not only mental but emotional maps acting as membrane for the transmission of affects. Vehicles for the inhabitation of the emotion, dwellings function as resting places along the map tour, places of lodging for the circulation of affects. Several such movements are possible and encouraged in a touring that produces a cumulative effect. The spectator/passenger was free to wander in this garden of emotions.

HAPTIC ROUTES

As it emerges out of these haptic routes, cinema has its spatial roots in the new 'fashions' of spatiality that marked the rise of early modernity, and, in turn, shaped the very 'design' of modern movement. Following the movement of 'Things to Come' that was taking place in cultural travelling, we traverse a terrain that extended from affective mapping to topographical view painting to landscape design and, eventually, panoramic vision and filmic site-seeing. As it was located and dislocated, vision was transformed along the route of urban mapping.[8] As space was haptically absorbed and consumed in movement by a spectator, a new

architectonics was set in motion: sites were set in moving perspectives, expanding both outward and inward. The new sensibility engaged the physicality and imagination of the observer who craved this mobilized space.

During the eighteenth century, the production of travel discourse began to grow and took on a variety of forms, from literary to visual and spatial configurations.[9] Journey literature, view paintings and garden views combined a sensualist theory of the imagination with the touch of physicality. A haptic consciousness grew. The broadening of visuality produced at this time essentially joined space with desire: it effectively 'located' affects in space and articulated desire as a spatial practice. There was an increased yearning for capturing sites in the form of '-scapes'. Scanning cityscapes, moving through and with landscapes, this opening of spatial horizons fashioned an expanded interior landscape. This 'collective attraction for views' was the force that shaped the cultural movement which proleptically led to the cinema (cited in Corbin 1995: 138). The new mechanisms for spatiovisual (e)motion, that is, expressed the desire for the moving image.

Cinematic motion descends from the fascination for views and the psychophysical hunger for space that led the subject from vista to vista in an extended search for urban and environmental pleasure to open mental maps. Spatial curiosity and the practice of site-seeing, consolidated in eighteenth-century culture, designed a route that ranged across topographical views and maps to the architectonics of gardens and led to the opening of travel to more people, the circulation of travel narratives and the rise of a leisure industry. This included the grand tour, with its voyage to Italy, as well as the amusement of peering into cabinets of curiosities that became the museum and browsing through the composition of natural settings or their depictions. Moving along the path of modernity from view painting to garden views, from travel sketches to itinerant viewing boxes, from grand tours to panoramas and other geographical '-oramas' to forms of interior/ exterior mapping, from the mobile views of train travel to urban street-walking and imaginary *flânerie*, the subject was 'incorporated' into motion pictures. It is this moving, haptic space that created the (e)motion picture and its spectator – a social body of 'passengers'. To sum it up, it was the very sense that space can be '*touching*'. As a lived experience, it 'moves'.

THE ART OF VIEWING THE CITY: *VEDUTISMO*

To understand the origins of the moving image's e*motion* – its inner 'transport' – we must continue to take a step back, and further explore the aftermath of early modernity, especially the flourishing of topographical representation of cities and of urban view painting, and their creation of an urban imaginary.[10] These forms of viewing space offered an experience that in Italian is called *trasporto*. This 'transport' refers to the sort of carrying that is a carrying away by emotion, as in the English expression 'transports of joy', and characterizes the affective pull as a 'drive' – an attraction. The *veduta* was an art of viewing that attracted one to site, providing such form of *trasporto*. Its effect was to carry away – transport – the spectator into the landscape or cityscape depicted, powerfully creating embracing atmosphere, mood, and the feeling of imaginative travel.

The art of viewing the city assumed different forms, from the display of architectural sites as emotional matters, in the tradition of the Neapolitan artist Salvator Rosa (1616–73), to a more descriptive mode that circulated widely as paintings, prints, illustrations published in travel accounts, and also as atlases and topographical mappings. Foregrounded by a growing interest in architectural forms, paintings of city views were recognized as an autonomous aesthetic category in the late seventeenth century. The influential Italian art of imaging the city was named *vedutismo*.[11] It evolved from a veritable pandemic of urban imaging and *furor geographicus* that took place from the fifteenth century onward, establishing a hunger – a 'taste' – for viewing sites. Inseparable from the history of travel culture, the *veduta* embodied a touch of space, and a taste for motion.

As an art of viewing, the Italian *veduta* used different codes in its description of the city than the Dutch city view.[12] In the *veduta*, the portrait of the city was staged. Masters of this type of representation included Canaletto (1697–1768) and Giovanni Paolo Pannini (c.1691–1765). Working closely with topographical representation, this genre of view painting emphasized the drama of location; the portrait of the city in Italian *vedutismo*, that is, tended toward a narrative dramatization of sites, characterized by a heightened sense and a tactile texture of place.

As they merged the codes of urban topography and landscape painting, city views also incorporated the cartographic drive, creating imaginative representa-

Figure 1.4
New York's *Washington, Madison, and Union Squares*, O. B. Bunce, 1874, woodcut.

Figure 1.4
New York's *Washington, Madison, and Union Squares*, O. B. Bunce, 1874, woodcut.

tional maps. The city was approached from different viewpoints. Factual accuracy was not the aim of these urban views, which exhibited an interest in rendering a mental 'image of the city' and proposed not a single 'cognitive mapping' but diverse observational routes.[13] Imaging a city, in fact, involves a cluster of multiple, diverse maps that are inhabited and psychically carried around by city dwellers within themselves. View painting inscribed this moving, inhabited, articulated inner space within its mapping of the city.

City views were part of the everyday narrative of urban life.[14] From the sixteenth century on, city views and maps were produced as objects of display suitable for wall decoration and thus became a feature of interior urban life. Urban views even migrated from forms of architectural decor and decoration all the way to the decorative arts. From the mid-eighteenth century on, they literally entered the public taste. They shaped table manners in the form of embellishment on plates, bowls, glasses, cups and trays, and illustrated the tops of dining room tables or were inscribed on their surfaces. They 'illuminated' pieces of furniture such as writing desks and decorated ladies' jewellery boxes and fans. City views travelled from the outside to the inside, mapping out the space of the urban interior.

The art of viewing followed the older touristic drive to embrace a terrain that led to the climbing of church towers, mountains and buildings to take in the panorama. From the beginning, the city view adopted this practice and transcended its real-life limits, as shown, for instance, in the exemplary *Bird's-eye View of Venice* attributed to Jacopo de'Barbari, produced back in 1500.[15] This multi-sheet mapping of the city was an impressively imaginative enterprise of topographic rendering, for the overall view was assembled from a number of disparate drawings made from different high points throughout the city. There is no clear focal point in this imaginary view, which is, rather, constructed as a *montage* of different vanishing points. The observer is not positioned at a set distance but appears free to wander in and around the space. This imagined dislocated view, made possible much later by the spatiovisual techniques of cinema, attempted to free vision from a singular, fixed viewpoint, imaginatively mobilizing narrative visual space.

In view painting, the city was part of a sequence of mental maps, an integral part of cultural travel and memory. A geographical rendering of the imagination, the bird's-eye view was an imaginary map for both those who knew and those who had never seen a city; both spectators encountered the site in mobilized form.[16] The wide vistas of prospect and profile views also functioned in a way that pushed perspectival boundaries. These vistas strove to overcome the limitations of perspective by creating a wider horizontal expanse, often made of aggregate views, that eroded the notion of a single, prioritized perspective.

Thus, the image of the Western city expanded, 'unlimiting the bounds of painting'.[17] Such expansion – rupturing the containability of borders and frames – made it impossible for the ideal city of Renaissance perspective to remain representationally intact, to be captured in a single image. Beginning in the eighteenth century, urban *vedute* were produced in several parts, even as different viewpoints. The image of the city underwent an intense process of fragmentation and multiplication before being refigured in the all-embracing views of the panorama, which extended the very borders of the frame. The urban organism shatters, dissolved in multiple views. The body of the city is cut into partial, serialized views and a fractured montage is set in motion in this imaginary urban mapping.

Such montages of views, combined with the panoramic impulse, spoke of things to come: motion pictures. By presenting multiple, mobile perspectives and suggesting a mobilized observer, these urban views exhibited a protocinematic attempt to expand the field of haptic vision. It was this cartographic mobilization of perspective, inscribed in the movement of urban imaging, that led to nineteenth-century panoramic culture, with its metropolitan transit, arcade life and railway travel, eventually becoming the very 'transport' of motion pictures.

MOBILE MAPPINGS: VIEWS IN FLUX

In early modernity, the techniques of observing architectural views articulated a relationship between space, movement and narrative, thus mobilizing spatial storytelling.[18] The flow of history entered representation. By representing the life of the site, view painting captured its affective atmosphere. Depicting space as inhabited by events and moving with the dynamics of the city, the rectangular space of the view was extended into film; before the film strip, architectural pictures began to tell stories in long formats. This enlarged perspective extended into the full view of nineteenth-century panoramas, where the subjects of history and narrative realism featured large.[19] In the evolution of perspectival practice, an aspect of tactile experience – space that is lived – became charted in observational, prefilmic 'moving' practices.

The multiple perspectives that rendered haptic space and made landscape inhabited turned urban sites into filmic '-scapes'. The techniques of observation themselves mobilized.[20] Drawing distant objects closer and pushing back close ones, the views filmically rendered space. Picturing space as an assemblage of partial views – a montage of spatial fragments linked panoramically by a mobile observer – cartographic art pictured (pre)filmic space. It pictured 'sensational' transitions from kinetic to kinesthetic to kinematic. The emotion of movement was made palpable.

As the views captured movement, they attempted to make it material and even graft it physically onto the picture surface. Such kinesthesia was also exhibited in the mobile cartographic activity that charted the sky and the movements of the waters, viewed in relation to currents and winds. These were forms of mapping that inscribed in their design an 'atmospheric' transport, charting the unmappable before visual technology could. The cityscape was expanding as the practice of the urban pavement extended to aerial flotation in a new perspective of shifting atmospheric spaces. Haptic wanderings were transferred from the feet to 'the wings of desire', well before motion pictures fully enabled their moving montage, created their own 'transport', and even celebrated their 'Voyage to Italy'.

In the voyage of modernity, a terrain of urban transformations led into filmic site-seeing.[21] In prefilmic times, urban space became documented at the meeting point of city and territory as aerial mapping, nautical cartography and fluvial topography merged with urban mapping. The resulting representations sought to capture motion with a moving image, following a course. Creating a beautiful mobile architectonics at the interstice of land and water, this type of cartography, drawn from direct travel experience, strove to materialize motion, making it not simply visible but especially tangible. It was precisely this passage that the filmic flow of images would haptically materialize, establishing its own cartographic course. Portable maps drawn on skin, the portolan nautical charts were consulted as they unravelled, prefiguring the materiality of the film strip and its own cartographic movement on the cinematic reel.

Fluvial prospect or profile views extended picture borders into a fluid prefilmic narrative format. The representations of nautical cartography and, by extension, fluvial topography reproduced the movement of vessels. After all, as Gertrude Stein put it, 'geography includes inhabitants and vessels' (Stein 1993: 470).

Figure 1.5
Voyage in Italy, Roberto Rossellini, 1953, frame enlargements.

Viewing an urban space by moving in and out of its bordering sea, or through its fluvial architexture, one experiences the sensation of cinematic emotion. As one moves with the flow of the current, the view develops into a flow of images (Dubbini 1987: 105).[22] When the point of observation shifts into a sequence of viewpoints that create a geographical route, this is a filmic route. A route where motion is emotion.

MOVING THROUGH INNER LANDSCAPES

As the travelling eye came into place, motion became clearly bound to emotion. Such *emotion* was consolidated within a grand epistemic resurgence of the sense of touch starting in the second half of the eighteenth century. Motion was craved as a form of stimulation, and haptic sensations were at the basis of this geographical impulse to expand one's inner universe. Urban viewing joined garden theory in the articulation of this interior landscape. The garden was a privileged locus in the pursuit of erotic, haptic, emotive space. Diversely shaped by associative philosophies, eighteenth-century landscape design embodied the very idea that motion rules mental activity and generates a 'fancying'. The images gathered by the senses were thought to produce 'trains' of thought.[23] This philosophy of space embodied a form of fluid, emotive geography. Sensuously associative in connecting the local and topographic to the personal, it enhanced the passionate voyage of the imagination. 'Fancying' – that is, the configuration of a series of relationships created on imaginative tracks – was the effect of a spectatorial movement that evolved further in cinema and the museum. It was the emergence of such sensuous, serial imaging (an affective 'transport') that made it possible for the serial image in film and the sequencing of vitrines in the museum to come together in receptive motion, and for trains of ideas to inhabit the tracking shots of emotion pictures.

The legacy of the picturesque, in particular, was 'to enable the imagination to form the habit of feeling through the eye' (Hussey 1927: 4). Sensational movements through the space of the garden 'animated' pictures, foregrounding the type of haptic sensing enacted by film's own animated emotion pictures. Not unlike cinematic space and the display of collections, picturesque space was, furthermore, an aesthetics of fragments and discontinuities – a mobilized montage of multiple, asymmetrical views.[24] These fragments turned into a passion for ruins and debris. Relics punctuated the picturesque ruined map, preparing the ground for more modern experiences of recollection.[25]

A memory theater of sensual pleasures, the garden was an exterior that put the spectator in 'touch' with inner space. As one moved through the space of the garden, a constant double movement connected external to internal topographies. The garden was thus an outside turned into an inside; but it was also the projection of an inner world onto the outer geography. In a sensuous mobilization, the exterior of the landscape was transformed into an interior map – the landscape within us – as this inner map was, itself, culturally mobilized. In this 'moving' way, we came

Figure 1.6
Interior of an
'atmospheric' movie
palace, the Loew's
Paradise Theatre, Bronx,
NY, 1929. Designed by
Eberson.

to approach the kind of transport that drives the architectonics of film spectatorship and of museum-going. No wonder moody, mnemonic architecture became the mark of the urban movie palace. The atmosphere of the 'atmospheric' movie theatre created a sensory affective remake. Here, one could walk, once again, in the imaginary garden of memory.

THE ARCHITECTURAL JOURNEY AND THE GARDEN OF MEMORY

The picturesque promenade extended into modern itineraries of re-collection. 'Picturesque' views were adopted and transformed into peripatetic vision by Le Corbusier and Eisenstein, who conceived of a filmic-architectural promenade in modern picturesque terms.[26] Claiming that 'architecture and film are the only two arts of our time', the architect affirmed: 'in my own work I seem to think as Eisenstein does in his films' (cited in Cohen 1992: 49).[27] Indeed, Le Corbusier and Eisenstein fashioned their thoughts similarly. Their itineraries follow the same mnemonic path, which engages the labour of imagination. From a moving perspective, in the architectural journey, one performs an imaginative traversal. As Le Corbusier put it, revealing his cinematic vision of architecture: 'The architectural spectacle offers itself consecutively to view; . . . you play with the flood of light' (Le Corbusier and Jeanneret 1964: 60).[28] In this filmic view, 'a true architectural promenade [offers] constantly changing views, unexpected, at times surprising' (Le Corbusier 1964: 24). An architectural ensemble, that is, is 'read' as it is traversed by light. This is also the case for the cinematic spectacle, for film – the screen of light – is read as it is traversed and is readable inasmuch as it is traversable. As we go through it, it goes through us and our own inner geography. A practice that engages psychic change in relation to movement was thus *architected*, in between the wall and the screen.

MOTION, EMOTION AND TOPOPHILIA

The desire to make a private 'album' of moving views for public consumption created the architecture of the cinema, an intimate travelling room. Cinema – a nomadic archive of images – thus becomes a home of 'moving' exploration. A haptic architexture. A topophilic affair.[29] A place for the love of place. A love of place that holds the residual texture of time – the very fabric of temporality. As we come to the close of our topophilic exploration of modernity's moving geography, we might stress that this landscape is, indeed, a work of the mind.[30] A cultural landscape is, in many ways, a trace of the memories, the attention, the imagination and affects of those inhabitant-passengers who have traversed it at different times. It is an intertextural terrain of passage that carries its own representation in the threads of its fabric, weaving it on intersecting screens. A palpable imprint is left in this moving landscape; in its folds, gaps and layers, the geography of cinema, heir of modernity, holds remnants of what has been projected onto it at every transit, including the emotions.

Space – including cinematic space – 'emoves' because, charged with layers of topophilic affects, it is invested with the ability to nourish the self. This psychic process involves making claims and demands on the site. In the history of mobilized space we have described, a traveller seeking a particular landscape may go there, imaginatively, *even filmically*, to be moved, replenished, restored, held and fed. In the hub of filmic travelling and dwelling, we are absorbed in the stream of *emotion*s and experience an embracing affective transport. As the history of film architecture shows, cinematic motion implies more than the movement of bodies and objects, as imprinted in the change of film frames and shots, the flow of camera movement, or any other kind of locomotive shift in viewpoint. Motion pictures move, not only through time and space or narrative development but also through inner space. Film moves, and fundamentally 'moves' us, with its ability to project affects and, in turn, to affect. The city is itself such a psychogeographic landscape. It is a collection of the mental, mnemonic and affective fabric – the maps – designed by its inhabitants and passengers. And it is akin to the museum, for, as we argued earlier, the city and the museum share the ability to function as permutable temporal landscapes and chance accumulation of relics. Film is part of this delicate urban fabric, the web of time. It enables us to redraw the maps and recollect the traces of urban psychogeography. As products of modernity, the cinema, the city and the museum are linked in this collective itinerary of recollection. They are mental 'projections' – topophilic places that can hold us in their geopsychic design and navigate our story. In this interface between the architectural wall and the film screen, memory places and affects are searched and inhabited throughout time in interconnected visual geographies, thus rendering, through cumulation and scanning, our fragile place in history. This modern architecture breathes in the passage and the conflated layers of materially lived space in motion. This architexture is an absorbing screen. It is a screen of moving pictures. An intimate art of viewing. An atlas of e*motion*. A *kinema*, indeed.

NOTES

1   On the subject of film and modernity, see, among others, Giuliana Bruno, *Streetwalking on a Ruined Map*, Princeton, NJ: Princeton University Press, 1993; Anne Friedberg, *Window-Shopping: Cinema and the Postmodern*, Los Angeles, CA: University of California Press, 1993; and Leo Charney and Vanessa R. Schwartz, eds, *Cinema and the Invention of Modern Life*, Los Angeles, CA: University of California Press, 1995.

2   For a more extended historical and theoretical mapping of haptic, 'moving' space, see Bruno, *Atlas of Emotion: Journeys in Art, Architecture, and Film*, New York: Verso, 2002.

3   See Bruno, *Atlas of Emotion*, and 'Collection and Recollection: On Film Itineraries and Museum Walks', in Richard Allen and Malcolm Turvey, eds, *Camera Obscura, Camera Lucida*, Amsterdam: Amsterdam University Press, 2003.

4   See Francis A. Yates, *The Art of Memory*, Chicago, IL: University of Chicago Press, 1966; Yates, 'Architecture and the Art of Memory', *Architectural Design*, 38 (12) (December 1968), pp. 573–8; and Mary Carruthers, *The Book of Memory: A Study of Memory in Medieval Culture*, New York: Cambridge University Press, 1992.

5   Marcus Tullius Cicero's version of the art of memory recounts how the Greek poet Simonides first discovered the spatial principles of the mnemonic technique – the placing of images in an architectural setting – when, using this principle, he was able to remember the names of all the guests in a banquet that had been killed by the collapse of the roof. His account of memory influenced Quintilian, and is outlined in his *De Oratore*, trans. E. W. Sutton and Harris Rackman, London: Loeb Classical Library, 1942. Marcus Fabius Quintilian's rendition of the subject is laid out in his *Institutio oratoria*, vol. 4, trans. H. E. Butler, New York: G. P. Putnam's Sons, 1922.

6   For an extension of this reading of the wax texture of memory see Plato, *Theaetetus*, trans. Harold N. Fowler, London: Loeb Classical Library, 1921; and Sigmund Freud, 'A Note on the Mystic Writing Pad', in *Complete Psychological Works*, vol. 9, London: Standard Edition, 1956.

7   *Carte du Pays de Tendre* [the map of tenderness] was published in Madeleine de Scudéry's novel *Clélie* (Paris: Augustin Courbé, vol. 1, 1654), and engraved by François Chauveau. On this map, which inspired my *Atlas of Emotion*, see also Claude Filteau, 'Le Pays de Tendre: l'enjeu d'une carte', *Littérature*, no. 36 (1979), 37–60, and Jean de Jean, *Tender Geographies: Women and the Origins of the Novel in France*, New York: Columbia University Press, 1991.

8   For a history of the urban imaginary, see, among others, Richard Sennett, *Flesh and Stone: The Body and the City in Western Civilization*, New York: W. W. Norton, 1994,

pp. 261–4. M. Christine Boyer, *The City of Collective Memory: Its Historical Imagery and Architectural Entertainments*, Cambridge, MA: MIT Press, 1994.

9 See, among others, Barbara Maria Stafford, *Voyage into Substance: Art, Science, Nature and the Illustrated Travel Account, 1760–1840*, Cambridge, MA: MIT Press, 1984.

10 See, among other references cited below, David Woodward, ed., *Art and Cartography*, Chicago, IL: The University of Chicago Press, 1987; P. D. Harvey, *The History of Topographical Maps*, London: Thames and Hudson, 1980; and Giuliana Massobrio and Paolo Portoghesi, *L'immaginario architettonico nella pittura*, Bari: Laterza, 1988.

11 On this subject, see, among others, Cesare de Seta, ed., *Città d'Europa: Iconografia e vedutismo dal XV al XIX secolo*, Naples: Electa, 1996; de Seta, 'Topografia urbana e vedutismo nel Seicento: a proposito di alcuni disegni di Alessandro Baratta', *Prospettiva*, no. 2, July 1980, pp. 46–60; de Seta, 'Bernardo Bellotto vedutista e storiografo della civiltà urbana europea', *Quaderni dell'Istituto di Storia dell'Architettura*, nos. 15–20, 1990–92, pp. 813–18; de Seta, *L'Italia del Grand Tour da Montaigne a Goethe*, Naples: Electa, 1992; Giuliano Briganti, *The View Painters of Europe*, trans. Pamela Waley, London: Phaidon, 1970; and *The Origins of the Italian Veduta*, Providence, RI: Brown University, 1978 (exhibition catalogue). A bibliography on view painting was compiled by Elisabeth Chevallier and published in the proceedings of the conference 'Archéologie du paysage', *Caesarodunum*, 1 (13), 1978, pp. 579–613.

12 On Dutch methods of description and mapping, see Svetlana Alpers, *The Art of Describing: Dutch Art in the Seventeenth Century*, Chicago, IL: University of Chicago Press, 1983.

13 On the notion of the mental image of the city, see Kevin Lynch, *The Image of the City*, Cambridge, MA: MIT Press, 1960. On cognitive mapping as developed from Lynch, see Fredric Jameson, 'Cognitive Mapping', in Cary Nelson and Lawrence Grossberg, eds, *Marxism and the Interpretation of Culture*, Chicago, IL: University of Illinois Press, 1988; and Jameson, *Postmodernism, or the Cultural Logic of Late Capitalism*, Durham, NC: Duke University Press, 1991, especially pp. 51–2.

14 See Christian Jacob, *L'empire des cartes: approches théorique de la cartographie à travers l'histoire*, Paris: Editions Albin Michel, 1992, especially chapter 1; and Joy Kenseth, ed., *The Age of the Marvelous*, Hanover, NH: Hood Museum of Art, Dartmouth College, 1991 (exhibition catalogue).

15 On this map, see Juergen Schulz, 'Jacopo de'Barbari's View of Venice: Map Making, City Views, and Moralized Geography Before the Year 1500', *The Art Bulletin*, 60 (3), September 1978.

16 Art historian Louis Marin claims that the bird's-eye view offers a 'snapshot of the city', in his *Utopics: Spatial Plays*, trans. Robert A. Vollrath, Atlantic Highlands, NJ: Humanities, 1984, p. 208.

17 On prospect views as precursors of panoramic vision, see Ralph Hyde, *Panoramania!: The Art and Entertainment of the 'All-Embracing View'*, London: Trefoil, in association with the Barbican Art Gallery, 1988. The expression cited is the title of the book's introduction. See also, Hyde, *Gilded Scenes and Shining Prospects: Panoramic Views of British Towns, 1575–1900*, New Haven, CT: Yale Center for British Art, 1985 (exhibition catalogue).

18   On perspective and cultural change, see Erwin Panofsky, *Perspective as Symbolic Form*, trans. Christopher S. Wood, New York: Zone Books, 1997.

19   See Stephan Oettermann, *The Panorama: History of a Mass Medium*, trans. Deborah Lucas Schneider, New York: Zone Books, 1997; and Schwartz, *Spectacular Realities: Early Mass Culture in Fin-de-Siècle Paris*, Los Angeles, CA: University of California Press, 1998.

20   Art historian Anne Hollander significantly refers to painterly scenic designs as 'moving pictures'. See Anne Hollander, *Moving Pictures*, Cambridge, MA: Harvard University Press, 1991, especially chapter 8.

21   With regards to the spectacular display of urban images, many examples can be found in Richard Altick, *The Shows of London*, Cambridge, MA: Harvard University Press, 1978.

22   See also Dubbini, *Geografie dello sguardo: visione e paesaggio in età moderna*, Turin: Einaudi, 1994, especially chapters 2 and 6.

23   See Stafford, *Voyage into Substance*, especially p. 4. See also John Dixon Hunt, *Gardens and the Picturesque*, Cambridge, MA: MIT Press, 1992.

24   On the picturesque as landscape aesthetics, see also, among others, John Dixon Hunt, *Gardens and the Picturesque: Studies in the History of Landscape Architecture*, Cambridge, MA: MIT Press, 1992; Malcolm Andrews, *The Search for the Picturesque: Landscape Aesthetics and Tourism in Britain, 1760–1800*, Stanford, CA: Stanford University Press, 1989; Sidney Robinson, *Inquiry into the Picturesque*, Chicago, IL: University of Chicago Press, 1991; David Watkin, *The English Vision: The Picturesque in Architecture, Landscape and Garden Design*, London: Murray, 1982; Monique Mosser and Georges Teyssot, eds, *The Architecture of Western Gardens: A Design History from the Renaissance to the Present Day*, Cambridge, MA: MIT Press, 1991; and Sylvia Lavin, 'Sacrifice and the Garden: Watelet's *Essai sur les jardins* and the Space of the Picturesque', *Assemblage*, no. 28, December 1995, pp. 17–33. The notion of 'picturesque' was first used by Alexander Pope in relation to the narrative impact of history painting and originally referred to a scene that would be apt for painting. See also William Gilpin, *Three Essays: On Picturesque Beauty; On Picturesque Travel; and on Sketching Landscape*, London, 1792; and Uvedale Price, *Essays on the Picturesque*, 3 vols, London, 1810.

25   For a re-vision towards a modern picturesque, see Kim Ian Michasiw, 'Nine Revisionist Theses on the Picturesque', *Representations*, no. 38, Spring 1992, pp. 76–100; Rosalind Krauss, *The Originality of the Avant-Garde and Other Modernist Myths*, Cambridge, MA: MIT Press, 1985, especially pp. 162–70; Caroline Constant, 'The Barcelona Pavilion as Landscape Garden: Modernity and the Picturesque', *AA Files*, no. 20, 1990, pp. 47–54; Yve-Alain Bois, 'A Picturesque Stroll around *Clara-Clara*', October, no. 29, 1984, pp. 32–62; and Robert Smithson, 'Frederick Law Olmstead and the Dialectical Landscape', in Nancy Holt, ed., *The Writings of Robert Smithson*, New York: New York University Press, 1979.

26   In 'Montage and Architecture', Eisenstein used the 'picturesque' views of Auguste Choisy (the architectural historian interested in peripatetic vision) to illustrate his conception of a filmic-architectural promenade, following Le Corbusier's own appropriation of this vision. On Choisy and Le Corbusier see Richard A. Etlin, 'Le Corbusier, Choisy, and

French Hellenism: The Search for a New Architecture', *Art Bulletin*, no. 2 (June 1987), pp. 264–78. On Eisenstein and architectural history, see Yve-Alain Bois's introduction to Eisenstein's 'Montage and Architecture'; and Anthony Vidler, 'The Explosion of Space: Architecture and the Filmic Imaginary', in Dietrich Neumann, ed., *Film Architecture: Set Designs from Metropolis to Blade Runner*, New York: Prestel, 1996.

27 This interview was the only one that Le Corbusier gave during his stay in Moscow in 1928.

28 On Corbusier and his cinematic viewpoint, see Beatriz Colomina, *Privacy and Publicity: Modern Architecture as Mass Media*, Cambridge, MA: MIT Press, 1994.

29 For an introduction to this term, see Yi-Fu Tuan, *Topophilia: A Study of Environmental Perception, Attitudes, and Values*, New York: Columbia University Press, 1990. Although I have found inspiration in this work, I have developed the notion of topophilia along a different path.

30 See Simon Schama, *Landscape and Memory*, New York: Vintage Books, 1995.

REFERENCES

Cohen, J.-L. (1992) *Le Corbusier and the Mystique of the USSR*, trans. K. Hylton, Princeton, NJ: Princeton University Press.

Corbin, A. (1995) *The Lure of the Sea: The Discovery of the Seaside 1750–1840*, trans. J. Phelps, New York: Penguin Books.

Dubbini, R. (1987) 'Views and Panoramas: Representations of Landscapes and Towns', *Lotus International*, no. 52.

Eisenstein, S. M. (1980, first written c.1937) 'El Greco y el cine', in F. Albera (ed.) *Cinématisme: Peinture et cinéma*, trans. A. Zouboff, Brussels: Editions complexe.

—— (1989, first written c.1938) 'Montage and Architecture' *Assemblage*, with an introduction by Y.-A. Bois, no. 10: 111–31.

Hussey, C. (1927) *The Picturesque: Studies in a Point of View*, London: Frank Cass.

Le Corbusier (1964) *Oeuvre complète*, vol. 2, ed. Willi Boesiger, Zurich: Editions Girsberger.

—— and Jeanneret, P. (1964) *Oeuvre complète*, vol. 1, ed. W. Boesiger, Zurich: Editions Girsberger.

Mumford, L. (1937) 'The Death of the Monument', in J. L. Martin, B. Nicholson and N. Gabo (eds) *Circle: International Survey of Constructivist Art*, New York: E. Weyhe.

Oxford English Dictionary (1989) vol. 5, Oxford: Clarendon Press.

Quintilian (1922) *Institutio oratoria*, vol. 4, trans. H. E. Butler, New York: G. P. Putnam's Sons.

Stein, G. (1993) 'Gertrude Stein, *Geography* (1923)', in U. E. Dydo (ed.) *A Stein Reader*, Evanston, IL: Northwestern University Press, reprinted from G. Stein (1955) *Printed Lace and Other Pieces (1914–37), The Yale Edition of the Unpublished Work of Gertrude Stein*, vol. 5, New Haven, CT: Yale University Press.

Chapter 2: Early Film and the Reproduction of Rio

Maite Conde

INTRODUCTION

In recent years, some of the notable intersections between cultural and urban studies have examined the relationship between the physical and spatial city and cinema, with a particular focus on how the development of cinema and the development of urban life were intrinsically related.[1] Here the actual physical space of the city provided not just important imagery for early films but also key infrastructures that would play a part in the emergence of film as a popular and mass medium. In turn, motion pictures helped to construct people's experiences of the city space. This work has mainly concentrated on early cinema and urban landscapes in Europe and the United States. There is still much to learn about how the space of the city, the lives of its inhabitants and the relationships between them, are represented and reproduced on the screen space beyond the Anglo-European context.

This chapter draws upon recent discussions of the cinematic city to provide some reflections on urban space and film in Brazil, exploring the relationship between early film practices and a particular urban transformation in Rio de Janeiro at the start of the twentieth century, intended to make it, to paraphrase Walter Benjamin (1978), 'Brazil's capital of the twentieth century'. This transformation was part of a broader reconfiguration. In 1889, slavery in Brazil was abolished and the Portuguese imperial monarchy was ousted and replaced with a new Republican regime that set about reinventing the country's identity. The peripheral character of Brazil was to be a thing of the past, as it turned its back on its rural slaveholding history and rewrote itself as a nation of order and progress. As the current capital, Rio de Janeiro was the symbolic centrepiece of this new identity and received a radical facelift with which to project the nation's new global design. The arrival and development of film was inextricably linked to these urban reforms; indeed, the medium was immediately seized upon as an ideal vehicle for displaying and projecting Rio's new identity. Yet, far from being a determining force, early forms of spectatorship and production quickly became engaged in a more troubled social and spatial dynamic. These involved tensions and negotiations between the discursive dimension of the civilizing space of the city and its material reality. It is this complex relationship between early cinema and Rio's urban changes that this essay charts, exploring ways in which the medium was imbricated both in reproducing the Republic's new global design while also helping to chart alternative spatial practices.

RIO: THE CINEMATIC CITY

In December 1895, the Lumière brothers arranged a public screening of the *cinematograph* at the Grand Café on the Boulevard des Capucines in Paris. Barely six months later, on the evening of 8 July 1896, the *cinematograph* was shown for the first time in a small theatre in the centre of Rio de Janeiro. By this time, pre-cinematic forms of entertainment, such as the *kinetoscope*, the *vitascope* and the magic lantern were already familiar in the city. The rapid appearance of these forms in Brazil was facilitated by regular routes of transatlantic commerce which had imported foreign manufactured goods through the main port of Rio since the 1850s. The routes intensified following the advent of the Republic as the new government embraced a policy of economic liberalism, exchanging raw materials such as coffee for foreign technological and consumer goods. By the twentieth century, Rio had the fifteenth busiest port in the world, surpassed in the Americas only by Buenos Aires and New York. Increasing numbers of the city's population were able to purchase up-to-date fashions, taste foreign foods and see the latest technological marvels. This gave rise to what critic Brito Broca (1975) termed a *mundanismo* – a worldliness, which pervaded Rio, shaping the ways in which people ate, dressed and spoke and the ways in which they experienced the city.

The centre of this worldliness was a small street in the heart of Rio called the Rua do Ouvidor (see Figure 2.1). European merchants had made the Ouvidor their home since the early 1800s, introducing foreign goods and items into the capital. English tea-shops, French cafés, department stores and novelty shops were all located here, and it was here that everything 'novel and civilized made its first appearance in Brazil, from ice-cream to gas lighting' (Needell 1987: 164). Commentators praised the street as a site of luxury and commerce: 'The Ouvidor shines and radiates. Its commerce displays an ostentation of luxury, of elegance and variety' (cited in Gomes 1980: 40).[2]

With its seductive display of consumer goods, the Ouvidor was a shrine to commerce, a blatant manifestation of the expansion of foreign commodities and goods in Brazil. Historian Jeffrey Needell (1987) compares the Ouvidor to the Parisian arcades famously analysed by Walter Benjamin. For Benjamin these arcades were spaces of extreme cultural ambivalence, their architectural design – streets covered with roofs of glass and iron, blurring strict divisions between light and dark, private and public spaces. Although the Ouvidor was an open pedestrian street not a covered space, it still contained its own cultural ambivalence. Its amalgamation and collection of foreign items and products made it a 'passage'

Figure 2.1
Photograph of Rua do
Ouvidor (Ouvidor Street),
Rio de Janeiro, Marc
Ferrez, c.1905.

Rua do Ouvidor.   *Marc Ferrez*

between Brazil and the outside world. Alice Gonzaga (1996: 52) describes the
Ouvidor as a space in-between Brazil and the rest of the world.

In its symbolic, iconographic and commercial density, Ouvidor offers a parallel
with the World's Fairs that were popular at the end of the 1800s. World's Fairs
gathered together different objects from around the world and showcased them
for the public gaze. The objects displayed became fetishes – they gained an
ideological value linked to their representation. This value was above all visual,
and implied a fiction or a fantasy – a fantasy of universal belonging or worldliness.
Needell (1987: 164) notes that the actual space of the Ouvidor presented a similar

fantasy for its visitors: 'a place for the expression of a fantasy of cultural identification with the rest of the world'.

Yet, not all *cariocas* (people from or living in Rio) shared this fantasy. Needell describes the Ouvidor, not as a public space but as a meeting point for the city's privileged few. Trams linked the area to elite suburbs and residential areas. As writer Afranio Peixoto (1937: 183–4) observed at the time, the street acquired an uncanny private and intimate aspect:

> A narrow street where, on Saturdays, we would gather as if in a procession or a crowded church, seeing people bump into and greet each other. In that small colonial alleyway, everyone saw each other and they hugged one another tightly, like young love-struck things. There was an intimacy, a familiar aspect to the city in that communal salon and small corridor, where relatives saw and greeted one another, and planned things to do beyond that place.

The Ouvidor was a space where shoppers could find friends and meet loved ones, a familiar space, almost an extension of the salon society that had dominated colonial Brazil. It was on the Ouvidor that the first movie shows took place in Brazil. This is hardly surprising since cinema appeared 'as another foreign import', on the very same ships that carried imported goods into the country (Paranaguá 1985: 9). Cinema was quickly inscribed into the Ouvidor's broader social and cultural environment. Movies were shown in fashionable coffee shops, known as the *café concertos*, recreations of France's *café chantants*; and, in German Beer shops, giving rise to the *cinemas cervejarias*, and in *salões de novidades* – novelty salons, where they were exhibited next to other foreign technological inventions such as the phonograph, the electrograph and X Ray machines (Araújo 1976: 126).

The early films that *cariocas* were watching were characterized by what Tom Gunning (1986) has termed 'a cinema of attractions'. Unlike storytelling or narrative forms, the cinema of attractions was 'an exhibitionist cinema' based on an aesthetics of astonishment that appealed to the audience's fascination with the new technology (Gunning 1986: 57). Ana López (2000: 52) has observed that in Latin America, the 'aesthetics of astonishment was complicated by the ontological and epistemological status of the apparatus'. López argues that 'the cinematic attraction is attractive in and of itself and an import' (ibid.). Descriptions of the first movie shown in Brazil emphasize cinema's foreign and imported status as its main appeal. On 13 July 1896, for example, a journalist for the newspaper *A Notícia* described film as a medium that 'has recently been causing the most astonishing admiration in Paris and all of Europe' (cited in Ferreira 1986: 19). Another reviewer in *A Cidade do Rio* wrote: 'yesterday we assisted the inauguration of one of the most marvelous spectacles that is currently exciting audiences in the main European capitals' (ibid.). These commentators were more fascinated by 'cinema's ability to allow spectators to share and participate in the experience of a new medium that was exciting audiences elsewhere around the world' (López 2000: 52) than with the new technology itself.

The newspaper *Jornal do Commércio* in 1897 remarked on the capacity of movies 'to parade in front of our very eyes, in their exact dimensions, the Parisian boulevards, with their continual coming and going, men, women, children cars, buses, animals, everything' (cited in Araújo 1976: 9). As López (2000: 52) observed:

> With its *vistas* of sophisticated foreign cities and customs (ranging from Lumière's rather sophisticated workers leaving the factory and magnificent locomotives to Edison's scandalous kiss), the imported views could produce the experience of an accessible globality among the urban citizens . . . many of them less than a generation away from the old world.

In 1905, one Brazilian exhibitor, Paschoal Segreto, exploited cinema's international appeal by constructing his own version of Hale's Tours, which had attained popularity internationally. Hale's Tours placed spectators in the role of passengers with a screen displaying passing panoramas in exhibition venue which often replicated train carriages. Segreto dubbed his own tours – the *Estrada de ferro mundial* – 'the global railway', promising to take spectators on 'journeys around the world in 25 minutes'. Travel was paramount to early cinematic experience in Brazil, and film was imagined and marketed as a medium that could facilitate global journeys. These journeys were clearly 'an object of representation' and 'the most popular and developed of film' (Bruno 2002: 76). But they were also both object and subject informing the broader matrix of aesthetic experience – an experience of worldliness that linked Brazil and the rest of the world, along with the expansion of trade and commerce. Cinema thus developed within and articulated a new logic of circulation at the height of historical imperialism.

Cinematic images of distant civilized places seemed to fulfil the fantasy that progress was on course in Brazil. While this experience was both desirable and delightful, it also created a profound ambivalence and source of anxiety. 'The cinema's complex images of distance and otherness problematized the meaning of locality and self', as López (2000: 53) considers. And, whereas

> the cinema fed the national self confidence that its own modernity was in progress by enabling viewers to share and participate in the thrills of the experience of modernity as developed elsewhere. On the other hand, to do so, the national subject was also caught up in a dialectics of seeing: viewers had to assume the position of spectators and become voyeurs, rather than participants.
>
> (ibid.)

Consequently, the cinema of attractions in Latin America depended on an awareness of the film as image, and of the act of looking itself. It also produced a highly self-conscious form of spectatorship that was generated by and, in turn, reinforced a distance between the world on the screen and that of Brazil.

As Paulo Emílio Salles Gomes has pointed out, this distance was imbued in forms of spectatorship in quite practical ways. At its inception, 'cinema vegetated in Brazil both as a commercial activity generated towards the exhibition of foreign movies and as a local venture' (Salles Gomes 1996: 9). After 1906, the country experienced a boom in cinematic activities leading to what scholars have called the *belle-époque* of Brazilian cinema (1908–12): a golden age when domestic movies were preferred over foreign imports.[3] In 1907, author Joaõ do Rio observed: 'In every square of the city there are cinemas bringing together thousands and thousands of people' (cited in Araújo 1976: 205); and, a 1910 editorial from the magazine *Fon-Fon!* noted, 'in Rio the cinema has become part of the population's daily habits' (cited in Gonzaga 1996: 104). However, these testimonies reveal that the *Belle époque* of Brazilian cinema was not nation-wide but predominantly based in Rio.

RIO'S *BELLE ÉPOQUE*

Critics attribute this mushrooming of cinematic activity to the industrialization of electricity. In 1906, a reservoir was opened on the outskirts of Rio providing the electricity that promoted the growth of entertainment and leisure in the capital. The development of electricity was part of a wider programme of improvements begun in 1902 intended to 'modernize' the capital. They included a sanitation process aimed at eliminating epidemic diseases such as the plague, yellow fever and smallpox which rendered the capital insalubrious, particularly for foreign visitors. This period also saw a drastic reconstruction of Rio's infrastructure: the tight streets and alleyways which made the transfer of consumer products to and from the port so difficult were widened and extended, new boulevards, gardens and parks were built and colonial buildings were destroyed and replaced with modern structures. By 1904 the city's new morphology was complete and the new capital was officially unveiled with an inauguration ceremony on 15 November 1905, on the anniversary of the proclamation of the Republic. The new city was 'a monument' to Brazil's new identity, observed Needell (1987: 39).

This new identity was not, strictly speaking, Brazilian. The blueprint for Rio's facelift was the redesign of Paris in the 1850s, now known as Haussmanization, that transformed the French capital into what Walter Benjamin (1978) called the 'capital of the nineteenth century'. Rio's boulevards, gardens and plazas were conscious reproductions of those in Paris. The Monroe Palace (1906), The School of Fine Arts (1908), and the Municipal Theatre (1909), reproduced the architectural motifs and structures of French Eclecticism exemplified by the *École des Beaux Arts*. In fact, the Municipal Theatre was a virtual replica of the Paris Opera, designed by the *école*'s Charles Garnier. The reproduction of Paris in Brazil went as far as the importation of flowers and sparrows from France to replace local flora and fauna (Sevcenko 1989: 31).

Under the aegis of Napoleon III and his prefect of the Seine, Baron Georges Haussmann, the reforms of mid-nineteenth-century Paris set out to modernize its infrastructure. Paris represented not just a modern city, but a universal urban paradigm which could be replicated elsewhere. In Brazil the transcendence of

Haussmann's city articulated the global designs of the Republic, and the materiality of the built environment was a central expression of the new nation's desire to become part of the modern Western world. The centre of Brazil's new, sophisticated city was the Avenida Central, renamed Avenida Rio Branco in 1912 (see Figures 2.2, 2.3 and 2.4). Avenida Central was Rio's main artery, connecting different parts of the city to the port. The capital's new grandiose buildings, such as the Municipal Theatre, were there, making it what Needell (1987: 40) calls a 'showcase for civilization'. This echoes the views of scholars influenced by Walter Benjamin, such as T. J. Clark (1984) and Vanessa R. Schwartz (1997), who emphasize the spectacular aspects of Haussmann's redesign of the French capital. An emphasis on the visual underpins sociologist Gilberto Freyre's (1968) description of Rio's reforms in *The Mansions and the Shanties*, where he describes the reconstruction of the Brazilian capital as a process of *desasombramento* – of unshadowing. For Freyre, this 'unshadowing' was central to Rio's new structures: narrow alleyways were replaced with grand boulevards, literally opening the city up to the visual gaze.

The turn of the century also brought important developments to the popular press in Brazil: the introduction of phototypy, which enabled the reproduction of illustrations and pictures in magazines and newspapers. This promoted the publication of illustrated journals, such as *Illustração brasileira* (1900), *A notícia illustrada* (1901), *A avenida* (1903) and *Kosmos* (1904), all of which carried numerous pictures of the capital's reforms. The magazine *A avenida* was founded in honour of Rio's new Avenida Central, and dedicated all its pages to the new city, carefully documenting each stage of Rio's reconstruction with impressive pictures of new buildings and parks. The same period also saw the extensive

Figure 2.2
Avenida Central, Rio de Janeiro, Augusto Malta, c.1902.

Figure 2.3
Avenida Central, Rio
de Janeiro, Augusto
Malta, *c.*1904.

Figure 2.4
Avenida Central, Rio
de Janeiro, Augusto
Malta, *c.*1906.

Figure 2.5
Map of Rio de Janeiro
City Centre, 1912.

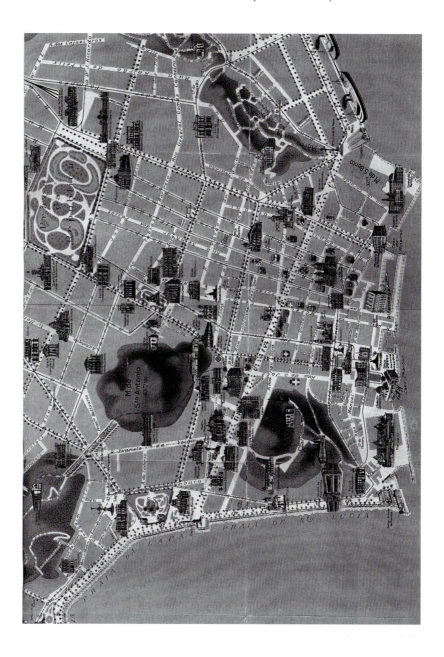

production of postcards and official photo albums by photographers Marc Ferrez
and Augusto Malta and the production by the municipal government of a new
genre of maps, known as monumental maps which carefully plotted Rio's visual
sites along its new boulevards. All of these visual forms played their part in
depicting Rio's new geography as a spectacular attraction, an object 'to be looked
at' (see Figure 2.5).

Cinema immediately became part of this new spectacular city. Exhibitors migrated from the older Rua do Ouvidor to the newer and more fashionable Avenida Central and at least 20 movie theatres opened there in 1906, creating a cinematic hub that would later be renamed *Cinelândia* (Araújo 1976: 24). Just as film became implanted in the new city, so filmmakers too played a part in constructing the capital's modern identity. Following the reconstruction of Rio, films rarely focused on iconographic exotic landscapes such as Corcovado or the Sugar Loaf. Tropical visions gave way to urban images as filmmakers turned their gaze towards Rio's streets. The city's changes also became an extremely popular subject for filmmakers, with films such as *Melhoramentos do Rio de Janeiro* (*The Improvements of Rio de Janeiro*, 1906) and *Erradicação da febre amarela no Rio de Janeiro* (*The Erradication of Yellow Fever in Rio de Janeiro*, 1909). Salles Gomes has proposed practical reasons as to why the cinematic lens focused on these new areas. The older streets were 'too narrow and dark to feature in films that required natural light' (Salles Gomes 1996: 40), suggesting an almost natural relationship between the movie camera and modern urban spaces.

The engagement between cinema and the new space of the city had important implications for the content and reception of film in Brazil. Spaces that were associated with the country's past were considered unsuitable for the cinema and abstracted from the new and modern identity to be projected to spectators. This abstraction was, itself, part of the reconstruction project. Reforms involved the destruction of the São Bento and Castelo hills – natural spaces were deemed an obstacle to modernization of the city – and the demolition of almost 600 colonial buildings. These were predominantly residential properties, and their displaced inhabitants, mainly blacks and former slaves, fled to shantytowns on the nearby hillsides. The new capital lacked any traces of the country's past – particularly its rural and slaveholding past. From its new and magnificent buildings to its flora and fauna, the capital was ironically devoid of features specific to the country's history. Modern Rio erased all links with the past, situating itself in 'a universal empty time' (Benjamin 1968).

Nicolau Sevcenko (1989: 38) points out that this process was matched by rigid urban strategies based on four key policies:

> The condemnation of the habits and customs connected to the memory of traditional society; the negation of any element of popular culture which disturbed the civilized image of the dominant society; a strict policy of expulsion of the popular classes from the centre of the city, available now for the exclusive use of the bourgeoisie strata and an aggressive cosmopolitanism profoundly identified with the Parisian lifestyle.

Popular customs and festivities connected to the memory of traditional society came under attack from the state. The marginal classes were outlawed from the city centre, which was reserved exclusively for the elite as Rio's new sweeping boulevards were policed for uncivilized vagrants and its new 'public' spaces were de-limited to those who complied with the constructed civilized image. The policing of streets and boulevards was an attempt to create, or recreate, the private and intimate environment that had characterized Ouvidor and colonial Brazil. This intimate public area depended on the opposition between modernity and tradition, civilization and barbarism, which became not only 'the cornerstone of intellectual debate' (Sevcenko 1989: 39), but also underpinned the foundations of the city and gave rise to the social and spatial segregation that still exists today.

With theatres located in the new centre, movie-going became an elite activity and filmmakers played their part in producing the social and spatial configurations of the city by portraying sanitized urban spaces. The movie camera became a tool for reproducing the civilizing project of the urban modernizing elite, disassociated from the barbarism of the national Others. If the myth of film's universalism had developed into class discourses elsewhere (Hansen 1990), it did not in Brazil, with slavery only recently abolished and traditional hierarchies and social and spatial divisions still in place. Although Rio's reforms were symbolic, as Needell (1987: 46) stresses, they also had the clear practical purpose of luring overseas commerce and a new white and European workforce to the tropics. In 1904, for example, one writer pointed out the essential role of the capital:

> The foreigner who disembarks here brings from his brief visit to our impoverished city a sad idea of all of our country. . . . To attempt to turn Rio de Janeiro into a modern comfortable and civilized city, then, is an undeniable and immediate necessity in our economic plight.
>
> (cited in Needell 1987: 46)

The reproduction of the capital was partly intended to transform it into a market-able commodity in order to attract foreign interest, and its depiction in maps, postcards, photo albums and films was intended to disseminate this commodity, not just nationally but internationally.

RIO'S TRANSITIONAL URBAN IDENTITY

Rio's attractions were not illustrated with images of tropical and exotic otherness, of a prodigious landscape waiting to be exploited, but as a modern city equal to any global metropolis. It was by subduing its prodigious and tropical nature into a more civilized construct that Rio was to be converted into a material object, a commodity. This strategy was clearly aimed at investors and immigrants who might otherwise shy away from 'exoticism', 'tropicalism' and difference. Despite its ornamental quality, this strategy can be judged to have been a success. European immigrants arrived in abundance, foreign investment soared and new foreign commercial firms all established themselves in Rio's new city centre.[4] This suggests that the urban image projected was mirrored by the people and investment it conjured up, not vice versa. Representation created the referent. The movie camera was clearly significant, both as a means of narcissistically projecting Rio's new, modern identity to its own urban citizens, and of fetishistically displaying it for others. While the ideological imperatives that underlined Rio's reconstruction were by no means benign, this belief in progress and modernity placed tradition and the old elite in an ambiguous position. The new commercial culture fostered an emerging entrepreneurial middle class whose desire for financial gain required them to cater to a larger public.

These ambiguities featured in the cinema as Brazilian filmmakers and exhibitors, unable to compete in an international arena dominated by superior European films, realized the financial advantages of developing the new medium as a popular national form of entertainment. They developed new tactics whereby the movies could both reproduce elite urban pretensions and incorporate established popular practices and histories. In 1906, exhibitors introduced new entrance prices. Holders of first-class tickets were entitled to the best seats in the house while second-class ticket holders were seated in the upper sections of the theatre. First-class ticket holders were additionally provided with pre- and post-show entertainment in sumptuous *salas de espera* or waiting rooms, complete with orchestras and refreshments. Access to the waiting rooms meant that these affluent spectators could avoid bumping into second-class spectators, either in the streets outside or within the movie theatre. These ticketing strategies led to segregated viewing practices that replicated those in the new city itself, but they also ensured that movie exhibitors could satisfy the elite classes while also catering for a broader popular audience. This led to the production of new kinds of films that managed to display the civilized city while drawing on popular cultural forms which exposed the contradictions of its spectacular image in a tropical setting.

By the time the new city was launched, spectators in Brazil were becoming used to what Gunning (1986: 63) has called 'transitional narratives', located between the cinema of attractions and fully fledged narratives.[5] Brazilian filmmakers blended urban vistas with popular culture.[6] Antonio Leal's 1909 film *Nas entranhas do morro do castelo* (*In the Belly of Castelo Hill*), for example, depicted Rio's reforms but it also drew upon urban legends that were circulating at the time about hidden treasures excavated during the city's reconstruction. Another film by Leal, made in 1908, *O comprador de ratos* (*The Buyer of Rats*), dealt with the campaign to eradicate yellow fever when the government announced that it would buy dead rats by the pound. The inhabitants of Rio's poor neighbourhoods developed a thriving industry, breeding rats to sell to the government. The practice was popularized in newspapers and cartoons and became the subject of a popular song, *O vendedor de ratos* (*The Rat Seller*). These new narrative films, like the cultural forms they drew upon, incorporated emerging urban spatial practices, through which marginalized classes negotiated their own transition to the new city.

At the heart of these transitional films lay the idiosyncrasy of reproducing a modern city in the context of underdevelopment, which soon gave rise to a genre of urban comedies popular between 1908 and 1912, known as *filmes de revista*. Júlio de Ferrez's 1908 film *Nhô Anastácio chegou de viagem* (*Mr Anastácio*

Arrived on a Trip), for example, narrates the misadventures of a country bumpkin visiting the monuments, parks and palatial buildings of the new city in the course of a mistaken identity love plot. Fiction is mixed with a tour of the capital's new sites and the film emerges as a travelogue, a cinematic translation of the monumental maps that charted Rio's spectacular spaces. *Zé Bolas* and *As Aventuras de Zé Caipira* (*The Adventures of Country José*) both made in 1908, repeated what was proving to be a highly successful formula, detailing the adventures of rural migrants in the new capital. The genre was named after Brazil's popular vaudeville theatre, known as the *teatro de revista*, which also relied for its comedy on the conflict between the traditional rural customs of their characters and modern Rio, with its Europeanized ways.

As Elias Thomé Saliba (2001) points out, the city–country dialectic ran across the spectrum of cultural production. By 1900, 25 per cent of Rio's population came from Brazil's rural north-east. These migrants were crucial to the development of a new urban mass culture and central to an emerging film spectatorship. Film-makers integrated their experiences in narratives and through extratextual practices by incorporating north-eastern music and songs performed live by popular singers standing behind the screen. The cinema became an important space for new migrants, presenting them with practices and traditions from their rural homelands and characters they could identify with, while allowing them the vicarious pleasure of laughing at the hillbilly's inappropriate ways in the new urban context. These transitional narratives, arguably, helped spectators negotiate their own passage from the country to the city.

López (2000: 65) believes that these comedic transitional narratives supported the discursive triumph of positivism, because they rendered the traditional, rural figure 'nostalgically obsolete, a cultural remnant willed into history, while the modernity of the city is presented as natural, inevitable and national'. However, they did so in a problematic way because they also offered metaphorical challenges to the urban ideal of Rio and the Republic. Despite their outward complicity, these films incorporated banned traditions, songs and dances to construct what Miriam Hansen (1990: 90) calls an 'alternative public sphere', one that functions not against official discourses but because of, and in spite of, them. This working against the grain was not exclusive to the cinema, as filmmakers were practising what literary critic Antonio Cândido (1995) and social anthropologist Roberto da Matta (1991) have termed a 'dialectic of roguery' – a Brazilian cultural ethos through which the marginalized use official and dominant discourses to their own advantage.

In the dialectic of roguery, the marginalized do not just make do, they manipulate and divert official discourses to expose order or disorder. This subversive tactic was crucial to urban film comedies where apart from the rural protagonist, the *dramatis personae* included a tableau of caricatures of other people familiar to audiences, particularly authority figures involved in constructing Rio's modern and European identity. While *Zé Bolas* focused on the urban escapades of a rural migrant, it also featured his encounters with politicians and Europeanized urban inhabitants. The film pokes fun at their superficiality in a ludic and irreverent attack on the civilized space of the city, satirizing the ineffectual activities of the proponents of Rio's new identity.

RIO'S URBAN GROWTH, ETHNICITY AND MASS CULTURE

The satire of politics and society was central to an expanding popular press. Film comedies had strong links to satirical political magazines published in Rio in the early 1900s. *Zé Bolas*, for example, was written and produced by writers responsible for the political-satirical magazine, *Careta*, that appeared in 1906. The film capitalized on the popularity of the magazine, and can be seen as an extension of it and, perhaps, also as an offshoot of a cultural practice popular at the time, the *jornal falado*, literally the spoken press, in which features were re-enacted live on stage for largely illiterate audiences. The growth of magazines such as *Careta* testify to the increasing politicization of mass culture. Francisco Foot Hardman (2002: 301) ties this growing political consciousness to the development of a new urban public, comprised not only of rural migrants but also of members of a new international workforce. Immigration to Brazil intensified following the birth of the Republic as a result of the government's attempt to attract a white industrial workforce. In 1890 alone, 106,819 international migrants arrived in Brazil, mainly from Europe, and many settled in the capital.

European immigrants played a crucial role in the development of mass cultural forms in Brazil. Indeed, the overwhelming majority of early filmmakers in Brazil were first-generation European immigrants. They had links to other filmmakers or distributors in Europe as well as in the US, and were thus able to secure a regular supply of imported 'vistas' for movie theatres in Rio. As noted above, these imported vistas catered to the worldly aspirations of Rio, but they also had a great appeal for immigrant communities for whom they carried particular affective meanings.

Many of the immigrants who settled in Rio at the beginning of the century were members of mutualist associations. In 1909, there were 438 mutualist associations in Rio alone with 282,937 members (Carvalho 2002: 143). These associations offered the kind of practical assistance later supplied by the welfare state and insurance companies as well as fulfilling important recreational functions. The centres staged plays, musical concerts, performances, song recitals and poetry readings which included food, drink, card games and competitions and movie shows. In 1898, for example, the newspaper *Gazeta de Notícias* noted that film exhibitor Cunha Sales had organized a 'great festival in honour of the Portuguese Club' (Araújo 1976: 105) which included a number of specially selected movies: *Desfile das carruagens na cidade do Porto* (*Processions of Carriages in Porto*), *As grandes touradas em Lisboa* (*The Great Bull Fights in Lisbon*) *Banhistas na praia de Belém* (*Bathers on the Beach at Belem*) and *Jardineiros Portugueses* (*Portuguese Gardeners*). The movies offered Brazilian spectators the opportunity of travelling the world in tune with the new *mundanismo*. In contrast to promoting a modern and civilized space devoid of past culture and tradition to the city's new immigrants, this new genre of films transported them back to their previous homes.

These cinematic journeys often incorporated extratextual cultural elements, especially music and song. The period saw the emergence of *filmes cantados*, literally sung films in which singers would perform standing behind the screen, a practice also adopted in the *filmes de revista* discussed earlier. Examples of such films are *La educanda do Sorrento* (1909), *Dueto da mascote* (1909), *La farfalle* (1909), *Salve aurora* (1910), *Si fossi* (1910), and *Carezze e bacci* (1910). Many of these films were recordings of European opera performances, and as Brazilian film critics (Araújo 1976; Salles Gomes 1996) have observed, they catered for the cultural and European pretensions of Rio's urban elite, yet they were also popular among immigrant audiences, especially Italians. Indeed, screenings were often supported by performances by Italian singers, such as Enzo Banino, Amica Peliser and the duet Santucci and Cataldi, present in Brazil as part of an extensive network of travelling performers and European troupes. The cinema's intersection of visual, textual and musical practices helped immigrant audiences forge their own links with past spaces and aided their transition to Rio.

The mediatory functions of film mirrored the role of the Rio mutualist associations and many were directly linked to them, recording social and recreational events. The film *Círcolo operário Italiano* made by Affonso Segreto in 1899 documented celebrations of the anniversary of Italy's unification. Other films, as Araújo (1976: 116) discusses, recorded political activities such as: *Círcolo Operário em São Paulo* (*Workers' Group in São Paulo*, 1899), *Largo de São Francisco por ocasiaõ de um meeting* (*São Francisco Square During a Meeting*, 1899), *Passagem do círcolo operário Italiano no largo de São Francisco de Paula* (*Demonstration of the Italian Workers' Group in São Francisco de Paula Square*, 1900), *Círcolo Italiano operário* (*Italian Workers Group*, 1910) and *Festa da união dei Italiani* (*Festival of the Italian Union*, 1911). Given the links immigrants had with other filmmakers and distributors internationally, these early political films likely travelled to other countries contributing to new political urban spaces.

Robert Stam (1997: 63) notes that many early political films featured Rio's black population, visually projecting a community that crossed racial boundaries. Other films that featured the city's black population were the *filmes carnavalescos* that documented Rio's carnival celebrations, such as *O carnaval da Avenida Central* (*Carnival on Central Avenue*, 1906) and *Pela vitória dos clubes carnavalescos* (*In Honour of the Victory of the Carnival Clubs*, 1909). These movies were also connected to Rio's new immigrant communities, particularly Neopolitan groups who also celebrated carnival, resulting in complex cultural affiliations and identities. Mixed social gatherings form the basis of the 1908 film *Os capadócios da cidade nova* (*The Imposters of the New City*) which showed the old Praça Onze, a square popular among blacks and Portuguese, Italian and Spanish immigrants. Neverthe-less, while blacks might have featured in some silent movies, 'Afro-Brazilians did not feature prominently in the symbolically white cinema of the first few decades of the century' (Stam 1997: 63), a reflection of the country's wider attempt to project a global and civilized identity that was, ultimately, seen as white.

One real-life event involving Rio's black community did capture the imagination of journalists and filmmakers. On 22 November 1910, João Candido, a black corporal, led a group of soldiers in a revolt against corporal punishment in what became known as the *Revolta da chiabata* (*The Whip Revolt*). The abused soldiers, largely black, commandeered several warships recently acquired from England. João Candido took control of the cruiser *Minas Gerais*, demanding an end to corporal punishment with its vestigial memories of slavery. The Republican government was at the mercy of the black soldiers and agreed to grant them amnesty if they returned the ships. The government then reneged on its promises, arresting the rebels and murdering many of them. The event generated widespread media interest. Magazines closely reported the events, carrying daily news of the mutiny and extensive photographic documentation. Filmmakers also reconstructed the event in movies such as *Revolta da esquadra* (*Squadron Revolt*, 1910) and *Revolta no Rio* (*Revolt in Rio*, 1910) and in 1912 Italian immigrant Carlos Lambertini made *A vida do cabo João Candido* (*The Life of João Candido*) after Candido had become a popular hero. The naval ministry confiscated the film, making it the first officially censored movie in Brazil.

The reconstruction of real-life events figured in other movies of the time, forging a genre known as *Filmes criminosos* – crime films. *Os estranguladores* (*The Stranglers*, 1908), *A mala sinistra* (*The Sinister Suitcase*, 1908), *Um drama na Tijuca* (*A Drama in Tijuca*, 1909), and *O crime da mala* (*The Suitcase Crime*, 1912) among others, restaged gory crimes that had already been extensively popularized by newspapers and magazines. Once again urban society was the focus of attention, but its gaze was turned away from the sanitized and ideal city centre and towards an underclass of criminals and outlaws.

Documentation of these events in both press and film gave the impression of a dangerous rise in crime, threatening the new and civilized image of Rio. Sidney Chalhoub relates the popularization of crime to a growing emphasis on the need to control and discipline a rapidly expanding urban society. Chalhoub (1986: 163), however, notes that popular crime stories often depicted criminals as unwitting victims in a society beset by unemployment and lack of housing. Criminality was linked to what was depicted as a wider illegality – predicated on the poor living conditions of increasingly marginalized people. What emerged was an ambiguity in popular attitudes towards crime. The criminal often benefited from this wave of sympathy, his acts of violence understood to flow from a wider structural violence or, as in João Candido's case, from old struggles.

Early narrative films in Brazil thus combined the spectacular depiction of urban space with popular narrative forms. In the process, movies helped to position spectators as modern subjects, able to negotiate urban society. Yet, by drawing on other cultural traditions, practices and forms of address, the films also interrogated the new space of the city, pointing to alternative trajectories within it.

NOTES

1 See, for example, David Clarke, ed., *The Cinematic City*, London: Routledge, 1997; James Donald, *Imagining the Modern City*, London: Athlone, 1999; Giuliana Bruno, *Streetwalking on a Ruined Map*, New Jersey: Princeton, 1993; and the special issue of *Wide Angle* on 'Cityscapes', 20, no. 1 (1998).

2 Unless otherwise noted, all translations from Portuguese language sources are my own.

3 See Vicente de Paula Araújo, *A Bela época do cinema brasileiro*; Paulo Emílio Salles Gomes, *Cinema: Trajetória no subdesenvolvimento*; Roberto Moura, 'A Bela época' (Primórdios – 1912), in Fernaõ Ramos, ed., *História do cinema brasileiro*, São Paulo: Art editora, pp. 13–20.

4 Britain's investments in Brazil rose from £37,407,300 between the years 1863 and 1888 to a staggering £112,774,433 between 1889 and 1914. For more on foreign investment in Rio during this period see Needell, *Tropical belle-époque*, pp. 39–40. Immigration also increased. In 1880 the city's census recorded a total of 30,000 immigrants living in Rio as opposed to 106,819 recorded in 1900. For more details see Sevcenko, *Literatura como missaõ*, p. 39.

5 Tom Gunning writes that after the decline of the 'cinema of attractions' around 1905, early narrative forms developed enabling filmmakers to experiment with a narrative film language that would become standardized as the 'Classical Hollywood narrative style' around 1915–17. This transitional period of more than a decade was volatile and ambivalent.

6 During the early days of Brazilian cinema, films were referred to as 'vistas'.

REFERENCES

Araújo, V. de P. (1976) *A Bela Época do Cinema Brasileiro*, São Paulo: Perspectiva.

Benjamin, W. (1968) 'Theses on the Philosophy of History', in H. Zohn (ed.) *Illuminations*, trans. H. Zohn, New York: Schocken Books, pp. 253–65.

—— (1978) 'Paris, Capital of the Nineteenth Century', in P. Demetz (ed.) *Reflections: Essays, Aphorismos and Autobiographical Writings*, trans. E. Jephcott, New York: Schocken Books, pp. 146–63.

—— (1983) *Charles Baudelaire: A Lyric Poet in the Era of High Capitalism*, trans. H. Zohn, London: Verso.

Broca, B. (1975) *A vida literária no Brasil – 1900*, Rio de Janeiro: José Olympio.

Bruno, G. (1993) 'Cultural Theory and the City Films of Elivira Notari', in *Streetwalking on a Ruined Map*, Princeton, NJ: Princeton University Press.

—— (2002) *Atlas of Emotion: Journeys in Art, Architecture and Film*, London: Verso.

Cândido, A. (1995) *On Literature and Society*, trans. and ed. H. Becker, Princeton, NJ: Princeton University Press.

Carvalho, J. M. de (2002) *Os bestializados: O Rio de Janeiro e a República que naõ foi*, São Paulo: Companhia das letras.

Chalhoub, S. (1986) *Trabalho, lar e botequim: O cotidiano dos trabalhadores no Rio de Janeiro da belle-époque*, São Paulo: Brasiliense.

Clark, T. J. (1984) 'Paris in the Art of Manet and his Followers', in *The Painting of Modern Life*, Princeton, NJ: Princeton University Press.

Clarke, D. (ed.) (1997) *The Cinematic City*, London: Routledge.

Donald, J. (1999) *Imagining the Modern City*, London: Athlone.

Elsaesser, T. and Barker, A. (eds) (1990) *Early Cinema: Space, Frame, Narrative*, London: British Film Institute.

Ferreira, P. R. (1986) 'Do Kinetoscópio ao omniographo', *Filme Cultura* 47: 14–22.

Foot Hardman, F. (2002) *Nem pátria, Nem patrão: Memória operária, cultura e literatura no Brasil*, São Paulo: Unesp.

Freyre, G. (1968) *The Mansions and the Shanties: The Making of Modern Brazil*, trans. H. de Onís, New York: Knopf.

Gomes, D. (1980) *Uma rua chamada Ouvidor*, Rio de Janeiro: Fundação Rio.

Gonzaga, A. (1996) *Palácios e poeiras:100 anos de cinema no Rio de Janeiro*, Rio de Janeiro: Funarte.

Gunning, T. (1986) 'The Cinema of Attractions: Early Film, its Spectator and the Avant-Garde', *Wide Angle* 8 (3–4): 63–70.

Hansen, M. (1990) 'Early Cinema – Whose Public Sphere?', in T. Elsaesser and A. Barker (eds) *Early Cinema: Space, Frame, Narrative*, London: British Film Institute, pp. 228–47.

López, A. M. (2000) 'Early Cinema and Modernity in Latin America', *Cinema Journal* 40 (1): 48–78.

Matta, R. da (1991) *Carnivals, Rogues and Heroes: An Interpretation of the Brazilian Dilemma*, Notre Dame: University of Notre Dame Press.

Needell, J. (1987) *A Tropical Belle-Époque: Elite Culture and Society in Turn-of-the Century Rio de Janeiro*, Cambridge: Cambridge University Press.

Paranaguá, P. A. (1985) *Cinema na America Latina: Longe de deus e perto de Hollywood*, Porto Alegre: L&PM Editores.

Peixoto, A. (1937) *As razões do coração*, São Paulo: Companhia Editora Nacional.

Saliba, E. T. (2001) 'A dimensão cómica da vida privada na República', in N. Sevcenko (ed.) *História da vida privada no Brasil*, São Paulo: Companhia das Letras, pp. 289–367.

Salles Gomes, P. E. (1996) *Cinema: Trajetória no subdesenvolvimento*, Dimensão São Paulo: Paz e Terra.

Schwartz, V. R. (1997) *Spectacular Realities: Early Mass Culture in Fin-de-Siècle Paris*, Berkeley, CA: University of California Press.

Sevcenko, N. (1989) *Literatura como missaõ: Tensões sociais e criaçaõ cultural na Primeira República*, Dimensão São Paulo: Brasiliense.

Shiel, M. and Fitzmaurice, T. (eds) (2001) *Cinema and the City: Film and Urban Society in a Global Context*, Oxford: Blackwell.

Stam, R. (1997) *Tropical Multiculturalism: A Comparative History of Race in Brazilian Cinema and Culture*, Durham, NC: Duke University Press.

FILMOGRAPHY

As aventuras de Zé Caipora (*The Adventures of Country José*) (1908) dir. Antonio Serra, Photo-Cinematographica Brasileira.

Banhistas na praia de Belém (*Bathers on the Beach at Belem*).

Os capadócios da cidade nova (*The Imposters of the New City*) (1908) dir. Antonio Leal, Photo-Cinematographica Brasileira.

O carnaval da Avenida Central (*Carnival on Central Avenue*) (1906).

Círcolo Italiano operário (*Italian Workers Group*) (1910) dir. Joaõ Stamato.

Círcolo operário em São Paulo (*Workers' Group in São Paulo*) (1899) dir. Afonso Segreto.

Largo de São Francisco por ocasião de um meeting (*São Francisco Square During a Meeting*) (1899) dir. Afonso Segreto.

O comprador de ratos (*The Buyer of Rats*) (1908) dir. Antonio Leal, Photo-Cinematographica Brasileira.

O crime da mala (*The Suitcase Crime*) (1912) dir. Francisco Serrador.

Desfile das Carruagens na cidade do Porto (*Processions of Carriages in Porto*).

Um drama na Tijuca (*A Drama in Tijuca*) (1909) dir. Antonio Serra, Photo-Cinematographica Brasileira.

Erradicação da febre amarela (*The Eradication of Yellow Fever in Rio de Janeiro*) (1909).

Os estranguladores (*The Stranglers*) (1908) dir. Antonio Leal, Photo-Cinematographica Brasileira.

Festa da união dei Italiani (*Festival of the Italian Union*) (1911) dir. Joaõ Stamato.

As grandes touradas em Lisboa (*The Great Bull Fights in Lisbon*).

Jardineiros portugueses (*Portuguese Gardeners*).

A mala sinistra (*The Sinister Suitcase*) (1908) dir. Antonio Leal, Photo-Cinematographica Brasileira.

Melhoramentos do Rio de Janeiro (*The Improvements of Rio de Janeiro*), (1906) dir. Antonio Leal.

Nas entranhas do Morro do Castelo (*In the Belly of Castelo Hill*) (1909) dir. Antonio Leal, Photo-Cinematographica Brasileira.

Nhô Anastácio chegou de viagem (*Mr Anastácio Arrived on a Trip*) (1908) dir. Júlio Ferrez.

Passagem do círcolo operário Italiano no Largo de São Francisco de Paula (*Demonstration of the Italian Workers' Group in São Francisco de Paula Square*) (1909) dir. Afonso Segreto.

Pela vitória dos clubes carnavalescos (*In Honour of the Victory of the Carnival Clubs*) (1909).

Revolta da esquadra (*Squadron Revolt*) (1912).

Revolta no Rio (*Revolt in Rio*) (1912).

A vida do cabo João Candido (*The Life of João Candido*) (1912) dir. Carlos Lambertini.

Zé Bolas (*José Bolas*) (1908) dir. Eduardo Leite, Photo-Cinematographica Brasileira.

Chapter 3: Visualizing the Urban Masses

Modern Architecture and Architectural Photography in Weimar Berlin

Sabine Hake

This essay examines the photographic representation of Erich Mendelsohn's building, Mossehaus (1922), and its transformation into an icon of Weimar modernism in architectural publications, photo-books and the illustrated press. In so doing, it sheds new light on the mediations between the social and the spatial that implicate photography in the ideologies of the urban. As will be argued, these ideologies were especially pronounced in the representation of the buildings and urban projects associated with *Neues Bauen*. But if the new architecture was perceived as an expression of modern society, and the big city as the home of the masses, what can we say about the role of photography in realigning the social and the spatial imagination in accordance with the technologies of massification? More specifically, what was the role of these mass-produced images in introducing new definitions of urban culture, in advancing alternative notions of social class, and in providing a visual vocabulary and perceptual matrix for the New Berlin? These are some of the questions that animate the following reflections on Mossehaus and the contribution of architectural photography to the changing topographies of class.

Bertolt Brecht (2000: 164) once famously said 'that the "simple reproduction of reality" says less than ever about that reality. A photograph of the Krupp works or of the AEG yields almost nothing about these institutions. Reality as such has slipped into the domain of the functional'.[1] And in a critical review of New Vision photography, Walter Benjamin (2003a: 775) asserted that photography 'can no longer record a tenement block or a refuse heap without transfiguring it. Needless to say, photography is unable to convey anything about a power station or a cable factory other than, "What a beautiful world!"'.[2] Having identified the false claims on the real made in the name of photography, Brecht and Benjamin probably would have said the same about any photograph of Mossehaus, the headquarters of the Mosse publishing company and one of Erich Mendelsohn's most famous buildings. In the visual archives of Weimar Berlin, such individual images – of famous buildings, streets and squares – have come to serve as conduits to an urban culture romanticized in the myth of 'the golden twenties', theorized in reflections on urban subjectivity and Weimar flânerie, and scrutinized in numerous studies on German mass culture and modernity. But how can we move beyond the indeterminacy of the image, as diagnosed by Brecht, and gain access to its meanings within a specific social and cultural context? How can we avoid the aestheticizing effects observed by Benjamin and consider formal qualities as part of a broader cultural shift toward vision and visuality? And in what ways must we link the profound changes in the organization of urban life and the structure of class society to the new cult of surfaces associated with modern entertainment and consumer culture and the surrender to visual spectacle brought about by new visual mass media such as photography and film?

As I hope to show on the following pages, the photographic representation of the physical structures that constitute a big city offers revealing insights into the ways a society imagines itself: through its definitions of public and private space; through its organization of housing, commerce and industry; and through its attitudes toward tradition, innovation and change. But no photograph of the big city exists in isolation; it is also part of an extended dialogue – carried out across different art forms, media technologies and interpretive registers – about that which remains inaccessible to direct representation: the underlying structure of urban society which, in the divided political landscape of Weimar Berlin, invariably means class society. As soon as we approach the individual photograph through the conditions of its emergence and expose it to the kind of semiotic analysis of cultural material described by Clifford Geertz (1973: 3–32) as 'thick description', we can retrace the processes of inscription that are of particular relevance for understanding architecture's overdetermined function as a symbol of modern mass society.

Accordingly, the following case study of Mossehaus illustrates how the photographic representation of one particular building can be used to gain access to the historical process through which the meaning of photographs was, in fact, established and continuously revised. But what made the photographs of modern buildings so important to the self-understanding of post-war German society and the self-representation of Berlin as the quintessential German metropolis? In what ways did photography contribute to the visual iconography of massification? What was the role of photography in promoting the aesthetic visions and social utopias of *Neues Bauen* (New Building), the architectural movement spearheaded by Bruno Taut, Walter Gropius, Mies van der Rohe and Erich Mendelsohn?[3] In what ways did photography contribute to the self-representation of the New Berlin, that ambitious programme of rationalist city-planning initiated by Martin Wagner during his tenure as building councillor? These are some of the questions that animate the following remarks on the photographic representation of modern architecture as a symbol of modern mass society. Using Mossehaus as a case study, I proceed in a diachronic and synchronic fashion. After a brief discussion of the hidden affinities between modern architecture and architectural photography, I focus on the historical circumstances, cultural practices and artistic interests that contributed to the elevation of Mossehaus to an icon of Weimar modernity. As I will argue, the image of Mossehaus allowed for a visualization of the future of the metropolis as the home of the modern masses; but it also validated the perspective of the creative individual as personified by the modern architect and photographer.

MODERN ARCHITECTURE AND PHOTOGRAPHY

Critical awareness of the precarious nature of meaning in photography must be considered a distinguishing mark of Weimar photography. Nowhere can we see the contingent nature of photography more clearly at work than in the photographic representation of the German capital. During the 1920s, Weimar Berlin evolved into a laboratory for new ways of seeing, with film and photography spearheading the mechanization of perception diagnosed through such diverse terms as 'the shock of the new' and 'the snapshot quality of things'. The artistic developments initiated by New Vision photography, especially in photomontage and photo collage; the growing reliance of the illustrated press on photo reportages and photo essays; and the popular appeal of photo-books with their evocative captions and commentaries, corroborate a much-discussed fact of Weimar visual culture: namely, that photographs needed texts in order to be understood. In the mainstream illustrated magazines, Friedrich Seidenstücker, Hans Casparius and countless lesser press photographers chronicled the rituals of daily life in the modern metropolis and trained their lenses on the newest social group, the white-collar workers, to take over the streets. Meanwhile Egon Erwin Kisch and a corps of anonymous worker photographers provided photo reportages to the left-wing *Arbeiter Illustrierte Zeitung* that uncovered the sharp class divisions in German society. Committed to the project of New Vision, Laszlo Moholy-Nagy and Otto Umbehr (Umbo) explored the spectacle of the crowd and the mysteries of the street through the technical possibilities of the camera. Meanwhile, old-school Berlin photographers such as Max Missmann, Waldemar Titzenthaler and others continued to portray buildings and streets with the sense of order and stability that had prevailed in the pre-war years. However, as that order was dissolving, even the static order of buildings could no longer be represented without the discursive apparatus that subsequently made architectural photography a particularly powerful tool in the social imaginary of Weimar society.

Under these conditions, Weimar photography did much more than establish a social typology and urban iconography. Photographers contributed actively to the making of the urban masses as a discursive and aesthetic phenomenon and established the framework for the emergence of a homogeneous white-collar society. Instead of retracing this process through the social typologies established by Seidenstücker or the critical interventions made by Kisch, my discussion focuses on the visualization of mass society through one of its main locations and central tropes: urban architecture. With their respective perceptual registers, architecture and photography played an essential part in the social and spatial imagination of historical change. The images of the New Berlin disseminated in daily newspapers, illustrated magazines, architectural journals and art books trained new modes of perception and aesthetic sensibilities and explored new forms of sociability, community and collectivism. The progressive political commitments of the architects associated with *Neues Bauen* linked their Berlin-based projects – from the public housing estates on the periphery to the office high rises in the old centre – to the rationalized forms of living regarded by many, including Wagner himself, as socialism without revolution. Not surprisingly, photographing buildings such as Mossehaus meant participating in a highly contentious debate: about the ideology of architectural form, about architecture as an agent of social change, and about the metropolis as the home of the modern masses.

The photographers, both known and unknown, who captured the spirit of the New Berlin provided Weimar contemporaries with a material representation of their future, with the individual building treated as an extension of the new mass individual and a visualization of the new body politic. Translating spatial elements into visual terms, they made visible the social utopias of Weimar society, thus completing the cycle of conception, construction and representation on which *Neues Bauen* depended. In recognition of the various contexts that constituted Weimar Berlin as a photographic corpus, we must approach this visualization of mass society through the three photographic practices – photo reportage, art photography and architectural photography – which, from the beginning, defined the form and function of city photography. Likewise we must read these images through the corresponding institutional practices – the illustrated press, the art establishment and the architectural profession – that determined their discursive functions more than any particular artistic influence. All three sets of practices aligned the urban experience with specific modes of presentation: the illustrated magazines through image–text relations that anchored photographic meaning in the larger narratives of Weimar mass culture and modernity; the art books through formal techniques that transformed the metropolis into a laboratory of new sensations, experiences and identities; and the architectural publications through critical readings that turned modernist architecture into an object of aesthetic appreciation and social transformation.

Because of the overriding concern with representation and representability, most photographers of the New Berlin adhered to a realist aesthetic, and that despite growing awareness of its aesthetic limitations and epistemological pitfalls. Photographic realism offered the (illusory) promise of immediacy in a predominantly literary culture haunted by the crisis of language and the decline of literature as a master discourse. However, assuming this function meant compensating for the indeterminacy of the image by adding captions or texts and overcoming its singular perspective through the multiperspectivism of photo montage and photo collage. It was in this context that modern architecture, as an overdetermined trope of massification, provided the materials, as it were, through which to analyse the relationship between the social and the spatial and thus make visible the process of massification.

Modernist buildings have been an integral part of the photographic self-representation of Weimar Berlin from the very beginning, and this is no coincidence. The public perception of *Neues Bauen* depended to a large degree on the presentation of its most famous buildings in illustrated magazines, cultural journals, photo-books, and, to a lesser degree, in feature films. Part of the increasing mediatization of modern life, architectural photography played a key role in advertising *Neues Bauen* as the most ambitious project of social change. Making sense of the metropolis as the home of the modern masses meant presenting architectural interventions and innovations as the preconfiguration, in formal terms, of more fundamental social changes. Photographers turned their attention to the static order of stone, glass, concrete and steel; but in showcasing new buildings, they also reflected on the much more dynamic (and elusive) architecture of social groups and classes. Through lighting, contrast and frame composition, they transformed Weimar Berlin into an object of aesthetic appreciation, visual pleasure and cultural consumption. This highly mediated iconography of the New Berlin not only trained new ways of seeing and envisioning the metropolis. By assuming the photographic point-of-view, literally and figuratively speaking, Weimar city-dwellers learned to equate the images of a city-in-progress with the dream of a future society unburdened by economic and social determinants.

SHOOTING MOSSEHAUS

During the 1920s, the streamlined façade of Mossehaus emerged as one of the most recognizable icons of Weimar modernism, a symbol of the new spirit of mobility, functionality and adaptability and hence a key site in the visual imaginary of an emerging white-collar society. Photographed for tourist guides and photo-albums, discussed in architectural surveys and cultural magazines, and adapted as a trademark by the company's advertising business, Mossehaus in 1927 was one the few new buildings to be included in Walter Ruttmann's famous *Berlin – die Symphonie der Großstadt* (*Berlin, Symphony of the Big City*, 1929).[4] Two years later, Mossehaus became the only individual building chosen to represent the New Berlin in all three popular photo-books about Weimar Berlin: Mario von Bucovich's *Berlin* (1928), Sasha Stone's *Berlin in Bildern* (*Berlin in Pictures*, 1929), and Laszlo Willinger's *100 × Berlin* (*Berlin One Hundred Times*, 1929).

But what distinguishes Erich Mendelsohn's Mossehaus from, say, Emil Fahrenkamp's equally unique Shellhaus? A first clue can be found in the historical events that made the façade renovation necessary in the first place. Located on the corner of Jerusalemer Straße and Schützenstraße in the famous *Zeitungsviertel* (newspaper district), Mossehaus was the headquarters of the Berlin-based publishing company Mosse. The newspaper district had seen plenty of street fighting during the revolutionary uprisings in the first half of January 1919, an indication also of the central role of media conglomerates such as Scherl, Ullstein and Mosse in sustaining the precarious balance between democratizing tendencies and imperial power structures durig the Wilhelmine Empire. Spartacists had taken over the editorial offices of the *Berliner Tageblatt*, the influential daily newspaper founded by Rudolf Mosse in 1871. In response, government troops had surrounded the armed revolutionaries and, with the help of considerable fire power, regained control of this highly symbolic place in the city's topography of power. The price to be paid for this victory of law and order? A heavily-damaged building that required major repairs to an ornate neo-Renaissance sandstone façade completed in 1903 by Cremer & Wolffenstein.[5]

Confirming Manfredo Tafuri's (1976: 100) damning remark that Germans in 1918/19 chose 'architecture rather than revolution', the Weimar Republic was founded on a precarious compromise between the newly empowered Social Democrats and the old political and military elites. Soon after order was restored in the capital, Hans Lachmann-Mosse, the son-in-law of the company's founder, approached the architect Erich Mendelsohn to come up with a design that would express Mosse's identity as a liberal, progressive publishing house more adequately than the old historicist façade. Lachmann-Mosse, who had a personal interest in modern art, chose the young Mendelsohn after seeing a photograph of the Einstein Tower in the *Berliner Tageblatt*.[6] The Mosse commission marked the beginning of a spectacular career that made Mendelsohn one of the most respected new architects working in the Berlin of the 1920s. Mendelsohn and Mosse-Lachmann, both of whom belonged to the city's German-Jewish liberal bourgeoisie, continued to collaborate on several other architectural projects until the world economic crisis and the rise of anti-Semitism and National Socialism put an end to their endeavours (Mendelssohn 1982: 398–401). While a series of bad business decisions forced Lachmann-Mosse in 1932/3 to sell his almost bankrupt company to Max Winkler's infamous Cautio GmbH, Mendelsohn found himself increasingly marginalized within the German architectural establishment and, in 1933, had no choice but to leave Berlin, first for Istanbul and Tel Aviv, and eventually for Southern California (James 1997: 88–102).

Under the circumstances, replacing Mossehaus's damaged historicist front with a modernist exterior was a highly symbolic act that required specific strategies of mediation and integration. Here Mendelsohn, together with assistant Richard Neutra, came up with a highly original solution: he used a protruding entrance canopy and a three-storey entrance bay of curving window bands to create the distinct curved corner that would soon become the distinguishing mark of his department stores and office buildings. Three additional floors ended in a roof line reminiscent of an ocean liner, another characteristic feature of Mendelsohn's contribution to what is often referred to as the functionalist style. Contemporaries hailed the aerodynamic design as a perfect expression of the modern cult of movement, dynamism and functionality. The black ceramic tiles of the cornice and the shiny window bands only heightened this effect, as did the clear simple lines that translated the acceleration of urban life, as symbolized by the shift from pedestrians to motorists as the paradigmatic urban subjects, into the building's rhythmic order of horizontals and verticals.

The transformation of Mossehaus into an icon of Weimar modernity must be examined within two equally important developments, the erasure of the memories of war and revolution through the cult of surface phenomena and the promotion of white-collar diversions and mentalities by the powerful culture industry.

During the first days of the uprisings in January 1919, images of the revolution made it onto the cover pages of most daily newspapers and illustrated supplements. For obvious reasons, the street fighting in the newspaper district and, in later issues, the destruction of Mosse's editorial offices was given particular attention. In all cases, selecting the right image involved choosing the right perspective. Thus on the cover of *Weltspiegel* (1919), the illustrated supplement to the *Berliner Tageblatt*, the uprisings were depicted from the point-of-view of the government troops, with the heading 'Berlin under the sign of terror' establishing the soldiers as the legitimate defenders of a terrified populace (see Figure 3.1).

Figure 3.1
Street fighting in the newspaper district, *Weltspiegel* 2/3, 1919, front page.

By contrast, the few independent photographers who, like Willy Römer (1984: 16), spent those fateful January days on the side of the Spartacists took his photographs from inside Mossehaus, a choice that clearly shows his solidarity with the insurgents (see Figure 3.2).[7] Interestingly, on the tenth anniversary of the occupation of the newspaper district, several illustrated magazines reprinted these dramatic images from 1919, presumably in order to highlight the difference between the chaos of the immediate post-war years and the political and economic stability achieved during the mid-1920s.[8] However, the juxtaposition of past failures and present achievements also brought back the spectre of revolution: this time through the images of a class-conscious urban proletariat and radicalized Communist Party marching on the streets of Berlin. In the same year, *Der rote Stern*, the new illustrated supplement of the KPD newspaper *Die rote Fahne*, reprinted the above-mentioned Römer photograph of armed revolutionaries seeking cover behind rolls of newspaper: a clear indication that the political conflicts of the pre-war period had not been resolved.[9]

Between these two pivotal moments in the photographic history of Weimar Berlin, the Mendelsohn building was established as an easily recognizable symbol for the Mosse concern and the liberal, cosmopolitan spirit of its signature publications. Their stories on modern architecture and urban life gave readers the opportunity to become active participants in the convergence and urban consciousness and white-collar mentality. The *Weltspiegel*, the biweekly illustrated supplement of the *Tageblatt*, regularly published photo reportages that, in the style of 'On the Roofs of Berlin' or 'Witnesses of the Night', celebrated white-collar society as a valid alternative to the traditional class divisions.[10] Self-serving

Figure 3.2
Street fighting in the newspaper district, Willy Römer, *Januarkämpfe Berlin 1919*, Berlin: Dirk Nishen Verlag, 1984.

reportages on the pleasures of window-shopping, bar-hopping, and people-gazing coexisted with more critical reportages on the infamous 'rental barracks' on Ackerstraße and other typical working-class settings.[11] Unlike the more conventional illustrated supplements, *Weltspiegel* also featured several photo essays on *Neues Bauen* in Berlin, from the public housing estates in Zehlendorf and the planned modernization of Potsdamer Platz and Alexanderplatz to the Karstadt department store on Hermannplatz and the Wernerwerk in the Siemensstadt; throughout, the work of Mosse's house architect was featured prominently (e.g., in a piece on Herpich Furriers on Friedrichstraße). Elaborate photo reportages on the annual Radio Exhibition (after 1924), the World Advertising Congress in 1928, and the World Trade Week in 1932 took advantage of the close affinities between the city as tourist attraction and exhibition space and the illustrated magazine as a training ground for distinctly urban sensibilities.

The Mosse publishing house showed a remarkable understanding of the functioning of the culture industry when it chose the Mendelsohn façade to present itself as a modern corporation and cultural institution. From 1923 on, a minimalist graphic rendition of the corner design served as a trademark for the company's profitable advertising business; sometimes Mosse also used a wide-angle shot that emphasized the building's similarities with an ocean liner (see Figure 3.3). The synergies between mass publishing and modern architecture extended even to the marketing of Mendelsohn as house architect and house author. Promoting the architect's vision of modernity became synonymous with providing new designs for living for the typical Mosse readers: the new technical and managerial elites and the large and diverse group of white-collar workers. Not surprisingly, Mosse published two of Mendelsohn's books and produced the first survey of his career, *Gesamtschaffen des Architekten* (1930, *The Architect's Complete Works*); all of these books were advertised in illustrated supplements such as *Weltspiegel*.

The significance of photography in increasing public awareness of architecture as a collective art form is also evident in Mendelsohn's own sojourns into criticism and photography, not least because of their discursive function in establishing the political significance of *Neues Bauen*. First the architect published *Amerika: Bilderbuch eines Architekten* (Mendelsohn 1993 [1926], *America: The Picture Book of an Architect*), a photographic travelogue of his 1924 visit to the United States that featured his photographs as well as the uncredited work of others, including travel companion Fritz Lang.[12] Working with light instead of glass, the architect-turned-photographer relied on symmetrical frame composition and graphic chiaroscuro effects to celebrate the modernist monumentality of New York skyscrapers and reveal the functionalist beauty of grain elevators in the Midwest. Mendelsohn again turned to photography when putting together an international survey of modern architecture, programmematically titled *Russland – Europa – Amerika* (1929), that places contemporary European culture between the alternatives of Americanization and Bolshevization. The juxtaposition of 'Russia and America, the collective and the individual, . . . and of America and Russia, the material and the spiritual' (Mendelsohn 1929: n.p.),[13] subsequently establishes

Figure 3.3
Mossehaus logo.

modern architecture as the artistic and social practice where the demands of individuality and collectivity could, in fact, be articulated and mediated. More specifically, it is the German movement of *Neues Bauen* which, for Mendelsohn, opens up a third way between capitalism and communism, an argument made in the book through its effective combination of images and texts.

'No more reading! Looking!' declared a New Objectivity pamphlet, asserting the inherent superiority of the image as an instrument for capturing and mastering modern urban life (Molzahn 1928). *Neues Bauen* would never have attracted such public interest and acquired such symbolic capital without its photographic reproduction on the pages of cultural journals, illustrated supplements, and, not to forget, trade publications. Familiarity with the newest architectural styles became an essential part of modern consciousness and a distinguishing trait of the educated city-dweller. But the transformation of building into visual icons also brought a growing dependence on writing as a necessary element in positioning *Neues Bauen* within the contemporary debates on modernity, urbanism and mass society. Literalization, the anchoring of photographic meaning through short captions or longer texts, was considered the most effective way of containing visual indeterminacy and ambiguity. Following Benjamin's call for 'the literalisation of the conditions of life',[14] Mendelsohn often relied on short texts in fixing the meaning of his buildings (Benjamin 2003b: 527). In fact, *Das Gesamtschaffen eines Architekten* presents Mossehaus twice, first on a film strip-like design placed alongside what many consider his most important essay on function and dynamism in architecture, and later in a narrow frame that showcases the distinct corner design in profile (see Figure 3.4). Here Mendelsohn's (1930: 28) comments link the building's perfect balancing of verticals and horizontals to the interplay of movement and standstill in the choreography of big city life:

> Just as the overall expression visibly echoes the rapid tempo of the street, the movement intensifying to an extreme toward the corner, at the same time, through the balance of its powers, it tames the nervousness of the street and

Figure 3.4
Mossehaus, in Erich
Mendelsohn, *Das
Gesamtschaffen des
Architekten: Skizzen
Entwürfe Bauten*, Berlin:
Rudolf Mosse, 1930, 28.

**DIE INTERNATIONALE ÜBEREINSTIMMUNG
DES NEUEN BAUGEDANKENS   ODER
DYNAMIK UND FUNKTION**

1923. VORTRAG IN „ARCHITECTURA ET AMICITIA", AMSTERDAM

Vor drei Jahren sprach ich hier über: „Das Problem einer neuen Baukunst."
Was damals, unmittelbar nach Krieg und Revolution, utopisches Gesicht und einzelner Glaube schien, ist heute allgemeines Problem geworden. — Was damals der jüngeren architektonischen Entwicklung als Problem entnommen wurde, tritt heute vielseitig als Forderung auf. — Was damals als gesetzmäßige Forderung aufgestellt wurde, ist heute schon sichtbare Übereinstimmung. Die Übereinstimmung des neuen Baugedankens, die Sie aus den mir zur Verfügung stehenden Produktionsergebnissen aller Länder ersehen werden, ist auf ihre allgemeingültigen Voraussetzungen zu untersuchen und die Verschiedenheiten ihrer zeitgemäßen Ergebnisse nach Möglichkeit auf den gleichen Nenner zu bringen. Diese vermeintliche Übereinstimmung schlechtweg „international" zu benennen, ist mehr eine begriffliche Bequemlichkeit als ein Gesinnungsdokument. — Im Gegenteil erscheint es in einer politisch so gespannten Zeit fast als frivol, den Beziehungen unter den einzelnen Staaten irgendeine gleichgerichtete Übereinstimmung unterstellen zu wollen. — Wie denn der Begriff der Internationalität in der Geschichte der Völker immer nur auftritt, wenn ihre struktiven Bindungen vernichtet sind und elementare Wehen die Dringlichkeit einer neuen, ursprünglichen Einstellung anzeigen. So gesehen, ist auch für uns eine Beschränkung ausschließlich auf die architektonischen Grundlagen nicht am Platz. Denn nur aus der Gesamterscheinung der Lebensformen, nur aus den Tatsachen der gesamten Wirklichkeit kann eine einzelne von ihnen ohne Gefahr der Kurzsichtigkeit und Eigenliebe herausgehoben werden. Wir stehen hart an der Wirklichkeit, sind also gezwungen, ihr Maximum auf uns zu nehmen. Wir Menschen von heute fürchten uns nicht davor. Wir ziehen gern die letzten Konsequenzen, um so schnell, so gründlich wie möglich zum Ziel zu kommen. — Große Staaten zerfallen in ihre Komponenten.

the passers-by. . . . By dividing and channelling traffic, the building stands, despite its tendency toward movement, as an immovable pole in the agitation of the street.[15]

Celebrating the modernist building as a work of art required its clear separation from the historical cityscape through framing, cropping, or masking. At the same time, such decontextualization called for extensive recontextualization within the aesthetic projects of *Neues Bauen*. The visual presentation of Mossehaus in the two most important book publications on *Neues Bauen* published during the Weimar years, Elisabeth M. Hajos's and Leopold Zahn's *Berliner Architektur 1919 bis 1929* (1929, *Berlin Architecture 1919–29*) and Heinz Johannes's *Neues Bauen in Berlin* (1931, *New Building in Berlin*) attests to these underlying dilemmas and confirms their origins in the revolutionary days of January 1919. In *Neues Bauen in Berlin*, whose Bauhaus cover design and sans serif typography suggest uncompromising commitment to modernism as a way of life, the Mendelsohn building is photographed from the opposite street corner, with the streamlined corner in the centre axis and the two symmetrical flight lines highlighted as its most significant features (see Figure 3.5). The one-point perspective and the converging diagonals integrate the building into the perimeter block as a powerful symbol of homogenization and standardization. Consequently, it is left to the accompanying text to ascertain how the building rises above the forces of levelling and assert its power as a work of art. In the words of Johannes:

> Expansion of the old publishing house and modernization of the corner, built during the revolutionary triumphs of the early post-war years. A new spirit (*Gesinnung*) is searching for expression. Forcefully the streaming masses of the new addition envelop the ossified façade of an exhausted eclecticism.
>
> (Johannes 1931: 16)

Using the same photograph of Mossehaus as Johannes, Hajos and Zahn, in *Berliner Architektur 1919 bis 1929*, offer a slightly different reading:

> The protruding ceramic ledge, which separates the old building from the new, sharply moves toward the corner, falls down and lands in the energetic four-meter wide canopy over the entrance. The building is no longer a passive observer of the cars driving by, of the ebb and flow of traffic; it has become a receiving, participating element of movement.
>
> (Hajos and Zahn 1996 [1929])

Where agency was once the prerogative of social classes, Hajos and Zahn suggest, the modernist building now assumes their place, as the materialization of a more democratic, egalitarian society. Where revolutionary masses once fought the forces of the reaction, Johannes implies, Mossehaus remains the vessel that preserves their revolutionary energy in the formal vocabulary of functionalism.

Figure 3.5
Mossehaus, in Heinz
Johannes, *Neues Bauen in
Berlin: Ein Führer mit 168
Bildern*, Berlin: Deutscher
Kunstverlag, 1931, 16.

BERLIN SW   **16**

12. MOSSEHAUS (Gebäude des Berliner Tageblatts)   **1921**
Jerusalemer Straße
Architekt: Erich Mendelsohn, Mitarbeiter: Arch. Richard Neutra und Bildhauer
R. P. Henning.

Aufstockung des alten Verlagsgebäudes und Neugestaltung der Ecke, entstanden
im revolutionären Ringen der ersten Nachkriegsjahre.
Eine neue Gesinnung sucht nach neuem Ausdruck.
Gewaltsam umspannen die strömenden Massen des neuen Baukörpers die
erstarrte Fassade eines übermüdeten Eklektizismus.

Confirming the identification of *Neues Bauen* with the disembodied gaze
of the urban masses, most architectural publications do not even identify their
photographers; the credits given to Sasha Stone or Laszlo and Lucia Moholy-Nagy
in Wagner's journal *Das Neue Berlin* (1929) are truly an exception here. Instead,
all attention is focused on the building as the expression of an individual's artistic
will. As a rule, photographs are presented together with elevations, cross-sections
and floor plans, all of which treat the new building as a self-contained, independent
entity. Further contributing to this decontextualized view of architecture, the
images are sometimes manipulated (e.g., through retouching or cropping) to
minimize the presence of other urban structures or elements – not to mention of
the conspicuous lack of pedestrians and vehicles. Separating the building from
the cityscape makes *Neues Bauen* available to the kind of allegorical readings which,
as demonstrated by Johannes and Hajos/Zahn, translate its formative role in the
process of massification into purely aesthetic terms. After all, the ultimate goal,
to quote *Reichskunstwart* Edwin Redslob (1996: vii) in the introduction to *Berliner
Architektur*, was to express the 'artistic will (*Kunstwille*) of our present time' through

the powers of architecture as a 'spatial art' (*Raumkunst*), a bold application of Riegleian categories to an architectural movement strongly committed to realizing the political will of the people.

Architectural photography, as my discussion of Mossehaus has shown thus far, served principally two purposes during the Weimar years: to present new buildings against the backdrop (and the contingencies) of urban life, and to promote modern architecture as an artistically relevant, socially significant, and economically profitable practice.[16] A third set of functions, the transformation of architectural structures and urban spaces into ambitious dreams of individual and collective agency, was frequently diagnosed but rarely analysed. Questions of discursivization (e.g., the literalization proposed by Benjamin) played a key role in the elevation of *Neues Bauen* to a symbol of modern mass society and proved instrumental in the promotion of its urban projects as an effective solution to the problems of the metropolis. All formal aspects of photography, from framing and lighting to questions of scale, angle, tone, contrast and perspective, were utilized to serve this overarching purpose. Capturing the dynamics of individual building and perimeter block, architectural photography restaged the complex relationships between city-dwellers and their built environment in aesthetic terms.

By presenting the building as both an individual work of art and a symbol of mass society, photography established itself as the perfect medium for propagating the unifying social and aesthetic vision of *Neues Bauen*. Moreover, the textual anchoring of the images allowed for the reconciliation of two opposing tendencies in Weimar architectural culture: the cult of the modern architect as social visionary and the affirmation of the urban masses as the agents of history. And, to return to Mossehaus, it is precisely in the resultant replacement of collective resistance by individual achievement and the displacement of social activism into the dynamism of architectural form that we once again find confirmation of Tafuri's earlier diagnosis of 'architecture rather than revolution'. By articulating the tension between building and cityscape, architectural photography established a representational model for the changing dynamics of the social and the spatial that haunted Weimar urban culture, both in relation to the intensifying social struggles triggered by the crisis of traditional class society and to the bold programmeme of the New Berlin that was meant to overcome such crises of the classical metropolis.

WEIMAR BERLIN AND THE PHOTO-BOOK

On the remaining pages of this essay, I want to use the representation of Mossehaus in the photo-books of Stone, von Bucovich and Willinger to examine the positioning of *Neues Bauen* in the larger narrative of Weimar Berlin. Von Bucovich's *Berlin*, Stone's *Berlin in Bildern* and Willinger's *100 × Berlin* all bear witness to the process of aestheticization that transformed Mossehaus into a corporate icon and a symbol of the New Berlin, reason enough to take a closer look at their different photographic styles. To begin with the more traditional approaches, both von Bucovich

Figure 3.6
Mossehaus, in Mario von
Bucovich, *Berlin 1928: Das
Gesicht der Stadt*, Berlin:
Nicolaische Verlag,
1992, 55.

and Stone present Mossehaus as an integral part of the perimeter block and its mixture of old and new buildings. Von Bucovich (1992: 55) achieves this integrationist approach by shooting the streamlined façade from the perspective of Schützenstraße (see Figure 3.6).[17] Like von Bucovich, Stone (1998 [1929]: 57) avoids the high drama of the corner diagonal by assuming a position on the other side of Jerusalemer Straße (see Figure 3.7). But whereas von Bucovich demonstrates the successful integration of the old and the new by showing Mossehaus next to an eighteenth-century building, Stone places greater emphasis on the harmonious relationship between building and street traffic: that is, the participation of this modernist icon in the daily rituals of urban life. The reduction to the essential elements of architecture and photography is most pronounced in the approach taken by the young Willinger (1997 [1929]: 3). Here the narrow frame and skewed angles, so typical of Bauhaus photography, turn the curved window bands into an almost abstract reflection on surfaces and structures (see Figure 3.8).

Published in 1928/29, the high point and turning point in Wagner's ambitious programmes for the New Berlin, the three photo-books under discussion present Berlin within the familiar narratives of tradition and innovation, continuity and change, and rely heavily on frame composition to establish Mossehaus as an

Figure 3.7
Mossehaus, in Sasha
Stone, *Berlin in Bildern*,
Berlin: Gebr. Mann,
1998, no. 57.

iconic presence within these competing narratives. But positioning the building meant much more than frame composition and other formal means; it also included the placement of the image within the generic conventions of the photo-book. Weimar publishers promoted photo-books as the perfect hybrid form that allowed readers to participate in the visualization of urban culture and the proliferation of photographic consciousness, while preserving bourgeois modes of art appreciation.[18] In other words, the photo-books offered an inexpensive and convenient way to reproduce the art-book experience in a different perceptual register and decidedly contemporary medium. In their layout and design, all three

Figure 3.8
Mossehaus, in Laszlo
Willinger, *100 × Berlin*,
Berlin: Gebr. Mann,
1997, 3.

photographers combine formal allusions to the high-end art book with the representational conventions of the illustrated travel guides that take full advantage of the reader's familiarity with the city's famous monuments, streets and squares, thus making the inevitable moments of recognition an important aspect of the genre's popular appeal.[19]

With its 254 plates, beautifully reproduced and presented in an appealing square format, von Bucovich's *Berlin* appeared in Albertus-Verlag as the first volume in a proposed series on 'The Face of the Cities'; the only other volume, a portrait of Paris, was published in the same year. Aiming at a cultured, middle-class readership, the book included a preface by Alfred Döblin, who had himself initiated a radical reassessment of the conventions of realism through the highly fragmented view of Alexanderplatz in his famous novel of 1927. Similarly, the well-known art book publisher Epstein had planned to make Stone's *Berlin in Bildern* part of a series titled *Orbis Urbium: Schöne Städte in schönen Bildern* (Beautiful Cities in Beautiful Pictures) that apparently never materialized. Edited by the architectural critic Adolf Behne, and with a dedication to Martin Wagner, the book sought to advance the programmeme of the New Berlin within the continuities of Berlin history, as symbolized by its grand imperial architecture. Inexpensively produced by the Berlin-based Verlag der Reihe, Willinger's *100 × Berlin* (like von Bucovich's *Berlin*) appeared as part of a similar series on city portraits that only saw the 1929 publication of a second book on *100 × Paris*, this time with photographs by Germaine Krull. The accompanying German, French and English texts address a cosmopolitan readership fully conversant in modernist styles.

Participating in the intense debates on text–image relationships, all three books are prefaced by more general reflections on photography, architecture and the metropolis. In the introduction to von Bucovich's *Berlin*, Döblin addresses the politics of the visible when he concludes that 'Berlin is largely invisible. A strange phenomenon . . . Could it be that all modern cities are invisible – and that the things visible in them are only the remnants of the past'? (Bucovich 1992: 5). Less interested in questions of representation than in showcasing the New Berlin, Behne in his introduction to *Berlin in Bildern* describes how 'the task of the modern city-builder is not to place monumental buildings in favoured locations. He is no longer a tactician but a strategist of building in the city' (Stone 1998: 8). Whereas Döblin uses von Bucovich to reflect on the problem of representing the modern metropolis, Behne relies on Stone to reframe the very terms of urban thought, away from monumentality and historicity and toward functionality and rationality. Finally, in an openly political reading that reflects its author's left-wing sympathies, Karl Vetter in his introduction to Willinger (1997: xxv) describes Berlin as a city without tradition and, for that reason, the perfect setting for envisioning new possibilities and initiating social changes that advance 'the tendency toward the collective spirit and the common will'.

Notwithstanding their aesthetic and conceptual differences, von Bucovich, Stone and Willinger all present Mossehaus within a narrative trajectory which, reminiscent of a photographic *flânerie*, reclaims the metropolis for individual perspectives. The sequential arrangement of plates in the three photo-books under discussion imitates the act of walking in the city and, in so doing, suggests both a narrative of progress and an experience of agency. In view of the fact that von Bucovich, Stone and Willinger were not only foreign-born but also forced to leave Germany after 1933, we might even detect hidden affinities between the figure of the stranger and the condition of exile – as if individual agency were only possible within the terms of otherness. Von Bucovich, Stone and Willinger all organize their images in the form of a typical journey through Weimar Berlin.

They start out in the historical centre around Unter den Linden and proceed along landmarks and monuments such as the Reichstag, Brandenburg Gate, Old Museum, Opera House, Berlin Dome and Imperial Palace.

The absence of people and vehicles underscores the buildings' status as timeless works of art, far removed from the pressures of contemporary life. From the centre, the journeys typically advance in two directions, toward the remnants of the Old Berlin (e.g., Krögel, Scheunenviertel) and toward the New West, with Wittenbergplatz, Emperor Wilhelm Memorial Church and Kurfürstendamm as the most famous destinations. And the photographic excursions usually end on the city's periphery where the new public housing estates in Zehlendorf and Britz and the famous monuments to Prussian architecture in Potsdam confirm once again the compatibility of old and new in the self-understanding of Weimar Berlin. In all three photo-books, the spatial re-enactment of the cityscape is overlaid by a functional view of the modern metropolis, with the different urban functions of commerce, transportation and recreation represented through the city's centres of entertainment (Friedrichstraße) and consumption (Leipziger Straße), the pedestrian and automotive traffic on its major squares (Potsdamer Platz, Alexanderplatz), and the outdoor activities in its popular parks and lakes (Tiergarten, Wannsee). Often these typical urban activities are identified with the kind of quintessential urban architecture of train stations (Wittenbergplatz, Nollendorfplatz), department stores (Tietz, Wertheim, Karstadt), and entertainment complexes (Wintergarten, Aschinger) which, like the modernist office buildings and traffic squares, organize the modern masses according to the principles of standardization, homogenization, functionalization and massification.

'The true picture of the past flits by. The past can be seized only as an image which flashes up at the instant of its recognisability, and it is never seen again', observes Benjamin (2003c: 390) in his famous theses on the philosophy of history. If history is essentially imagistic, what are we to make of the problem of un/decipherability that seems to haunt Weimar Berlin more than other cities? And in what ways is this struggle over representation linked to the crisis of class society between the threat of a socialist revolution in 1919 and the terror of the racial community established in 1933? Despite the large amount and wide range of historical images in circulation, Weimar Berlin remains strangely fragmented and undecipherable as a photographic corpus. Berlin had no Eugene Atget to create a typology of urban sites and places; no Germaine Krull to approach familiar settings and situations with new eyes; and no Henri Cartier-Bresson to capture decisive moments in the life of its inhabitants.[20]

Unlike Paris, the German capital during the 1920s cannot be identified with a distinct photographic signature or aesthetic paradigm. Instead of individual photographers, powerful media conglomerates dominated the production and circulation of city images. As I have argued, Weimar Berlin asserted its photographic presence through the image–text relationships developed in illustrated magazines, trade publications and photo-books. The kind of architectural photography discussed on the previous pages was constituted through sharply divided spheres of reception and highly politicized mode of presentation that defined the central role of visual culture in the promotion of a homogeneous white-collar society. If we, as scholars of Weimar culture, are to overcome the problems of visibility addressed by Brecht and Benjamin at the beginning, we are well advised to read photographs within the larger contexts in which they were produced and consumed – and to take seriously their active contribution to the making of Weimar mass culture and modernity.

NOTES

1 For overviews of Weimar photography, see Ute Eskildsen and Jan-Christopher Horak eds, *Film und Foto in den zwanziger Jahren*, Stuttgart: Gerd Hatje 1979; and Herbert Molderings, *Fotografie in der Weimarer Republik*, Berlin: Dirk Nishen 1988.

2 The reference is to Albert Renger-Patzsch's *Die Welt ist schön* (1928).

3 For historical overviews of architecture and urban planning in Weimar Berlin, see Karl-Heinz Hüter, *Architektur in Berlin 1900–1933*, Stuttgart: Kohlhammer 1988; and Jochen Boberg, Tilman Fichter, and Eckhart Gillen eds, *Die Metropole: Industriekultur in Berlin im 20. Jahrhundert*, Munich: C. H. Beck 1986.

4 Examples include Hans Brennert and Erwin Stein eds, *Probleme der neuen Stadt Berlin*, Berlin-Friedenau: Deutscher Kommunal-Verlag 1926 and Max Osborn, *Berlin 1870– 1929: Der Aufstieg zur Weltstadt*, Berlin: Gebr. Mann 1994, 198. The latter was first published in 1926 in Leipzig.

5 Interestingly, one web site about the 1992–93 renovation of Mosse House by Peter Kolb, Bernd Kemper, and Dieter Schneider states that the original building was damaged during the First World War. See www.galinsky.com/buildings/mossehaus/.

6 The renovation, completed in 1923, took place under the difficult conditions of the post-war inflation and, in ways equally conducive to allegorical readings as the street fighting in the newspaper district, brought into relief the tension between architectural visions and construction problems. In March 1922, the main contractor's inexperience with reinforced concrete caused a tragic accident when collapsing floors and ceilings injured 24 office workers, 13 of them fatally.

7 For the same scene shot from a different perspective, see the front of Mossehaus on the cover of Mosse's own *Weltspiegel*, January 1919, under the heading 'Berlin under the sign of terror'. For an account of these revolutionary days, see *Die Revolution in Berlin November-Dezember 1918*, Berlin: Dirk Nishen Verlag 1989.

8 See, for instance, the cover of *Berliner Illustrirte Zeitung* 38.2 (1929).

9 See *Der rote Stern* 6.1 (1929), cover page.

10 See 'Auf den Dächern von Berlin', *Weltspiegel* 26 (1929), 2 and 'Zeugen der Nacht', *Weltspiegel* 17 (1929), 4.

11 See 'Berlin as Welt-und Fremdenstadt', *Weltspiegel* 34 (1926) and 'Berlin, die Weltstadt der Arbeit', *Weltspiegel* 43 (1927).

12 About half of the photographs in *Amerika: Bilderbuch eines Architekten* were taken by Mendelsohn; the others seem to have been either taken by friends (e.g., by Fritz Lang) or reprinted from other publications. The English translation gives no credits.

13 The book was advertised in *Weltspiegel* 30 (1930).

14 Translation modified.

15 For a critical review that takes issue with the decorative arrangement of the photographs, see Adolf Behne, *Das Neue Berlin* 12 (1929), 245.

16 On architectural photography, see Rolf Sachsse, *Photographie als Medium der Architekturinterpretation: Studien zur Geschichte der deutschen Architekturphotographie im 20. Jahrhundert*, Munich: Saur 1984.

17 The reprint published in 1992 contains only 107 of the original 254 photographs included in the 1928 edition published by Albertus Verlag.

18 See Leesa L. Rittelmann, 'Constructed Identities: The German Photo Book from Weimar to the Third Reich', Ph.D. dissertation, University of Pittsburgh, 2002.

19 For example, see *Berlin: Nach 40 photographischen Aufnahmen* (n.p., n.d.) published in the series 'Die deutsche Stadt im Bild' by the Deutscher Kulturbild-Verlag in the early 1930s; which includes images of Europahaus, Shellhaus, and so forth.

20 This does not mean that Atget was not an important influence; see the publication *Eugène Atget: Lichtbilder*, text by Camille Recht, Leipzig: Jonquières 1930.

REFERENCES

Benjamin, W. (2003a) 'The Author as Producer', in M. W. Jennings, H. Eiland and G. Smith (eds) *Selected Writings*, vol. 2, 1927–1934 trans. R. Livingstone *et al.*, Cambridge, MA: Harvard University Press.

—— (2003b) 'A Small History of Photography', in M. W. Jennings, H. Eiland and G. Smith (eds) *Selected Writings*, vol. 2, 1927–1934, trans. R. Livingstone *et al.*, Cambridge, MA: Harvard University Press.

—— (2003c) 'On the Concept of History', in M. W. Jennings and H. Eiland (eds) *Selected Writings*, vol. 4, 1938–1940, trans. E. Jephcott *et al.*, Cambridge, MA: Harvard University Press.

Brecht, B. (2000) 'The Threepenny Lawsuit', in M. Silberman (ed. and trans.), *Bertolt Brecht on Film and Radio*, London: Methuen.

Bucovich, M. von (1992) *Berlin 1928: Das Gesicht der Stadt*, preface Alfred Döblin, afterword Hans-Werner Klünner, Berlin: Nicolaische Verlag.

Geertz, C. (1973) 'Thick Description: Toward an Interpretative Theory of Culture', *The Interpretation of Cultures*, New York: Basic Books.

Hajos, E. M. and Zahn, L. (1996) *Berliner Architektur 1919 bis 1929*, Berlin: Gebr. Mann: first published in 1929 by Albertus Verlag.

James, K. (1997) *Erich Mendelsohn and the Architecture of German Modernism*, Cambridge: Cambridge University Press.

Johannes, H. (1931) *Neues Bauen in Berlin: Ein Führer mit 168 Bildern*, Berlin: Deutscher Kunstverlag.

Mendelsohn, E. (1929) *Russland – Europa – Amerika*, Berlin: Rudolf Mosse.

—— (1930) 'Die internationale Übereinstimmung des Neues Baugedankens oder Dynamik und Funktion' [1923], *Das Gesamtschaffen des Architekten*: *Skizzen Entwürfe Bauten*, Berlin: Rudolf Mosse.

—— (1993) *Erich Mendelsohn's 'Amerika'*, trans. Stanley Appelbaum, Toronto: Dover: first published (1926) *Amerika: Bilderbuch eines Architekten*, Berlin: Rudolf Mosse.

Mendelssohn, P. de (1982) *Zeitungsstadt Berlin: Menschen und Mächte in der Geschichte der deutschen Presse*, Frankfurt am Main: Ullstein.

Molzahn, J. (1928) 'Nicht mehr Lesen! Sehen!', *Das Kunstblatt* 12(3): 78–83.

Redslob, E. (1996) 'Introduction', in E. Hajos and L. Zahn, *Berliner Architektur 1919 bis 1929*, Berlin: Gebr. Mann.

Römer, W. (1984) *Januarkämpfe Berlin 1919*, Berlin: Dirk Nishen Verlag.

Stone, S. (1998) *Berlin in Bildern*, A. Behne (ed.), afterword M. Neumann, Berlin: Gebr. Mann: formerly published in 1929 by Vienna: Epstein Verlag.

Tafuri, M. (1976) *Architecture and Utopia: Design and Capitalist Development*, trans. B. Luigia La Penta, Cambridge, MA: MIT Press.

Weltspiegel (1919) Issue 2/3.

Willinger, L. (1997) *100 × Berlin*, preface K. Vetter, afterword H. Geisert, Berlin: Gebr. Mann: first published in 1929 by (Berlin) Westend: Verlag der Reihe.

Part II

Remembering and Reinventing the City

Chapter 4: *Beautiful Dachau's* Contested Urban Identity

Alan Marcus

INTRODUCTION

Joseph Anton Sedlmayr was a provincial artist who was born in Munich in 1797, and died there in 1863. He devoted much of his life to painting in the region of Upper Bavaria. At the age of 30, he was appointed to the position of overseer of the Royal Painting Gallery, Königliche Gemäldegalerie, and in 1840 completed a painting featuring an idyllic Bavarian town, located just outside Munich. That canvas, seen in Figure 4.1, is of the town of Dachau. Sedlmayr's painting captures the *Zeitgeist* of German romanticism, portraying the community in a dreamlike way, suggesting a harmonious synthesis between the urban and natural worlds. With a wooden bridge crossing over the river Amper in the foreground, the Schloss Dachau is seen on the hill above, a summer palace of the Wittelsbach family who ruled Bavaria from 1180 to 1918. Founded in the eighth century, Dachau, today with 40,000 inhabitants and serving as a commuter town to Munich, located 16 kilometres away, has become a major district town, a *Grosse Kreisstadt* of the administrative region of Upper Bavaria. In 2005, the city celebrated the 1,200th anniversary of the first reference to its existence, when in AD 805, the lady Erchana of the Aribons bequeathed her property in 'Dahauua' to the Diocese of Freising.

There is a sharp contrast between the elegant Renaissance palace, Schloss Dachau, situated with its walled gardens atop Schlossberg hill, and the town's more infamous landmark below – the SS-constructed *Konzentrationslager* (KZ) Dachau concentration camp, with its panoptic surveillance design. In what Paul Jaskot (2000: 1) refers to as an 'Architecture of Oppression', the SS 'linked state architectural policy to the political function of incarcerating and punishing supposed enemies of National Socialist Germany'. In fact, the forced labour camp at Dachau grew out of a penal tradition stretching back several centuries. Its problematic incorporation within the town, and function as a popular tourist attraction, is the subject of this chapter.[1] We will also consider issues associated with Dachau's sense

Figure 4.1
Painting of the town of
Dachau, J. A. Sedlmayr,
1840.

of *Gemeinschaft* (community), in terms of how visitors relate to one another within the camp, how the camp visitors relate to the city's residents, and how the city has perceived itself as it has alternated between rejecting and incorporating the concentration camp and its mass of visitors.

Known as an artists' colony in the late nineteenth and early twentieth centuries, Dachau was an unlikely location in which to site the Nazis' first state concentration camp two weeks after Hitler came to power in March 1933. Yet, even Dachau's bohemian environment produced celebrated writers such as Ludwig Thoma (1867–1921) who published anti-Semitic texts in addition to his popular works, such as *Ein Münchner im Himmel* (*A Municher in Heaven*, 1911). Since the war, the picturesque town has suffered a stigma of association that has left a lasting impression on its identity and post-war town planning. Tuan (1977: 179) reminds us that 'place is an organized world of meaning', and due to the long-standing segregated arrangements for visitors to the camp, many do not realize that Dachau is also the name of the medieval town. In charting the maturation of a city within a city, this chapter investigates the way the inclusion of the former camp within the modern city of Dachau has resulted in the transfiguring of both entities, redefining their design and social meaning.

A 30-minute documentary filmed in Spring 2006, *Beautiful Dachau*, observes the way visitors interact with the different areas of the camp (Figure 4.2). The film provides a research tool that methodologically underpins areas of this study. It also explores the relationship between Dachau's *Altstadt* (the old town) and East

Dachau, where the concentration camp and much of the city's new residential and commercial zoned growth is situated. The Nazis decided to establish the KZ camp in Dachau precisely because it was close to their political base in Munich, just a 20-minute train ride away. *Reichsführer-SS* Heinrich Himmler was aware of a large and disused former gunpowder and munitions factory outside Dachau, which could be converted into a prison camp. On 20 March 1933, Himmler, as Munich's Acting Chief of Police, used a press conference to announce the opening of KZ Dachau. The brutality of its regime was underscored when on the second day under SS administration four Jewish prisoners were led out of the camp and shot 'while trying to escape' (Distel and Hammermann 2005: 63).

The title of the film was taken from a colourful poster on a bus shelter near the entrance to the camp, announcing 'Beautiful Dachau: things to see and do'. This single phrase encapsulates the challenge of rebranding a town and marketing its tourism potential when yoked to the legacy of a site of mass murder. An article on KZ Dachau in a 1936 issue of the Nazi Party's illustrated weekly also referred to the camp as 'beautiful' and 'immaculate' (Marcuse 2001: 28). The practical and aesthetic appeal of this integrated design approach to the symmetrical layout of the main camp with its carefully organized areas underscores Weber's (1995: 109) point that 'one type of value intrinsic to form involves pleasure derived from the perception of order'. Dachau was a school for torture and systemized terror, which served both as a model for the whole concentration camp system and as a flagship for training future commandants. From its inception, KZ Dachau was a place for 'protective custody' incarceration for those at odds with National

Figure 4.2
KZ Dachau entrance gate, still from *Beautiful Dachau*, 2006.

Socialism. Political dissent in the new state was not tolerated and Dachau played a key function in harshly underscoring the threat of severe punishment.

Those sent to Dachau were branded 'politicals', 'racials', 'criminals' and 'anti-socials' – they included political prisoners, Jews, Jehovah's Witnesses, clergymen, homosexuals, criminals, Sinti and Roma, Spanish Civil War veterans, Austrians, French, Italian, Czech, Soviets and prisoners from other occupied territories (Berben 1975: 11). KZ Dachau, which was reconstructed in 1937–8 to accommodate the increase in prisoners, was exclusively a camp for males until towards the end of the war when 7,000 mostly Jewish women were deported there by the SS (Distel and Hammermann 2005: 167). During this period in 1944–5, over 100,000 prisoners were sent to Dachau and its sub-camps, primarily from the occupied countries (ibid.: 169).

KZ Dachau's first camp commandant, Theodor Eicke, instigated the camp's strict regime under the axiom that 'tolerance is weakness', and went on to become 'Inspector of Concentration Camps and Leader of the SS Guard Units'. The *SS-Totenkopfverbände* (Death's Head Formations) was the name given to all SS concentration camp guard units. Among the many SS camp commandants who trained at KZ Dachau were Hermann Baranowski (Sachsenhausen), Max Koegel (Ravensbrück), Josef Kramer (Bergen-Belsen and Auschwitz II-Birkenau) and Rudolf Höss (Auschwitz).

Emblematic of the horrors associated with Dachau were the human experiments conducted by SS doctors, including malaria, seawater drinking, freezing and high-altitude experiments, carried out in specially constructed vacuum chambers. Numerous prisoners perished or were disfigured by the tests. Prisoners at Dachau deemed mentally ill or 'unfit for work' were given lethal injections, or left to die in Barrack 30 for 'Invalids'. Estimates of the number of people killed at Dachau, the *Todesernte* ('death harvest'), vary from 31,000 to 50,000 or more. Meticulous records were kept, but many prisoners were never officially registered, such as over 4,000 Soviet prisoners sent to KZ Dachau in 1941–2 for execution (Distel and Hammermann 2005: 156). From its opening in 1933 until December 1944, an average of four persons died a day in Dachau. During its last four months of operation in 1945, that number increased to 100 persons each day (Marcuse 2001: 49).

THE SS TRAINING CAMP

Although visitors to the camp can now walk through the same portal the *Häftlinge* (prisoners) once entered, they still do not engage with a fundamental component of the visual experience. Camp prisoners first had to enter the main gate of the adjoining SS Training Camp, then pass through a second gate near the Command-centre building, before finally entering the *Jourhaus* gate with access to the inner prison compound, a 250 × 600 metre rectangular enclosure (Figure 4.3). It was then that new prisoners underwent the brutal and humiliating *Empfangszeremonie* (reception ceremony) at the hands of the SS guards. 'Social control was maintained . . . through a series of distinctly spatial strategies' (Jackson 1989: 100), and this

Figure 4.3
Aerial photo of KZ
Dachau and the SS
Training Camp, 1945.

journey taken by the prisoners underscored the relationship between the two camps.

The SS camp was a major base and garrison for two SS formations: the *Totenkopfverbände* and the *Waffen-SS*. The camp trained and educated SS officers and gradually became a virtual city with a full range of facilities and a large number of buildings for offices, factories and housing, all immaculately maintained. The base also served as the Officer-Cadet Training School of the SS Business Administration Department, which taught courses in law, economics, finance, bookkeeping and SS administration. In keeping with attempts to mould the body beautiful, it had a sizable sports ground (Richardi 1998: 112). There were also a number of SS factories and workshops with prisoner workforces instigated by Himmler's ambition to make the SS self-sufficient. This policy was given further impetus in March 1942 when Himmler placed the Office of SS Economic Administration in charge of the concentration camps. The Paymaster's Office of the Waffen-SS was based at the camp, as was the Waffen-SS school for medics, the SS training kitchens, the SS main services camp, the SS main arsenal, the SS manufacturing sites, the SS weapons workshops, the clothing works for the Waffen-SS, the SS riding school and various other SS departments.

The former SS Training Camp retains many more buildings from its Third Reich period than the concentration camp, though none of these are open to the public. On the other side of the fence in the KZ, the prisoners' former barracks were torn down in 1965. Two model barracks have been rebuilt, and the others are identified by concrete borders and numbered markers where their foundations once stood. Those structures of the concentration camp that remain include the gatehouse, the 200-metre-long service building housing the museum exhibition,

Figure 4.4
The former SS Training
Camp and original
entrance road to KZ
Dachau.

the 'bunker' (a prison within a prison), the crematoria, watchtowers and barbed wire fences.

More importantly, a tall earthen embankment and wall built since the war separated the two camps until recently, precluding visitors from any spatial sense of the systemic relationship that formerly existed between the adjoining camps (see Figure 4.4). This wall was removed in 2005, after a long campaign by supporters of the camp's role as a memorial site. Without understanding the physical and ideological ties that bound the two camp areas together, the supposition is reinforced that the concentration camp was an isolated space for torture. In fact, it was an intrinsic part of the whole SS operation, including the training camp, its manufacturing enterprises using prisoner labour, and extensive administrative centres. The drilling and levels of physical fitness pursued in the training camp stood in dramatic contrast to the efforts made next door to degrade and destroy the human body. What is surprising is that the SS decided to site the crematoria beside their own barracks and factories, as seen in Figure 4.3, such that the chimney, *Kamin*, would belch out acrid smoke over the area the Waffen-SS lived, trained and worked in. Today the concentration camp has become a transfigured, reboundaried space, in which one's experience is still hemmed in by fences and a lack of public awareness about the former layout, redefining the strata of the camp's ideological and spatial meaning.

ARBEIT MACHT FREI

A portion of the massive former SS Training Camp, which was many times larger than the concentration camp, has been appropriated and turned into the Dachau

Golf Club, featuring a nine-hole course and clubhouse. The remainder of the training camp, encompassing roughly two-thirds of its former size, including the former SS barracks, officers' villas and assorted buildings, is surrounded by a high fence and used by the Bavarian police. Until recently, visitors to the concentration camp entered the memorial site by way of a temporary entrance on the Alte Römerstrasse – across the camp from the original entrance. In 2005, the memorial site was finally able to create a new access along a specially constructed short path beside the Würm canal and through the passageway which all prisoners formerly entered.

The camp's guardhouse, known as the *Jourhaus*, contains the iconic iron gate, *Das Tor*, in its passageway (Figure 4.2), emblazoned with the words 'Arbeit Macht Frei' (translated, 'work brings freedom' or 'work sets you free'). This gate was the sole entrance to the concentration camp, through which all persons and vehicles passed after being carefully searched and accounted for. As they went through the gate, prisoners were required to remove any head coverings. For a prisoner to be summoned to the guardhouse meant certain punishment or death (Richardi 1998: 254–5). Much of the camp was constructed with forced labour, and the gate itself was made by the prisoner Karl Röder. The current gate is actually a copy of the original, which disappeared after the war.

The inscription, *Arbeit Macht Frei*, is attributed to Reich Minister for Public Enlightenment and Propaganda, Joseph Goebbels, who approved it for the entrance to the Oranienburg concentration camp near Berlin. It was also used on the gate at Auschwitz and at other camps. The irony is that for many thousands of prisoners, work did not mean freedom, it meant being worked to death. The link between the incarceration and execution of prisoners in KZ Dachau, and the desire by the SS to employ them as forced labourers in its adjoining camp containing factories and workshops, goes to the heart of the Reich's paradoxical treatment of prisoners. As Jaskot (2000: 4) has observed, 'the function of the camps – to abuse the labour population but also to exploit its productivity – were sometimes conflicting, sometimes complementary goals'. KZ Dachau's utilitarian project found its counterpart in the appropriation of labour in the industrial town, which as Lewis Mumford (1938: 144) noted in his contemporaneous critique: 'rested on a doctrine of productive avarice and physiological denial; and it took the form of a wholesale disparagement of the needs of life'. Prisoners worked up to 11 hours a day, six days a week in the SS industries (Berben 1975: 91). KZ Dachau's layout and design allowed for both extermination through work (*Vernichtung durch Arbeit*) and mass execution. Thus, the basis of the plan for the camp closely followed the axiom that 'an architectural form is shaped by its intended function' (Gelernter 1995: 3).

The premise for this architecturally codified penitential practice can find its antecedent in the eighteenth-century English and German workhouses. Such institutions, which instilled the 'discipline of production' by combining punitive treatment with underpaid forced labour, became particularly popular in Germany, and by the end of the eighteenth century there were around 60 of them (Melossi and Pavarini 1981: 22, 47–8). The phrase *Arbeit Macht Frei* echoes earlier blurring of the distinctions between the German prison, the *Zuchthaus*, and the *Arbeitshaus*, used by the police for housing indigents. KZ Dachau took this hybridity to a new level when developing penitential town planning, situating zones for living, work and execution in close proximity, as the aerial photograph in Figure 4.3 reveals. It illustrates a paradigmatic process of production which employed punitive measures to further engender prisoner productivity in the SS factory enterprises. This methodological imperative became pervasive throughout the Dachau camp and sub-camp system, and at other concentration camps which increasingly provided forced labour for industry. One of the barracks inside the camp was converted into making airplane cables for Messerschmitt in order to avoid being bombed. KZ Dachau's novelty was its holistic architectural design combined with repressive camp practices, and this both permitted systematic persecution and provided conditions for exploitation of human labour.

RELATIONSHIP OF TOWN AND CAMP

The spatial connections between Dachau's camp and town and the city of Munich are themselves revealing. Not only is Dachau a short S-Bahn train journey from Munich, but the main road that runs from Munich's city centre to Dachau is called Dachauer Strasse and serves symbolically as an umbilical cord. The parentage, though, runs both ways. Munich gave birth to the camp, but KZ Dachau became the mother camp to some 120 sub-camps located throughout Munich and the surrounding area. Over 200,000 prisoners were processed through Dachau. At the time of its liberation on 29 April 1945 by the Rainbow Division of the US Seventh Army, Dachau held over 67,000 people, one-third of them Jews, with roughly 30,000 prisoners in the main camp and 37,000 in sub-camps. In many cases, the sub-camps which provided labour for SS factories, construction work, aeronautics, metal industry, machinery, railway and agriculture, were quite large and just as brutal (Berben 1975: 214–18). Their systemic and tragic role is often overlooked by locals and a wider critical assessment is needed. The Dachau sub-camp at Allach, for example, held 5,000 prisoners who were used as forced labourers for BMW to manufacture fighter planes. 30 thousand Jewish prisoners were sent as forced labourers to build underground factories at Dachau's Kaufering sub-camp complex, where more than 10,000 died. KZ Dachau was Munich's concentration camp, but because of the two different names, one is not commonly associated with the other, despite their shared history and proximity.

In fact, in the 1933 national election only 24 per cent of votes from the town of Dachau were cast for the National Socialists, compared to 44 per cent nationally. After seizing power, SS stormtroopers proceeded to occupy the Dachau town hall and raised a large swastika flag in front of the building, despite local objections. Members of the city council who were political opponents were quickly replaced with Nazi supporters. On the day that the concentration camp was first opened, the town's newspaper, *Dachau Zeitung*, announced that: 'For

Dachau [township] the camp will be economically very advantageous, since the large number [of prisoners] there will require guards and administrators, who will bring a substantial increase in customers to the hard-pressed Dachau business community' (cited in Marcuse 2001: 25–6). The town's leaders soon followed the Nazis' racist policies, confirmed in a letter in 1938 from the mayor of Dachau, Hans Cramer, stating that the town and surrounding areas were now *judenfrei* (free of Jews) (Richardi 1998: 131). Ironically, he was not including those Jews held at KZ Dachau. Following *Reichskristallnacht* (the Night of Broken Glass) in November 1938, 10,911 Jewish prisoners were brought to Dachau by the Gestapo (ibid.: 128).

In 1934, Dachau officially became a city and within a few years the town council requested that the SS areas, including the concentration camp and adjacent SS Training Camp, be incorporated within the city's boundaries. This act was formally approved by the Reich Governor in Bavaria, Franz Ritter von Epp, in a decree in March 1939 (Richardi 1998: 114–15). Originally, the camp was largely separated from the town by fields and agricultural lands, and was out of bounds to most townspeople; although there was a constant stream of official visitors and train-loads of prisoners arrived at the town's central station before being marched to KZ Dachau. Prisoners from the camp worked in 12 places across the town, including a large number in the Wülfert wurst factory and the Präzifix screw factory. They were marched through the city streets to and from work every day, but the townspeople were forbidden from interacting with them. There are records, though, of occasional acts of humanity, such as factory workers hiding bits of bread in machinery for their famished colleagues.

While the town derived economic benefit from its enlargement, including increased tax revenues, the post-war circumstances are more complicated. After Dachau's liberation, the Americans used it as an internment camp for Nazi prisoners. It became the site of the Dachau War Crimes military tribunals and by 1946 over 16,000 former SS men were held in the barracks. The trials ended in 1948 and the camp was then used for holding displaced persons, until the last of the refugees left in the mid-1960s. The US Army converted the adjoining SS Training Camp into a base, which it occupied until 1973, when it was turned over to the Bavarian State. Since then it has served as the Bavarian Police Academy and as a base for the Bavarian mobile police force, which continues to occupy the site to this day. The first museum in KZ Dachau was created in 1960 and the memorial site itself was opened in May 1965, 20 years after the camp's liberation. In 1974, the Bavarian State designated the Dachau Memorial Site a protected monument. Since then, 800,000 to one million people visit annually, two-thirds of them foreigners and the rest mainly German school children on class trips.

During the post-war period, the town gradually expanded towards the former SS Training Camp and concentration camp, which are now completely integrated within residential, leisure and industrial areas, known as Dachau-Ost. New industrial buildings sit on the SS plantations in which prisoners worked, adjoining the KZ camp. Other SS buildings next to the camp were replaced by the 'Roman Grove' condominium complex in the 1990s. The town has had an ambivalent relationship with the camp, to the extent that in 1955 they tried to have the crematoria removed, and in the 1970s there were local discussions about having the memorial site eradicated. The city did have a number of the SS buildings torn down, including the former commandant's villa in 1987, and the SS plantation's greenhouses in 1998, where a number of prisoners died. The attachment of meaning to place, and the instability which results from the destruction of the meaning of places is particularly significant when considering a site such as Dachau (Entrikin 1991: 57). Buildings are erased at the cost of erasing memory.

In his classic study, *The Image of the City* (1960), Lynch sets out the mental representations and constituent elements that visually and spatially define a built environment and give it 'place legibility'. These include paths, edges, districts, nodes and landmarks (Lynch 1960: 46–8). In the case of Dachau, the chief and symbolic node in recent history is the train station – which brought both the prisoners and many of today's tourists. Dominant paths include that which leads from the station to the camp, upon which millions of visitors are either bussed or walk, and the route the prisoners trod, re-launched in spring 2007 as the 'Path of Remembrance', subsidized by the Bavarian Cultural Foundation (Kulturfonds Bayern). The post-war street names assigned to the designated path from the train station to the camp include: Peace Way Street (Friedenstrasse), John F. Kennedy Square, and the 'Road Commemorating the Victims of the Concentration Camp' (Strasse der KZ-Opfer) (City of Dachau 2007). Such non-indigenous place-naming and sign-posting represents an attempt to ideologically codify and reconfigure the space for external consumption, while publicly providing a *mea culpa* acceptance of the neighbourhood's past (these streets are in predominantly residential areas).

Until now, the town of Dachau has suffered from poor place legibility in terms of enticing tourists. The road from the camp to the *Altstadt* and commercial centre is obscured to visitors by the layout of the town and the fact that most are unlikely to have a map (since special buses wait by the station to take them directly to the camp). Dachau's key 'city edges' include the physical barrier which remains between the former SS Training Camp and KZ Dachau, and between the SS camp and the rest of the city. Another edge lies no further west than Frühlingstrasse, just outside the station's Bahnhofsplatz – a porous and invisible edge which is, nonetheless, traversed by few tourists and might as well be a city wall. Equally, the city's two districts are largely defined by old Dachau and East Dachau. Finally, Lynch's (1960) landmark points of reference present the crux of the city's long-standing tourism identity dilemma: it would like to recover the stature of its former landmarks in the *Altstadt* – principally the *Schloss*, its gardens and St Jakob parish church dating from 1624 – but they have been completely usurped by the omnipotent presence of the camp.

There is currently no bus available from the camp to the town centre, whereas, in 1937, a city bus route was inaugurated between the town and camp, primarily to serve the SS and their families who lived there (Marcuse 2001: 36). To walk to the town centre takes roughly 20 minutes, but most visitors remain unaware of the old town located up the hill, which is hidden from view because of the positioning of the station. The visitors' experience of the camp is totally segregated from interaction with the main part of the town and its hotels, shops and restaurants. Visitors usually view the camp for a few hours before returning to Munich. One aim of the new 'Path of Remembrance', one imagines, is to encourage more visitors to walk the town streets of Dachau.

Dachau has been ghettoized in the popular imagination since the war – a sequestered place where terrible things were done, often described as out of view from public scrutiny or complicity. Such is the stigma, that a long-time resident of Munich – itself the former epicentre of Nazism – recently remarked that he would never consider having a Dachau postal address. Residents' car licence plates feature the letter code of the city, DAH, with its negative associations. Those born in the city have 'Dachau' permanently recorded in their passports as their place of birth. As an example of responding to what Goffman (1990) in his study of stigma terms 'spoilt identity', it is not uncommon for local residents to arrange for their children to be born in Munich, so that they can have that city on their birth certificate, even though they might then be baptized in Dachau. Local politician Getrud Schmidt-Podolsky makes the plea that Dachauers should be able to live 'normally despite the town's grim legacy' (cited in Ryback 2001: 112). Overt attempts to counter its link to the Third Reich are reflected in the fact that the main street running through the old town and in front of city hall has been renamed Konrad-Adenauer Strasse, after the first post-war Chancellor of Germany (1949–63), who established a stable democracy. Notably, Adenauer had been persecuted by the Nazis and twice imprisoned.

It is only in recent years that the town's tourism office has recognized the commercial potential of trying to entice the large number of tourists who visit the camp to see the rest of the city. Tourist spots are often disruptive, resented by locals and 'likely to be contested spaces because, like urban spaces, they lie at the intersection of diverse and competing social, economic and political influences' (Low and Lawrence-Zuniga 2003: 22–3). Historically, this is nowhere truer than in Dachau. The 'Beautiful Dachau' poster, and other publicity materials like it, are indicative of new efforts to capitalize on the draw of the totemic concentration camp and market the town as a single entity. In 2006, city posters included images and descriptions of the *Schloss* concerts and other aspects of Dachauer cultural life, alongside that of the concentration camp. A tourism officer pointed out that almost none of the 800,000 annual visitors to the camp actually set foot in the rest of the city (and hence spend little money locally) (Schneider 2006). The memorial site itself does not charge admission and resolutely rejects traditional tourist income-generating opportunities. It hires out audio equipment to visitors at a modest rate and sells a small number of site-specific books, but does not provide refreshments, let alone a cafeteria.

This approach stands in marked contrast to the commercialization of some other Holocaust-related sites, such as the Anne Frank House in Amsterdam, which charges admission to see the empty rooms. Like at Dachau, here too there is a void, with the rooms deprived of their furnishings. It also includes a thriving café and bookstore. Their web site markets an extensive range of 'products' that can be purchased online, along with tickets (Anne Frank Organization 2007). The web site has attractive images of the Anne Frank House facilities, accompanied by descriptions of the café, where 'you have a wonderful view of the Westerkerk and the Prinsengracht', and 'you can enjoy a hot beverage' and choose from a selection of foods. In order to increase the menu's appeal, it is noted that 'the dishes are not kosher'.

On the City of Dachau's (2007) web site, they now promote themselves as the 'City of Artists' and 'A Place of Learning and Remembrance'. A series of menus, colourfully illustrated, provide access to a walking tour of the old town, the city's art galleries and museums, a calendar of events, including the weekly markets, a palace concert schedule and information on the summer Dachauer Musik festival. 'Humans react to places according to their assigned meanings' (Norton 1989: 60), an aspect that has been cogently acknowledged in the city's attempts to reposition itself as a place of artistic and cultural interest. This portrayal harks back to the vision of the beautiful Dachau captured in Sedlmayr's painting (Figure 4.1), as a site of quiet elegance in harmony with its natural environment. Significantly, the city's web site also advertises two-night 'Package Deals' to the town, which include a range of accommodation, a guided tour, and extras such as an evening meal at

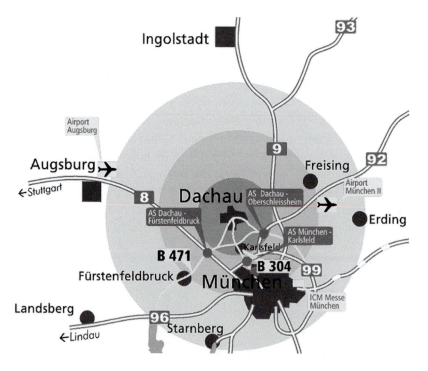

Figure 4.5
City of Dachau tourism web site map.

the Dachau Castle restaurant. A simplified map on the web site positions Dachau in equal font size to Munich, with circles radiating out to include surrounding cities, major roads and airports (Figure 4.5). With Dachau at the epicentre of the bull's eye graphic, the impression is of a city no longer overshadowed by the legacy of its concentration camp or quietly residing alongside its metropolitan neighbour, but rather demonstrating its regional importance and strategic appeal.

Even the Golfclub Dachau (2007), which occupies a substantial portion of the original SS camp, now advertises itself on an imaginatively designed web site. Although it does not mention the land's former association with the neighbouring SS compound, it charts the club's evolution from its original designation as the 'Golfclub München Dachau' formed in 1966. The initial choice of nomenclature, to include itself under the umbrella of Munich's sports orbit provided a reassuring link, encouraging Müncheners to travel out to the course. In 1983, the club modified its name to Golfclub Dachau, suggesting a renewed confidence in the stand-alone use of the name Dachau. The web site's virtual tour begins with a brief aerial shot of the course, with the conurbation of former SS buildings on its periphery, but omitting the concentration camp. It proceeds to zoom in and out of shots of long, heavily wooded fairways, and ends at the handsome clubhouse, with its new outdoor terrace dining facilities. The site's final web page features the 'Gastronomie im Golfclub Dachau', displaying images of a selection of traditional Bayerischer and international dishes that can be enjoyed on the dining terrace.

Corporate efforts to capitalize on the legions of visitors to the camp have occasionally backfired, such as in 1996 when McDonald's restaurant reportedly placed flyers under the windscreen wipers of cars parked outside the camp's gates in an effort to solicit new business (Mount 2000). The flyers read:

> Dear visitor, welcome to Dachau, welcome to McDonald's. Our restaurant's got 120 seats, about 40 outdoor seats and for our young guests an Indoor and Outdoor Playland. How to find us? Really simple. Just follow the picture! We're happy for your visit! Your McDonald's Restaurant, Dachau.

An article in the *New Statesman* reports that the public response that followed resulted in the chief executive of McDonald's Germany making a formal apology to the head of the country's Jewish community (ibid.). Greeted, as when visiting the town in 2006, by the bold visual image of a McDonald's billboard at the Dachau train station, together with others advertising popular beers, is illustrative of the city's contemporary struggle of perception between the horror conjured up by its name and its urban commonplace persona.

BEAUTIFUL DACHAU: THE TOURIST EXPERIENCE

The enduring physical beauty of the area has continued to attract artists, such as Otto Fuchs. 'If you look at the curves of the female form, you will see the Dachau landscape', remarks Fuchs, who first came to Dachau in 1938 and remained in the area after serving in the war (cited in Ryback 2001: 99). Yet, he acknowledges that 'regardless of what I paint or don't paint, for the rest of the world Dachau will always remain Dachau' (ibid.: 104).

Beautiful Dachau was designed as a large-screen video installation piece, which runs on a continuous loop, documenting the movement of people through architecturally juxtaposed and defined space, inviting the viewer to stand or sit and engage with it for a short period or for its duration. When it was first shown in the 'Visualizing TRANS Exhibition', organized by the University of Wisconsin at Madison, 20–28 October 2006, most spectators were seen to arbitrarily enter the film's narrative. In this setting, the film's lack of interviews or commentary worked to enhance 'the multisensory, multidimensional experience of the performance', much as Ockman (2000: 172) has described aspects of early cinema exhibition. In this respect, the film differs from the spectrum of previous documentaries related to this subject, including: *Nuit et Brouillard* (*Night and Fog*, 1955, 30 min.), filmed at Auschwitz, which uses commentary, archival photographs and footage and contemporary footage of the site; *Shoah* (1985, 544 min.), filmed at Treblinka, Chelmno and Auschwitz-Birkenau, which uses extensive interviews; *Gruesse aus Dachau* (*From Dachau with Love*, 2003, 77 min.), filmed in the town and camp of Dachau with interviews and commentary; and, *KZ* (2005, 97 min.), filmed in the town and camp of Mauthausen, using interviews and observational footage. The number of films that have examined the circumstances of the concentration camps are relatively small. As Floris Bakels (1993: 39), a prisoner of Dachau, explains that

> all those in a position to judge – i.e. former inmates – agree that it is impossible to describe a KZ adequately because it belongs to a different world, another planet. Not unlike the essence of dreams, which are equally hard to describe. This is probably the reason why so few people have ever attempted to make a KZ film, while POW camp films abound.

Through the use of historical witnesses film 'gives us history as triumph, anguish, joy, despair, adventure, suffering and heroism' (Rosenstone 1995: 59). Whether documentary or drama, 'film emotionalizes, personalizes, and dramatizes history' (ibid.). In not using witnesses or archival imagery, *Beautiful Dachau* does not adhere in the same way as previous documentaries do to the post-war genre of *Vergangenheitsbewältigungsfilm* – using film to come to terms with the past. The intention in *Beautiful Dachau* is in using a purist observational approach, it casts the viewer as witness to a contemporary engagement with Dachau's public space.

Without a narrator as guide, or dialogue to act as structural signposts, the viewer enters a liminal space populated by strangers and urban imagery, with the camp presented in the context of the town of Dachau and its mother city Munich. Modern urban life is seen thriving around the camp and penetrating its space with visitors' street fashions, multi-cultural mix of languages, sounds and body gestures. Kabakov's (1995: 256) view is that 'total' installation possesses an ability to position the spectator 'simultaneously as a "victim" and a viewer, who on the one hand surveys and evaluates the installation, and on the other, follows those associations, reflections which arise in him'. Operating in this vernacular, the immersive benefits of the format have the potential to situate the spectator as observer/participant, allowing them to physically move around freely and with the characters. Eschewing the inclusion of archival imagery associated with Dachau's past, represents an attempt to focus the film squarely on the now – relying on the viewer to provide the backlog of concentration camp imagery stored in their mental image bank, with scenes of abuse, incarceration, emaciation, SS 'medical' experimentation and stacks of corpses. To convey narrative, the film relies on the effect of visual and aural metaphor, such as when a group of officers in German uniforms tour the camp, or when the sound of marching on gravel turns out not to be German soldiers, but tourists walking en masse.

Beautiful Dachau observes today's visitors photographing the gate and posing cheerfully with their friends in front of it. What was once a totem for evil has become a popular tourist landmark. With the passage of 60 years and the deaths of most survivors of that period, many visitors to the memorial site are now either of school age or under the age of 50. The fact that Dachau's remit was not that of a mass extermination camp, a *Vernichtungslager*, like Auschwitz-Birkenau, and that its gas chamber was not used for killing (except in one possible human trial), might also with time have lessened the camp's horrific legacy for some of today's visitors.

As the film reveals, the old town is comprised of beautiful buildings, immaculate streets and public squares and spaces. Modern city life flourishes in its trendy cafés, shops and handsome hotels. The busy train station's platforms are regularly filled with commuters and tourists. Using the station as a hub, the city's buses either turn right to the camp, or left to the old town. After exiting the bus near the camp and walking along a path, tourists cross over a short bridge, walk through the main gate and disperse throughout the grounds. Most people first visit the museum and then gradually emerge to wander around, making their way to the crematoria on the far side of the camp. The *Appellplatz* (roll call square) seen in Figure 4.6 is situated in front of the *Wirtschaftsgebäude* (service building), which housed the kitchen, laundry, bathing facilities and storage rooms. The remainder of the camp is a vast space, where the 34 wooden *Blöcke* (barracks), each measuring 10 × 90 metres, once stood in two rows. It now presents a palpable site-specific void, carpeted in gravel.

The vision that the SS had of a 'beautiful', clean and model camp was symbolized by a ritualistic practice early every morning when 'special work units made up of invalids had to creep across the square, bent double, picking up every scrap of paper, every discarded matchstick' (Richardi 1998: 258). This description evokes the new moral order that the Nazis sought to champion, and the sublime, haunting qualities of its pristine spatial layout today. Experience of the sublime

Figure 4.6
Appellplatz, roll call square and 'service building', KZ Dachau.

could be 'both repulsive and desired', as Thomas (2000: 111) notes, with sublime sites having the potential to embody 'two opposing aspects affecting the psyche: physical conditions inspiring promise, and moral uplift countered by echoes of danger, death, hell and insanity'.

Visitors look minute in this spatial vacuum, where over 30,000 prisoners were held towards the end of the war, in a camp designed for 6,000. The *Lagerstrasse* central camp road was also known as 'The Avenue', and as visitors stroll down it some can be seen with a picnic basket or a dog on a lead, as if they were flâneurs in the similarly laid out formal gardens of Schloss Dachau in the *Altstadt* or in one of Munich's city parks. On either side of the Avenue are two columns of tall poplar trees (Figure 4.7), which stood with neat flower beds in front of the barracks during its time as a concentration camp. Together with the birch trees and other greenery that line the camp walls' periphery, these welcome signposts of nature hint at a more commonplace normality. As one former prisoner recalls the surreal setting: 'the almost idyllic image of the camp road, lined on both sides by poplar trees, and the plants in front of the barracks, contrasted sharply with the rest of the camp' (cited in Richardi 1998: 268).

Beautiful Dachau sets out to document the way in which a visit to the site provides a morphology of spatial engagement. As they enter the first portal to this space – the entrance gate, as seen in Figure 4.2, visitors are often expectant and the many teenage school groups are talkative and boisterous. After touring the catalogue of horrors in the museum, they move across the open space usually in pairs or small groups. Most experience the space as strangers – strangers to the space and to each other. The ambivalence of the stranger moving within the

Figure 4.7
The *Lagerstrasse* 'camp road' lined by poplar trees, with concrete borders denoting the 34 barracks.

camp's void, encircled by the city of Dachau's urban presence, creates a disjuncture of time and space which, as Clarke (1997: 4) has noted, replicates 'the ambivalence of the modern world'. While one might imagine that visitors to the camp are bound by a collective purpose – to pay homage to and witness an iconic site of mass murder, they behave much as they would on a city street: not making eye contact with others, or acknowledging each other's presence.

The festive atmosphere generated at the gate is replaced by a more restrained, sombre attitude in the open areas. In a space with numerous visitors, one is aware of absence. A place that was designed to house thousands of people now feels empty, much like the large building footprints of the Twin Towers in New York. With the numbered hut markers acting as emblematic headstones, the space in the camp has been transformed into that of an enormous, gravelled graveyard. *Beautiful Dachau* embraces the theme of spatial disconnection, which as Orr (2003) catalogues, is a common feature of a number of recent city films.

The emptiness of the space has been narrativized, though, with many visitors traversing it with headphones that convey stories of its former use and prisoners' experiences. The headphones can both inform the visitor about the space but also insulate them from engaging with its physicality or with each other. The ultimate objective of most visitors and the audio-recorded tour is the crematoria. At the far end of the camp, crossing the Würm canal over a small bridge, visitors make a journey that most prisoners only made when they were to be shot or hanged and their bodies placed in the ovens. The two crematoria are intact, one built in 1940 and a larger one constructed in 1942 to accommodate the increase in prisoners' deaths. The main crematorium, known as *Baracke X*, which was built by Polish priests who were prisoners trained as bricklayers, includes an undressing

Figure 4.8
Child posed in front of
the crematorium's ovens,
still from *Beautiful
Dachau*, 2006.

room, disinfection chamber, a gas chamber disguised as a shower room, the four-oven crematorium and a morgue (Berben 1975: 11). Each of the ovens was designed to accommodate seven to eight corpses at once. Here, in the same space where the liberators documented piles of emaciated bodies awaiting cremation, visitors now crowd around taking pictures of their friends and even their children posing in front of the ovens (see Figure 4.8). This response can appear peculiarly inappropriate, even flippant. But these photographic mementos may also serve as gestures of defiance and mockery.

Most visitors leaving the camp return on the special bus to the station, though in the writer's experience on a number of journeys none is overheard discussing any aspect of what they have just seen. On the short ride in what could be described as a casual and carefree atmosphere, tourists joked and conversed about what they would do next that day. Once again, their response perplexes the observer – does the void within the camp produce a void in people's response? Or, is the nature of their experience sufficiently profound and unexplainable that it is easier not to immediately discuss it? In spite of the remaining physical presence of the site and the graphic and tragic circumstances presented in KZ Dachau's museum, it can be difficult to tangibly appreciate those past events. Filmicly in this regard, Giuliana Bruno's (2002: 191) perceptive study, *Atlas of Emotion*, underscores the cultural process of visualization and evolution of the haptic bond between film and visiting a location – when sightseeing turns into site-seeing. Examples of first-person accounts correspond to this point, such as that of Floris Bakels (1993: 39), a Dutch lawyer who survived three years of incarceration in various camps and was prisoner number 99718 in Dachau when it was liberated:

> The *Häftling* is never sure of his life, truly not for one second of the day or night. Anything could happen at any time, and if one tried to imagine something really bad, something worse would really happen. We were deliberately and continuously terrorized on behalf of public authority. . . . We were *Häftlinge*, not people.

When visiting KZ Dachau today, such harrowing experiences can appear long distant. Yet, 'public remembrance is necessary for creating meaning in political culture', as Wolfgang Benz (2005: 33) asserts, and 'requires specific forms of ritual and concretization'. Viewing the visitors to the site, two significant thresholds are crossed and re-crossed – the entrance to the camp and the entrance to the crematorium. These two portals architecturally anchor the visitors' experience and act as *memento mori*. The specificity of place and the transmutation of meaning that the portals and the vast empty space in between them represent, reveal a journey of interpretation and recognition. In considering the monumentality of the site, one is reminded of the influential and prolific post-war architect, Paul Rudolph, who in his classic essay on 'The Six Determinants of Architectural Form' (1956) called for 'sequences of space which arouse one's curiosity, give a sense of anticipation, beckon and impel us to rush forward to find that releasing space which dominates, which promises a climax and therefore gives direction' (cited in Jencks and Kropf 1997: 214). The journey to, and experience of, KZ Dachau provides such an emotional response. Its crematoria now silent, now filled with boisterous crowds and clicking of cameras, adjoin the central vast, open space and the evocative International Monument sculpture designed by Nandor Glid, which represents twisted bodies caught on barbed wire, cogently provide an urban magnet which passionately engenders a monumental reckoning and humanistic plea inscribed with the words: 'Never Again'.

First there was an historic rural town that grew into a designated city and had the unusual circumstance of having a notorious concentration camp built on its periphery. It proceeded to develop a symbiotic engagement with the site during the course of its operation. Then occurred a schism and the simultaneous act of the city consuming the horror site within its residential and commercial zones, resulting in disavowal and the creation of a semi-divided city. Today, the city fathers have attempted to turn what once appeared to locals as a blight on the town's reputation and cultural history into an accepted space – even an asset. This unique transformation spanning the last 75 years has been emotionally, politically and spatially complex, problematized by conflicting local and national ideological forces, the attachment of shame, and the process of an urban integration accommodating the needs of the local populace and of millions of people visiting an international shrine and pilgrimage site.

NOTE

1   A shorter version of this essay appeared in *The Journal of Architecture*, 11 (5) (November 2006): 531–41.

REFERENCES

Anne Frank Organization (2007) Online. Available: www.annefrank.org/ (accessed 1 April 2007).

Bakels, F. (1993) *Nacht und Nebel, Night and Fog*, Cambridge: The Lutterworth Press.

Benz, W. (2005) 'Places of Remembrance, Culture of Remembrance', in B. Distel and G. Hammermann (eds) *The Dachau Concentration Camp, 1933 to 1945*, Dachau: Comité International de Dachau.

Berben, P. (1975) *Dachau, 1933–1945*, London: Norfolk Press.

Bruno, G. (2002) *Atlas of Emotion: Journeys in Art, Architecture and Film*, New York: Verso.

City of Dachau (2007) Online. Available: www.dachau.info/ (accessed 1 February 2007).

Clarke, D. B. (ed.) (1997) *The Cinematic City*, London: Routledge.

Distel, B. and Hammermann, G. (eds) (2005) *The Dachau Concentration Camp, 1933 to 1945*, Dachau: Comité International de Dachau.

Entrikin, J. N. (1991) *The Betweenness of Place*, London: Macmillan.

Gelernter, M. (1995) *Sources of Architectural Form*, Manchester: Manchester University Press.

Goffman, E. (1990) *Stigma: Notes on the Management of Spoilt Identity*, Harmondsworth: Penguin.

Golfclub Dachau e.V. (2007) Online. Available: www.gcdachau.de/ (accessed 10 February 2007).

Jackson, P. (1989) *Maps of Meaning*, London: Unwin Hyman.

Jaskot, P. (2000) *The Architecture of Oppression*, London: Routledge.

Jencks, C. and Kropf, K. (1997) *Theories and Manifestoes of Contemporary Architecture*, Chichester: Academy Editions.

Kabakov, I. (1995) *Total Installation*, Stuttgart: Cantz.

Low, S. M. and Lawrence-Zuniga, D. (eds) (2003) *The Anthropology of Space and Place*, Oxford: Blackwell.

Lynch, K. (1960) *The Image of the City*, Cambridge, MA: MIT Press.

Marcuse, H. (2001) *Legacies of Dachau*, Cambridge: Cambridge University Press.

Melossi, D. and Pavarini, M. (1981) *The Prison and the Factory*, London: Macmillan Press.

Mount, H. (2000) 'Ghost Town', *New Statesman*, 20 March. Online. Available: www.newstatesman.com/200003200056 (accessed 6 February 2007).

Mumford, L. (1938) *The Culture of Cities*, New York: Harcourt, Brace and Company.

Norton, W. (1989) *Explorations in the Understanding of Landscape*, New York: Greenwood Press.

Ockman, J. (2000) 'Architecture in a Mode of Distraction', in M. Lamster (ed.) *Architecture and Film*, New York: Princeton Architectural Press.

Orr, J. (2003) 'The City Reborn: Cinema at the Turn of the Century', in M. Shiel and T. Fitzmaurice (eds) *Screening the City*, London: Verso.

Richardi, H.-G. (1998) *Dachau – a Guide to its Contemporary History*, Dachau: Dachau Office of Cultural Affairs.

Rosenstone, R. (1995) *Visions of the Past*, Cambridge, MA: Harvard University Press.

Ryback, T. W. (2001) *The Last Survivor*, London: Picador.

Schneider, T. (2006) Personal communication with the author, 18 April.

Thomas, H. (2000) 'Sublimation', in I. Borden and J. Rendell (eds) *InterSections: Architectural Histories and Critical Theories*, London: Routledge.

Tuan, Y.-F. (1977) *Space and Place*, London: Edward Arnold.

Weber, R. (1995) *On the Aesthetics of Architecture*, Aldershot: Avebury.

FILMOGRAPHY

Beautiful Dachau (2006) dir. Alan Marcus, Granada Centre for Visual Anthropology/ Manchester.

Gruesse aus Dachau (From Dachau with Love) (2003) dir. Bernd Fischer, Egoli Tossell Film/Berlin.

KZ (2005) dir. Rex Bloomstein, Rex Entertainment/London.

Nuit et Brouillard (Night and Fog) (1955) dir. Alain Resnais, Argos Films.

Shoah (1985) dir. Claude Lanzmann, New Yorker Films.

Chapter 5: The Contested City

Beirut in Lebanese War Cinema

Lina Khatib

INTRODUCTION: BEIRUT BEFORE, DURING AND AFTER THE WAR

The city is a site for changing networks of power (Mahony 1997). Power relations are not only inscribed in spatiality, they are also 'spatially inscribed into cultural texts' like cinema (Shiel 2001: 5). As Mark Shiel argues, 'the fortunes of cinema and the city have been inextricably linked' (ibid.: 1). Perhaps nowhere does this statement ring true more than in the case of Beirut in Lebanese cinema. Lebanese cinema is a product of the landscape. The Civil War, which started in Lebanon in 1975 and ended in the early 1990s, left its mark on the physical appearance of the city, and on the cinematic imagination of Beirut. The representation of Beirut in pre-war and wartime Lebanese cinema closely follows the city's own war patterns.

Before the Civil War, Beirut was a cultural and economic centre in the Middle East. Its strategic location made it a link between the East and the West. It was also a host to mixed communities, a 'microcosm of Lebanon's pluralistic society' (Gavin and Maluf 1996: 33). Beirut's centre was its lifeline: 'when one arrived in Beirut one arrived in the center, when one left Beirut one left from the center' (Yahya 1993: 132). The centre of Beirut was its meeting space and the hub of its activity, harbouring 'the parliament, municipal headquarters, financial and banking institutions, religious edifices, transportation terminals, traditional souks, shopping malls and theaters' (Khalaf 2002: 246). During this period, Beirut featured in Lebanese cinema as the playground of the rich and famous, the setting for commercial action films and romantic comedies. In both sets of films, Beirut was a place of freedom and fantasy, the meeting place of lovers and the crossroad of the high powered.

The Civil War destroyed almost all of Beirut's centre. The markets were gone, the banks were abandoned, and most of the landscape was transformed into a vast collection of rubble. The city centre was deserted, its inhabitants reduced to warring militias who transformed its heart into what became known as the Green

Line dividing the Eastern and Western sections of the city. The spheres of destruction went beyond the centre, and the whole of Beirut came to be scarred by the war. The scars were physical and social as both the city's buildings and people shared the suffering. The metropolis that was a prime destination for the rich and famous of the Middle East became a ghost city, haunted by warring factions. 'Beirut' was no more; it was now either 'East' or 'West' Beirut – the East being the predominantly Christian side, the West the predominantly Muslim one. With the war, the image of Beirut began to change. The sight of buildings eaten up by bombs, abandoned shops and empty streets, transformed Beirut in war-time Lebanese cinema from a lived place into visions of an urban nightmare. This image of Beirut has become iconic, shared not only by Lebanese films but also by Western cinematic representations of the city. If there is an everlasting image of Beirut in Lebanese cinema, it is that of the broken city. In such images, Beirut is both a military and a symbolic battleground (Bollens 2000).

After the war, a major project of reconstruction began in Lebanon. As the city was re-unified, the focus of rebuilding was, unsurprisingly, the centre of Beirut. But reconstruction was not done through mere restoration. Although a selected number of streets in downtown Beirut were restored to their pre-war glory, most of the centre was simply cleared to make way for the erection of new buildings. 'The clearing of downtown created a collective homesickness for Beirutis even if they resided in Beirut. All manners of nostalgia and sentimentalized recollection were unleashed' (Sarkis 2005: 286). Beirutis wanted the city restored to its old self. Parents would tell their children about the lost souks in anticipation of their revival.

But the new face of the city was different from its old one. More than 15 years after the end of the war, most of Beirut's city centre remains empty, with the building project progressing significantly slower than anticipated. The emptiness of the centre mirrored the emptiness felt by the Lebanese people following the end of the war. With no national reconciliation taking place after the conflict, the war era was at risk of being swept under the carpet and forgotten about. The Lebanese were choosing not to confront their demons. The war became a saga not to be discussed. This action manifested itself in people's relationship with the city. Many buildings suffering from bomb damage were simply ignored: the 'physical marks of the war in Lebanon are still visible, habitable, coped with and normalized in the inattentiveness of daily life to their persistence' (Sarkis 1993: 119). As they walked through the streets of Beirut, it is as if the inhabitants selected to look straight ahead and not at the collapsing buildings surrounding them. Lebanese cinema has reacted to this avoidance strategy. While reconstruction was taking place, Lebanese cinema remained stubbornly focused on the devastated image of Beirut, whether by representing it graphically or by invoking it symbolically. This can be seen as a challenge to the post-war amnesia in Lebanese society. When the Civil War ended, the Lebanese people seemed to collectively want to leave it behind; it was too guilt-inducing as it did not have clear victims when all factions were involved in its execution. Cinema is one of the few arenas in Lebanon where the ugly reality of the war is confronted: over the last 30 years, the Civil War has been the predominant theme in Lebanese cinema (Khatib 2006).

Beirut in Lebanese cinema, therefore, presents a psychogeographic landscape. It is not a mere background space. It is another character with its own story to tell. It is 'immersed in narrative' (McArthur 1997: 20), its stories linked with those of its inhabitants. It is witness to their connections and divisions, their past and their present, and therefore plays an important role in countering attempts at recovering from the war by mere forgetfulness. In what follows, the chapter will start by analysing Lebanese cinema's focus on representing the disfigured face of Beirut. It will then discuss the representation of the mirroring of Beirut's fragmentation and the breakdown of society during the war. Finally, the chapter will offer an assessment of post-war Lebanese films set in present-day Beirut. Far from celebrating the resurrection of the city, the films offer a criticism of the way the city has been forced to forget its past.

THE DISFIGURED CITY

The Civil War redefined people's relationship with Beirut, and resulted in the 'redrawing of Lebanon's social geography' (Khalaf 1993: 18). The country in general, and Beirut specifically, came to be largely divided along religious lines, with communities from most of Lebanon's sects moving closer together to create homogeneous clusters. The change in place, therefore, reflected the change in people (Khalaf 1993). With the city being the centre of militia fighting during the war, Beirut was transformed from a 'playground' into a 'battleground' (Khalaf 1993: 107). Lebanese cinema reflected this change in territorial identity by foregrounding the representation of a wounded Beirut. By seeking out those areas of Beirut that highlight the material impact of war, Lebanese cinema excavates what Boyer (1995: 82) calls the *disfigured city*': 'the invisible city', or the 'abandoned segments' surrounding the figured city. He says: 'the disfigured city remains unimaginable and forgotten and therefore invisible and excluded' (ibid.). Dominant discourse on Beirut after the war focused on it as a city being resurrected. This discussion (propagated through the media and by those politicians and businesspeople involved in rebuilding the city centre) seemed to forget those segments of the city that were not considered worth preserving and consequently demolished, or that were ignored completely by the restoration project. The media, in particular, foregrounded the 'new and improved' Beirut, but they shied away from representing those abandoned areas of the city. While Boyer uses the term 'disfigured' symbolically to refer to the idea of lack of representation and imagination, in the case of Beirut, 'disfigured' can also be applied in the literal sense. Not only is war-time Beirut ignored in the Lebanese public imagination, the war-torn *body* of Beirut is disfigured and scarred.

Lebanese cinema uses different methods of highlighting this disfigurement, from lingering shots of physical destruction to shots of graffiti and other physical marks of war. It is as if Lebanese filmmakers are compelled to dwell on the image of broken Beirut, even if the city is not the overt focus of their films. *In the Battlefields* (2004), for example, is set during the war and narrates the stories of a 12-year-old Lebanese girl, Lina, whose family is torn apart, and of the family's teenage maid, Siham. The film follows Siham as she explores her identity and sexuality, and dreams of a future away from the harsh conditions inflicted on her by Lina's cruel aunt. But the film ends not with the long shot of Siham finally running away to start a new life (which would have made a logical conclusion to a film centred on her story), but with a sequence of Beirut's destroyed buildings (see Figure 5.1). While the director, Danielle Arbid (2006), insists that she did not want Beirut to be a 'character' in the film (Jaafar 2004), the shots of Beirut at the end function to symbolize the scars left on Lina and Siham by linking the interior drama with an exterior one. We see mid-shots of buildings on the verge of collapse and close-ups of others full of bullet holes intercut with wide shots of the city as a whole. The body of Beirut comes to mirror the bodies of its inhabitants. But this is not a causal relationship whereby 'nature' is mirrored in 'artifice'

> rather, there is a two-way linkage which could be defined as an interface . . . a model of the relation between bodies and cities which sees them not as megalithic total entities, distinct identities, but as assemblages or collections of parts . . . defining and establishing each other.
>
> (Grosz 1998: 47)

Perhaps the best illustration of this mutuality between bodies and cities is found in Maroun Baghdadi's film *Little Wars* (1982). The film revolves around the story of four young Lebanese men and women who are caught up in the war and who try to cope with it in different ways. While one of them decides that his

Figure 5.1
Scene of war-time Beirut, still from *In the Battlefields*, directed by Danielle Arbid, 2004.

only way of coping is by leaving the country, another, Nabil, realizes that the only way of survival in the city is through death. Posters of martyrs were a familiar feature of Beirut during the war. It was almost impossible to walk through the city while avoiding the gaze of the martyrs on the walls (see Figure 5.2). One of the most haunting scenes in *Little Wars* is one where Nabil decides to create martyr posters of himself and to declare himself dead. The film presents a right-to-left pan of a street in Beirut full of posters of martyrs. The shot of the poster-filled street in Beirut is cut to reveal Nabil in a room, empty but for the tens of black and white posters bearing his image on the walls (see Figure 5.3). It is in this way that Nabil's body is shown as merging with that of Beirut to form one entity, scarred by the war but unable to escape from it.

The city and its people shared a destiny during the war. Both lost their points of reference. The war changed the dynamics of interaction in Lebanese society, introducing new parameters of good and evil. It also forced Beirut to lose its prominent landmarks, its identity points. The Lebanese could no longer use the landmarks to orient themselves spatially, just as they could no longer rely on older forms of knowledge to orient themselves morally (Rykwert 2000). The Burj Square – also known as Martyrs' Square – in downtown Beirut was the most significant of such lost landmarks. The hub of interaction in the city, and its main transport link, the Square became the heart of the Green Line. Its gleaming statue that had been erected to glorify Lebanon's independence martyrs, was now punctured with bullet holes. The image of the 'new' Burj Square with its perforated statue became a symbol of the war, reproduced in the press, on television, and in cinema.

Lebanese films such as *To You Wherever You Are* (2001), *Once Upon a Time, Beirut* (1994) and *Around the Pink House* (1998) are examples of how the Square is used to comment on the destruction of the war. The first two films, set in the

Figure 5.2
Photographs of martyrs
on a Beirut street,
still from *Little Wars*,
directed by Maroun
Baghdadi, 1982.

Figure 5.3
Nabil surrounded by his 'martyr' photographs, still from *Little Wars*, directed by Maroun Baghdadi, 1982.

post-war present, contain nostalgic sequences using archival footage of the pre-war Square, a reminder of the loss created by the war. *Around the Pink House*, a film about the effects of reconstruction in downtown Beirut, shows us a still image of the Square in its opening credits. The photograph bounces up and down on the screen, in and out of sight. The first time we see the photograph, it is a postcard-like image of the pre-war Square with its leafy palm trees. However, each time it disappears and reappears, more (computer-generated) bullet holes cover it, until the original photograph is barely visible. *The Tornado* (1992) goes further in this focus on physical transformation by showing the reaction of an emigrant who has returned to Lebanon just after the end of the war, and who is shocked at his inability to recognize the city.

THE FRAGMENTATION OF THE CITY

As the city ceased to belong to all its inhabitants, the war changed the spatial patterns of life in Beirut. A number of Lebanese films depict the fragmentation of Beirut at the start of and during the Civil War. The fragmentation of the city in those films is a symptom of the fragmentation of Lebanese society: during the war, Beirut became 'a microcosm of Lebanon's fragmented political culture' (Khalaf 1993: 74). Films such as *West Beyrouth* (1998) and *In the Battlefields* deal with the breakdown of Beirut from a whole city into exclusive, homogeneous sectarian zones. *West Beyrouth* starts with the idyllic existence of a Muslim middle-class family, the Noueiris, living in Beirut. The only thing upsetting the harmony of this existence is the harmless clowning around of the teenage son Tarek at school.

This equilibrium is disturbed by the incident which catalysed the Civil War in Lebanon: on 13 April 1975, a bus carrying Palestinian passengers was attacked by right-wing Christian militants, killing 31 people and wounding another 30. The Noueiris are bewildered by the incident, not understanding its causes or its implications. Oblivious to the social and political cracks forming around them, they attempt to continue their life as usual. The father, Riad, talks of a planned family holiday in France, and the mother, Hala, insists on taking Tarek to school despite his assertion that school is now closed. Riad's misunderstanding of the situation leads him to distance himself as a Lebanese from the incident, saying it is 'between Palestinians and Israelis, nothing to do with us'. This statement echoes a sentiment that was prevalent in Lebanon during the war, where the conflict was referred to as 'the war of Others on our land'. *West Beyrouth* works to dispel this myth, forcing Riad to accept that the event of 13 April was not a mere 'incident', but a massacre.

Riad and his family's realization of what is going on, though, does not happen immediately. The family attempt to cling on to normality as much as possible, resisting notions of the city tearing itself apart. Instead, they try to recapture pre-war spatial patterns, when they had access to all parts of the city, as a counter strategy to the fact that it had now effectively been scissored in two. Hala, a lawyer, insists on going to work although the Palace of Justice is on the then-still-unnamed 'other' side of the city, while Tarek and his best friend Omar try to come up with ingenious ways of crossing the border, even if it means being held up by a militia. As the family drive through Beirut in their car, they are surrounded by military jeeps. A militant with a kaffiyah around his neck (to signify his Muslim affiliation) stops the car and asks for Riad's identity card (in Lebanon, before the introduction of new identity cards after the war, ID cards stated the bearer's sectarian affiliation). The militant tells Riad that the Christians are 'not letting anyone *in*' (see Figure 5.4). This statement is significant as it points out the division of the city into two zones. If there is an 'in', then there must be an 'out':

> *Riad:* But we're from here.
> *Militant:* Only Christians can cross.
> *Riad:* But we're from Beirut.
> *Militant:* Beirut is no more, it's East and West.
> (Hala wonders which one they are in.)
> *Riad:* West, I guess.

The conversation between Riad and the militant illuminates changing notions of place. The notion 'here' became contested. Beirut during the war, and as reflected in the film, was both close and distant to its inhabitants. It was still their city, but it also became a city of Others. As the war progressed, the gap between 'us' and 'them' widened. The contest over place was not only *between* militants and civilians, but also *among* militants and civilians, where each side claimed its own segment of the city that was dissociated from the Other. Beirut became the focal point of nationalistic ethnic conflict: a 'platform for the expression of conflicting sovereignty claims' (Bollens 2000: 3). The division of Beirut into a Muslim

Figure 5.4
Checkpoint on the East/West Beirut border, still from *West Beyrouth*, directed by Ziad Doueiri, 1998.

side and a Christian side transformed the city into 'an assortment of cloistered zones representing reawakened religious identities and communities: a series of enclosed territories founded upon the logic of exclusion and separation' (Yahya 1993: 128). In war-torn Beirut, each ethnic group claimed the city as their own (Bollens 2000).

While *West Beyrouth*, set at the outbreak of the war in 1975, represents the transition to this stage of exclusion, *In the Battlefields*, set in 1983, depicts Beirut as the divided city, focusing completely on life on the Eastern side. East Beirut in the film is shown as having a distinct life from that of West Beirut. Like Berlin in *Wings of Desire* (1987), in Beirut, virtually the only thing East and West shared was the sky. As Maha Yahya (1993: 132) states, the Green Line became 'the stoneless "Berlin Wall" of Beirut'. *In the Battlefields* focuses on the life of a middle-class family living in the then Christian East Beirut. The film does not focus on the representation of the war, but on the internal turmoil felt by the family members, especially the 12-year-old daughter Lina. The war is present in the film but not in the foreground. Instead, the breakdown of the family, with a gambling father and a tyrant aunt, is a metaphor for the breakdown of Lebanese society. But since the film focuses on life in East Beirut, and does not represent the other side of the city, it reflects the experience of people living on the East side during the war who had very little contact with those from West Beirut. The film highlights the ambivalence of this experience, and is an example of how each community during the war saw its territory as an unpolluted utopia (Khalaf 2002: 248).

The people in charge of East Beirut (the militants) featured in *In the Battlefields*, do not feel the need to leave their space. They express their satisfaction with the way their community survives on its own, and their preparedness to do whatever it takes to maintain the community's autonomy. The fact that they perceive themselves as Lebanese, highlights the re-definition of nationalism from being an inclusive sentiment, to one based on religion and ethnicity. Ethnic nationalism is by definition exclusive and fragmentary (Bollens 2000: 6). The Beirut of *In the Battlefields* is a place of multiple exclusions, its inhabitants kept apart by fear of the Other (Khalaf 2002: 247). This fear is voiced in one scene where the family and their neighbours have to stay in an underground shelter to escape from the shelling of their side of the city by Muslim militants. One of the neighbours says how he heard that the other side have recruited 'two-metre tall' Somalis to attack the Christian side. The film references the myths of the monstrous Other that circulated in Beirut during the war, where warring factions would attribute to the 'enemy' superhuman qualities that justified their own 'resistance' and presented the war as a necessity for self-preservation.

In the Battlefields, like *West Beyrouth*, illustrates the 'retribalization' of Lebanon in general and Beirut in specific: 'the reinforcement of kinship, confessional, and communal loyalties' (Khalaf 2002: 262–3) that pre-date the nation. Both films portray how the fragmentation of the city created multiple boundaries between different ethnic and religious groups (Yahya 1993). Khalaf (1993: 138) asserts that 'borders are usually more porous and malleable . . . On the other hand, boundaries conjure up images of confinement and exclusion'. Beirut in the films was transformed from a whole into several 'medieval cities' separated from one another by invisible walls (Yahya 1993: 134). Those invisible walls were supplemented by visible markers of demarcation. Yahya (1993: 128) asserts that 'particular fragments of territory become representative of different groups of citizens, as various physical structures give visible articulation to new identities'.

Each warring side had its own such structures: from its choice of graffiti to its selection of martyrs posters. Beirut was no longer controlled by its people collectively, but by different militias, their control of the space enforcing their psychological control over the population. The militias set about expelling 'outsiders', resulting in the homogenization of their areas. Beirut became a city contested, 'located on the fault line between cultures' (Bollens 2000: 5). This contest manifested itself in the way 'each militia imposed its own vision of the city' (Yahya 1993: 133). Neighbourhoods came to imply not only proximity but also group cohesion and attachment to the territory and separation from the Other (Herbert and Thomas 1997). However, viewing *West Beyrouth* and *In the Battlefields* together, one cannot help but draw similarities between the lives of people on both sides. Perhaps the most salient link is the separation between militants and civilians, where each community seems to be oppressed by its supposed 'protectors'. In *West Beyrouth*, terrifying Muslim militants interrupt Tarek and Omar's forays into the city. In *In the Battlefields*, Christian militants enter the shelter where the families are huddled to carelessly inform them that they have taken over the roof of the building to launch missiles from, making the building an almost definite target for counter-bombing.

IN SEARCH OF POST-WAR BEIRUT

There is still no consensus in Lebanon on the exact date the war ended. Some say it ended in 1990, while others say it was 1992. But there is a sentiment shared by a number of filmmakers such as Ghassan Salhab, Khalil Joreige and Joana Hadjithomas that the war has never ended. Those filmmakers only started making feature films after the war. Their films are set in the present, but feature the war both implicitly and explicitly. The explicit focus on war, such as in Salhab's film *Beirut Phantoms* (1998), is understandable when perceived from the director's point of view, that the war needs to be discussed in the public arena and confronted before Lebanese society can truly claim to move on (Salhab 2004). However, it is the implicit focus on the war in post-war cinema that is of interest here, the way war features in the background, in the actions of the characters, and in the city they inhabit. *A Perfect Day* (2005) and *Around the Pink House* represent this through a shared concern with the 'difficulty of living in the present in Beirut' (Joreige 2005) that is the result of post-war amnesia.

A Perfect Day is set in a present-time Beirut haunted by the war, 'a dystopian present defined by a sense of historical past' (Easthope 1997: 133). The post-war anomie felt by the young people in the film is sublimated through their attachment to material things: cigarettes, cars, alcohol and mobile phones. According to Joreige (2005), the characters represent post-war addiction that is filling an otherwise unfillable void. Khalaf (2002: 260) sees such actions as being the result of how 'victims of collective suffering . . . rage with bitterness and long to make up for lost time and opportunity'. The film portrays Beirut as a living nightmare: a bleak place often shot in the dark. While Beirut had become claustrophobic during the war as people's movement within the city was restricted, in *A Perfect Day* the claustrophobia is maintained, albeit differently. The film has several mid-shots of traffic jams in Beirut, where cars seem to be closing in on each other and where almost every driver is inundated with street vendors selling newspapers and cigarettes. The crowded streets of Beirut are also framed by seemingly endless advertising billboards. The martyrs posters of the war have disappeared from the walls, but they are now replaced with those of pop stars. We often see the main character, Malik, roaming around the city in his car, eyes barely open after many sleepless nights. Malik never manages to escape the watchful eye of the pop stars who peer at him from every wall, bridge and billboard. The pop stars are notable for their surgically enhanced appearance: fake hair, fake lips, fake breasts and fake noses. They seem to mirror the fakeness of Beirut after the war. Its reconstruction was seen by many as cosmetic, empty and inauthentic.

The reconstruction of Lebanon saw its greatest scale in downtown Beirut. The focus on the city centre emerged from its perception as the missing national centre that will bring the different factions in the country back together as one. As Bollens (2000: 4) argues, 'the management of war-torn cities holds the key to sustainable coexistence of warring ethnic groups subsequent to cessation of overt hostilities'. However, the process of reconstruction was contested. On one hand, it was seen as a chance for Beirut to become a modern economic centre; on the other hand, reconstruction provided hope of restoration of the city centre into its pre-war self. The result of this contest is that the little that has been rebuilt in the city centre of Beirut has elements of both visions. It is traditional and modern at the same time. But what was not anticipated by the Lebanese people who welcomed the reconstruction was their own exclusion from this space. The new downtown Beirut, with its exclusive apartments, designer shops and expensive restaurants, is beyond the means of most Lebanese. The only thing they can afford is to walk through the city in wonder, strangers in their own land.

The last shot in *Around the Pink House* 'reveals the new Beirut, a giant construction site, from which the poor are being excluded' (Walsh 2000). Borhan Alawiyeh's film *To You Wherever You Are*, also comments on this exclusion. In the film, one of the old inhabitants of Beirut, Ahmad Beidoun, says:

> The restoration that has taken place, despite the good appearances, has excluded 'you'; you have no past here. When you think of the past, it contradicts the current buildings. They now have no age, no depth, no relation to you. The youth excludes you. We the old become tourists, like in Rome or Larnaca.

Therefore, it is not just the economic factor that is sidelining the Beirutis, it is also the erased connection with the past. As Khalaf (2002: 309) argues, 'what we are witnessing at the moment is a multilayered negotiation or competition for the representation and ultimate control of Beirut's spatial and collective identity'. This is expressed in Hadjithomas and Joreige's film *Around the Pink House*. The film stresses the importance of place against 'de-territorialization' (Shiel 2001: 11). The film tells the story of an old, colonial-style pink house in Beirut that was selected for demolition in the aim of constructing a modern shopping centre in its place, triggering a conflict between those in favour of modernism and those in favour of tradition. The film focuses on the inability of the state to produce space:

> The city does not function in the film as a choreographed spectacle celebrating the scientific, cultural, intellectual, political and economic grandeur of the . . . nation-state. Rather, the film's representation of the city registers the traces of power, the decaying colonial infrastructure and the increased role of capital in the production of space. Multiple historical layers come together in the space of the city.
>
> (Narkunas 2001: 154)

The film begins with a still image of pre-war Burj Square. The camera zooms out to reveal the image as a picture carried by a man standing in the middle of a traffic jam in downtown Beirut, signalling the transformation of the landscape from an idyllic to a congested one. A news bulletin is heard from one of the cars' radios, stating how reconstruction in downtown Beirut has stopped the traffic and how 'the sound of construction has replaced the sound of bombs'. *Around the Pink House* proceeds to offer further comments on the city's changing character. We hear a man in the traffic jam saying 'it's no longer a city, it's an amusement park'. Unlike most Lebanese films, the film is not set in a recognizable area in Beirut. Joana Hadjithomas (2006) says: 'We built the city in *Around the Pink House* in a place that did not exist. It's a fictional city. There is a link between this theme and the rebuilding that was taking place in Beirut at the time.' Selected areas in down-town Beirut were chosen for preservation and restoration in the aim of retaining 'Beirut's memory', while most of downtown has been cleared in preparation for the building of modern buildings. In *Around the Pink House*, the businessman who wants to demolish the house to build a shopping centre in its place wants to retain the house's façade so the shopping centre can be built around it, because 'the façade is our memory' (see Figure 5.5). 'Beirut's memory' is therefore selectively reduced to token links with the past, forcefully severing the identity of the new city from its old one.

It is this forceful severing of the relationship with the past that links Joreige and Hadjithomas' films. The director, Hadjithomas (2006), explains that

> our films talk about the present and how we can live in it. This present is linked to the past and to memory. But how come we are not able to live in the present? Maybe we are severing our relationship with the past in a too artificial a way. It's like being on a treadmill, you run and you run and you are not progressing. When we wrote *A Perfect Day*, we felt that we are dead in this city and are not having much influence on the society around us or on the city itself. Maybe the relationship with the past is what is preventing us from moving on.

The reconstruction of Beirut is a symptom of the post-war amnesia experi-enced in Lebanon and that Lebanese cinema tries to counter. By insisting on linking present-day Beirut with the war past, the films perform an important role in the process of national recovery. Lebanese cinema – during and after the war – does not offer a romantic vision of Beirut, and seems incapable of ignoring the city as a witness to what has been. Whether by highlighting Beirut as a disfigured city, by re-presenting the social divisions of the war, or by commenting on the need

Figure 5.5
Plans for preserving the façade, still from *Around the Pink House*, directed by Joana Hadjithomas and Khalil Joreige, 1998.

for post-war reflection, the films use Beirut as a trigger of memory. As Dolores Hayden (1999: 144) observes:

> Places trigger memories for insiders, who have shared a common past, and at the same time places often can represent shared pasts to outsiders who might be interested in knowing about them in the present. Places also permit people who have lived in them to re-experience their pasts while simultaneously experiencing the place in the present. They may stimulate individual memory while mirroring current circumstances.

Beirut emerges as a city contested between dominant discourse and the resistant voice of cinema. The stubborn image of war-torn Beirut stands as a reminder of the cruelty of war, and of its remaining legacy. It is a necessary image fighting against the sanitizing of the war and the induced forgetfulness of its monstrosity.

REFERENCES

Arbid, D. (2006) Interview with the author, Paris, 3 April.

Bollens, S. A. (2000) *On Narrow Ground: Urban Policy and Ethnic Conflict in Jerusalem and Belfast*, Albany, NY: State University of New York Press.

Boyer, M. C. (1995) 'The Great Frame-Up: Fantastic Appearances in Contemporary Spatial Politics', in H. Liggett and D. C. Perry (eds) *Spatial Practices*, London: Sage, pp. 81–109.

Easthope, A. (1997) 'Cinecities in the Sixties', in D. B. Clarke (ed.) *The Cinematic City*, London: Routledge, pp. 129–39.

Gavin, A. and Maluf, R. (1996) *Beirut Reborn: The Restoration and Development of the Central District*, London: Academy.

Grosz, E. (1998) 'Bodies-cities', in S. Pile and H. Nast (eds) *Places Through the Body*, London: Routledge, pp. 42–51.

Hadjithomas, J. (2006) Interview with the author, Beirut, 22 April.

Hayden, D. (1999) 'Landscapes of Loss and Remembrance: The Case of Little Tokyo in Los Angeles', in J. Winter and S. Emmanuel (eds) *War and Remembrance in the Twentieth Century*, Cambridge: Cambridge University Press, pp. 142–60.

Herbert, D. T. and Thomas, C. J. (1997) *Cities in Space, City as Place*, London: David Fulton Publishers.

Jaafar, A. (2004) 'Domestic Battlefields: Danielle Arbid on *Maarek Hob*', *Bidoun*, Issue 2 (Fall) www.bidoun.com/issues/issue_2/02_all.html#article.

Joreige, K. (2005) Introduction to the screening of *A Perfect Day*, London Film Festival, 26 October.

Khalaf, S. (1993) *Beirut Reclaimed: Reflections on Urban Design and the Restoration of Civility*, Beirut: Dar An-Nahar.

—— (2002) *Civil and Uncivil Violence in Lebanon: A History of the Internationalization of Communal Conflict*, New York: Columbia University Press.

Khatib, L. (2006) 'The Voices of Taboos: Women in Lebanese War Cinema', *Women: A Cultural Review*, 17 (1): 65–77.

Mahoney, E. (1997) 'The People in Parentheses: Space Under Pressure in the Postmodern City', in D. B. Clarke (ed.) *The Cinematic City*, London: Routledge, pp. 168–85.

McArthur, C. (1997) 'Chinese Boxes and Russian Dolls: Tracking the Elusive Cinematic City', in D. B. Clarke (ed.) *The Cinematic City*, London: Routledge, pp. 19–45.

Narkunas, J. P. (2001) 'Streetwalking in the Cinema of the City: Capital Flows Through Saigon', in M. Shiel and T. Fitzmaurice (eds) *Cinema and the City: Film and Urban Societies in a Global Context*, Oxford: Blackwell, pp. 147–57.

Nowell-Smith, G. (2001) 'Cities: Real and Imagined', in M. Shiel and T. Fitzmaurice (eds) *Cinema and the City: Film and Urban Societies in a Global Context*, Oxford: Blackwell, pp. 99–108.

Rykwert, J. (2000) *The Seduction of Place: The City in the Twenty-First Century*, London: Weidenfeld & Nicolson.

Salhab, G. (2004) Interview with the author, Beirut, 14 April.

Sarkis, H. (1993) 'Territorial Claims: Architecture and Post-War Attitudes Toward the Built Environment', in S. Khalaf and P. S. Khoury (eds) *Recovering Beirut: Urban Design and Post-War Reconstruction*, Leiden: E.J. Brill, pp. 101–27.

—— (2005) 'A Vital Void: Reconstructions of Downtown Beirut', in L. J. Vale and T. J. Campanella (eds) *The Resilient City: How Modern Cities Recover from Disaster*, Oxford: Oxford University Press, pp. 281–98.

Shiel, M. (2001) 'Cinema and the City in History and Theory', in M. Shiel and T. Fitzmaurice (eds) *Cinema and the City: Film and Urban Societies in a Global Context*, Oxford: Blackwell, pp. 1–18.

Walsh, D. (2000) 'War and Peace', *World Socialist Web Site*, www.wsws.org/articles/2000/may2000/sff3-m26.shtml.

Yahya, M. (1993) 'Reconstituting Space: The Aberration of the Urban in Beirut', in S. Khalaf and P. S. Khoury (eds) *Recovering Beirut: Urban Design and Post-War Reconstruction*, Leiden: E.J. Brill, pp. 128–65.

FILMOGRAPHY

Around the Pink House (1998) dirs. Joana Hadjithomas and Khalil Joreige, Mille et Une Productions.

Beirut Phantoms (1998) dir. Ghassan Salhab, GH Films/Idéa Productions/Optima Film.

In the Battlefields (2004) dir. Danielle Arbid, Quo Vadis Cinema/Versus Production/Taxi Films.

Little Wars (1982) dir. Maroun Baghdadi, NEF Diffusion.

Once Upon a Time, Beirut (1994) dir. Jocelyne Saab, Aleph Producciones S.A./Balcon Production/Hessischer Rundfunk/ARTE.

A Perfect Day (2005) dirs. Khalil Joreige and Joana Hadjithomas, Mille et Une Productions.

To You Wherever You Are (2001) dir. Borhan Alawiyeh, Ardèche Image Production.

The Tornado (1992) dir. Samir Habchi, Arab Film Distribution.

West Beyrouth (1998) dir. Ziad Doueiri. Doueiri Films/Centre National de la Cinématographie/Ciné Libre/3B Productions.

Wings of Desire (1987) dir. Wim Wenders, Road Movies Filmproduktion/Argos Films/Westdeutscher Rundfunk.

Chapter 6: *Tribute in Light*

Iconography of a Memorial

Dietrich Neumann

Between 11 March and 13 April 2002, every evening from dusk until midnight, 88 custom-made Xenon searchlight projectors sent two shafts of light vertically into the New York sky (see Figure 6.1). They had been installed next to the site of the World Trade Center, whose twin towers were destroyed six months before in the terrorist attacks of 11 September 2001. This installation served as a temporary and ephemeral memorial to those who died in the attacks and to the towers themselves, by evoking their form and position in the skyline. The unforgettable spectacle of the two bluish beams of light reaching upwards into the night sky was witnessed simultaneously by hundreds of thousands in the city and its suburbs, and published around the world. It soon became one of the most powerful iconic images of the new century. In Spike Lee's beautiful film, *The 25th Hour* (2002), the lights provide a haunting backdrop for the story about a deeply conflicted American life. The memorial installation has been brought back every year on 11 September, following a decision by the Lower Manhattan Development Corporation that secured its yearly return until 2008 (Dunlap 2004).

The *Tribute in Light* was the collaborative work of a number of artists and architects, mainly two teams on the creative side, the architects John Bennett and Gustavo Bonevardi of PROUN Space Studio, and artists Julian LaVerdiere and Paul Myoda, as well as the architect Richard Nash Gould, and the lighting designers Paul Marantz and Jules Fisher. General Electric, the Deutsche Bank and AOL Time Warner provided the funding for the first 31 days of the memorial (Eboy 2001: 34).

During the initial run in March and April 2002, *The New York Times* established an online discussion forum (now archived), which collected 292 electronic mails sent between 7 March and 14 May 2002. The vast majority of contributors used terms such as 'beautiful', 'profound', and 'overwhelming' when describing their impressions, and many asked for the installation to become permanent. It appeared as the perfect combination of the ephemeral and the monumental, the literal and the metaphorical, as a 'beacon of hope' or 'lights of

Figure 6.1
Tribute in Light, Julian
LaVerdiere and Paul
Myoda, digital rendering.

reason'. Some contributors recognized an imaginary weapon, 'like a sword in the hand of the city itself', 'a warning to them, no matter where they hide', while another reader vehemently rejected this particular reading: 'I suspect that we are being manipulated to keep up the fervent patriotism and unquestioning war fever.'

Among the few negative voices five criticized the memorial for its waste of energy, and two for its danger to bird migration. Only three letters out of 292 referred to the installation's historic iconography. On 16 March one email cited widespread 'amnesia' for the fact that the creators of this 'flippant spectacle' were not aware of plagiarizing Speer's installation and 'completely oblivious to the cynical use of their luminous war-swords'. A few days later, on 19 March another reader warned that the memorial could 'be considered offensive by the survivors of the Holocaust. While we remember the victims of 11 September, we should also spend a minute remembering other victims of intolerance.' On 11 March 2002, one reader had asked: 'Did it occur to anybody that *Tribute in Light* is reminiscent of Albert Speer's *Cathedral of Light*, which was used for the 1936 and 1937 Nazi Party Rallies? If so, does it matter?' (New York Times 2002).

This is, of course, a perfectly reasonable question. In fact, it aims right at the heart of any discussion about the public construction of meaning and the power of images. To what extent does it matter if artistic tools and icons have been used in different cultural contexts before, especially if that previous use is little known in the new environment? The following short look at earlier uses of similar imagery suggests, I believe, that such historic context can indeed enrich an understanding of the *Tribute in Light*.

Shortly after the bright carbon arc light had been invented in the mid-nineteenth century, it was put to practical use: beams of light attracted crowds of onlookers to public spaces at night and allowed building construction to continue after dark. The World's Fairs of 1889 in Paris and 1893 in Chicago proudly displayed powerful searchlight beams, illuminating various exhibition buildings from high vantage points (Figure 6.2). It was not long before focused beams of light were being used for warfare. During nocturnal surprise attacks by land and sea technologically less advanced enemies were blinded and turned into easy targets, as for example in the French colonial wars in Sudan in 1884 (Schivelbusch 1986: 61).

When exactly searchlight beams were discovered as an artist's tool for nocturnal displays in their own right is hard to tell. An early instance is the moment when the American fleet under Admiral Dewey in 1899 returned triumphantly from its victory in the Spanish American war. The ships' arrival in New York City was celebrated with a festival of urban illumination. Among its most impressive parts were the beams sent upwards from searchlights on both sides of the East River, forming what 'looked like the ribs of a vaulted arch' high above the incoming fleet (*The New York Times* 1899). This triumphal arch of unprecedented proportions reflected the monumental satisfaction that the victory over the Spanish fleet near the Philippines had brought to the US – it signalled not only a recognition of the US as a major naval power, but also a vast expansion of its sphere of influence, thanks to the establishment of military bases in Cuba, Puerto Rico and the Philippines, as well as the annexation of Hawaii.

A strong, steady beam of electric light as a memorial for the tragic loss of many lives was introduced for the first time after the sinking of the Titanic in 1912. The Seaman's Church Institute in New York City established a 'Titanic Memorial Lighthouse Tower' on its roof in 1913, which sent a steady beam of green light out over the New York Harbor, visible as far away as Sandy Hook (*The New York Times* 1912, 1913, 1929). A year later, the First World War began in

Figure 6.2
Searchlight beams from
the Eiffel Tower during
the Paris World's Fair,
Georges Garen, 1889,
illustration.

Europe and bomb attacks by enemy aircraft became a feature of urban warfare. Searchlights above London, for example, would continuously roam the skies to detect small planes and dirigibles. British artists such as Muirhead Bone, Joseph Pennell and others, captured in their art work the stunning visual beauty of these lights in the urban context. At the same time, lighting engineers were using the constantly evolving technology of searchlight beams for spectacular effects at

Figure 6.3
San Francisco, Panama
Pacific Exposition, 1915,
postcard.

celebratory events. The Panama Pacific exposition of 1915 in San Francisco saw the introduction of colourful searchlight displays, in particular Walter D'Arcy Ryan's *Scintillator*, which sent coloured light beams across the nocturnal sky in constantly changing patterns (Figure 6.3). Many contemporary reports confirmed the awe-inspiring, sublime beauty of this spectacle, which celebrated the opening of the Panama Canal, the control over which the US had just secured with a series of shrewd political manoeuvres.

Discussions about memorials for the fallen soldiers began everywhere in the US immediately after the First World War ended in 1918 (Shanken 2002). Many critics felt that after too many 'unsightly relics of former wars' and a 'tidal wave of cemetery monuments', a new paradigm for memorials was needed: 'mere shafts of granite and statues of bronze, be they ever so artistic, are inadequate to express the tribute we would pay to our soldiers of democracy' (Candler 1919: 195–6). One of the artists who tried a new approach (after having created a number of conventional memorial sculptures herself), was the New York sculptor and millionaire heiress Gertrude Vanderbilt (Mrs Harry Payne Whitney), who suggested a tall lighthouse tower for downtown Providence, Rhode Island in 1925. Its 'memorial beam' was supposed to be visible for 30 miles. After long discussions among Providence's architects, Gertrude Vanderbilt's memorial design was not executed, but a competition was launched, whose text suggested an open-minded approach by requesting proposals for a $300,000 commemorative 'building, monument or whatever'. The winner, however, was the architect Paul Cret with an utterly conventional, fluted victory column, but several participants in the exhibition were inspired by Gertrude Vanderbilt's idea. William Lescaze, an acquaintance and neighbour of Gertrude Vanderbilt in New York City (and on his way to becoming one of the premier modern architects in the US) suggested an extraordinary luminous, crystalline tower, rising from a cubic concrete plinth. This little-known design hints at earlier expressionist work in Germany, and reveals a serious desire to find a modern formal language for the task of a memorial. Another architect, the local modernist Albert Harkness, adopted Gertrude Vanderbilt's idea and designed a classical base from which a strong searchlight sent a vertical beam into the night sky (Neumann 2004).

Solutions such as these inspired the international Columbus Memorial Lighthouse competition during the following year, in 1928. Sponsored as a joint effort by all American countries to commemorate the arrival of Christopher Columbus in the Caribbean in 1492, the competition invited architects to design a symbolic lighthouse near the city of Santo Domingo in the Dominican Republic. Among the hundreds of entries from all over the world were many in which translucent towers emitted horizontal and vertical beams of light. The winning entry came from the unknown British architect J. L. Gleave and proposed to arrange vertical floodlights in such a way as to send the image of a gigantic cross into the nocturnal sky, ideally to be reflected from the clouds above (Kelsey 1930). The memorial was not realized until 1992, long after its designer had died. The enormous, 688-feet-tall El Faro a Colón contains a chapel with a monumental tomb and – what some believe to be – the mortal remains of Christopher Columbus. When illuminated, the gigantic cross in the sky, created by 149 searchlights, can be seen as far away as Puerto Rico. (Due to economic constraints the lights are rarely turned on.)

Following earlier traditions, the World's Fairs continued to attract crowds at night with spectacular lighting displays. One of the most impressive and influential displays could be seen on top of the Ford Building during the second year of Chicago's Century of Progress exposition in 1934. On the flat roof of the circular, ten-storey structure by Albert Kahn, 24 strong searchlights were placed, sending

Figure 6.4
Chicago 1934, Ford
Pavilion with searchlights
at the World's Fair.

a 200-feet-wide beam of light thousands of feet vertically into the sky (Figure 6.4). Such installations were noticed with great interest in Europe. Architects and artists there had developed a fascination with the nocturnal aspects of architecture, and with the idea of light beams as a new artistic tool. The Russian sculptor Naum Gabo, for example, designed a display of fixed light beams sent by hidden searchlights into the night sky above Berlin for a 'Light Festival' in 1928 (Neumann 2002). The term *Lichtarchitektur* (light architecture) was much used in the intense debates about the future of modern architecture, which seemed to be continuously moving towards increasing lightness and immateriality. Many architects suggested that glimpses of this future were best seen at night when, due to electric lights switched on inside and illuminated advertising on the exterior, buildings seemed to be dissolving entirely into an abstract symphony of colour and light.

The National Socialists, who had taken over power in Germany in 1933, almost immediately usurped such avant-garde ideas. Eduard von Trappen, the leading lighting designer in National Socialist Berlin, was involved in the most important decisions. Together with the architect Albert Speer, who was responsible for the execution of Hitler's megalomaniac visions for the German capital, von Trappen experimented with powerful searchlights for political events. The Nazi Party Rally in Nuremberg on 7 September 1934 saw the first application of vertical searchlights, which found a climax in 1936 with the so called *Lichtdom* (Light Cathedral) at the final celebration of the Olympic Games on 16 August, the swearing-in ceremony for the local party officials (*Reichswalterappell*) in Nürnberg, and Mussolini's visit to Berlin on 28 September. On this latter occasion the vertical searchlights on both sides of the street were lowered towards the centre, until they crossed and created a long baldachin above the street, evoking crossed swords or fasces (Kosfeld 1997).

Albert Speer later recalled the impression of the *Lichtdom* at the *Reichsparteitag*:

> The actual effect far surpassed anything I had imagined. The 130 sharply defined beams, placed around the field at intervals of 40 feet, were visible to a height of 20 to 25 thousand feet, after which they merged into a general glow. The feeling was of a vast room, with the beams serving as mighty pillars of infinitely high outer walls. Now and then a cloud moved through this wreath of lights, bringing an element of surrealistic surprise to the mirage. I imagine that this 'cathedral of light' was the first luminescent architecture of this type, and for me it remains not only my most beautiful architectural concept, but, after its fashion, the only one which has survived the passage of time.
>
> (Speer 1970: 59)

Just as the National Socialist preference for Neo-Classicism as the main style for public buildings paralleled contemporary practice in France or the US (probably Hitler's most important cultural reference points), the adoption of the newest lighting technologies also has to be seen in a broader context. Contrary to what Albert Speer remembered, the dematerialized architecture of the *Lichtdom*, with its particular arrangement of searchlights and their spatial effects had clear predecessors in lighting and architectural concepts of the Weimar Republic and the US. The fact that the Nazis had usurped the idea of luminous spectacles did not keep architects and designers from simultaneously continuing their interest in their utopian artistic potential. In 1934, an anonymous author, using the pseudonym of 'Dr Gamma', suggested 'an architecture that . . . will at night find its essential fulfillment by its metamorphosis into sheer luminosity'. He imagined above the existing city of Berlin 'a dream city . . . one out of light and luminous relationships – A *Lichtraumarchitektur* (Light Space Architecture)' (Gamma 1934: 1001–3). Laszlo Moholy-Nagy, the former Bauhaus teacher, similarly wrote in 1936, from his exile in London: 'The time has come for someone to make use of the third dimension and . . . to create actual structures of light in space' (cited in Kostelanetz 1970). In all likelihood, the immediate model for Albert Speer had been the vertical light beams emerging from the Ford Pavilion at the 1934 Chicago World's Fair.

While, of course, none of Speer's predecessors are free from political subtexts, and the calculated use of the mind-numbing effects of the technological sublime has a long tradition, there were also important differences. Speer's light cathedrals were meant less as a spectacle to be viewed than as an interior space of unfathomable size to be experienced by participants whose strictly choreographed positions were an important part of the arrangement. The rectangular space conjured up above Nürnberg's Zeppelin field and the oval cylinder above the Olympic Stadium in Berlin, were illusionary interior spaces, carefully separated from the luminous city centres nearby, purged of colour and movement, and striving for a technologically infused modernity supposedly closer to Gothic Cathedrals

Figure 6.5
Nazi Party Congress
Grounds, Zeppelin
Airfield, Albert Speer,
1934, illustration.

than contemporary entertainment (Figure 6.5). The fact that the light cathedrals were an important tool in fostering the semi-religious following that helped Hitler in the build-up to the war and the Holocaust gives those images a particularly ominous meaning.

Immediately after the war, the well-developed vocabulary of nocturnal spectacles was used at countless occasions around the world for victory celebrations. London's 'Victory Lighting' in the summer of 1946, for example, transformed the centre of the city into a luminous 'fairyland' combining the floodlighting of buildings with illuminated fountains and fireworks. Lighting designers deliberately chose searchlight displays 'in spite of [their] ominous implications . . . [as] it was perhaps most fitting that at least one implement of war should be employed to demonstrate the arts of peace'. The lights were operated by the Anti-Aircraft Command of the Royal Artillery, which now could show its 'skill in a happier way by suggesting patterns of royal colours' (Ames 1946: 117–30). Two stationary blue searchlight beams formed a gigantic 'V' for 'Victory' above Buckingham Palace, whose façade was floodlit in red, white and blue.

In Los Angeles, a veritable '*Lichtdom*' of strong searchlights converged above the Los Angeles Memorial Coliseum as a 'Tribute to Victory' on 27 October 1945. However, in order to avoid any resemblance with Speer's installations, giant 'colour wheels' with glass discs of different hues were attached to the projectors for constantly changing rainbow effects (Figure 6.6).

The use of searchlight beams for political ends continued in the 1950s. During the height of the cold war, in 1956, the 'Freedom Lights' were installed at the

Figure 6.6
Victory Celebration, at
the Los Angeles Stadium,
1945, illustration.

top of the Empire State Building (Bracker 1956: 27). These four searchlight beacons were mounted at the ninetieth floor, one on each of the building's four sides. Each beacon revolved anticlockwise at an angle of five degrees above the horizon until it faced the building, at which point it swung to an upright position, before returning once again to the horizontal. One beam always pointed skyward at any given time. The design of this theatrical installation had been developed by America's most prominent industrial designer, Raymond Loewy. Much was made in contemporary accounts of the comparison between the Statue of Liberty welcoming with her torch earlier immigrants arriving by sea, and the Empire State now welcoming modern travellers arriving by air with its beacons. By 1964, when the building was about to lose its status as the city's tallest skyscraper to the World Trade Center, its owners looked for a way to reclaim its dominance of the skyline. The revolving beacons were turned off and, for the first time, the top 30 floors of the structure were floodlit (Lelyveld 1964: 63).

Robert Venturi and Denise Scott Brown made use of the established iconography and popular appeal of searchlight beams several times in their oeuvre. In 1972–73, batteries of skyward searchlights were key elements in their master plan for Philadelphia's 'Celebration 76' exposition (with Steven Izenour) (Brownlee 2003: 68). In 1979, they proposed a single vertical beam of light as a new

> sculptural presence in Fairmount Park to celebrate the Tercentenary of William Penn's founding of Philadelphia. . . . This form of sculpture – this shaft of light – like the Eiffel Tower, the St. Louis arch or the Jet d'Eau in Geneva, would enhance the identity of the city through its scale and symbolism.
>
> (Venturi 2003)

Even more significant for the context of this essay is their rarely published 1996 design for the Second World War memorial in Washington. The design consisted of a small sculptural installation at the rainbow pool with a world map and explanatory texts, and the triumphant nocturnal gesture of two bundled searchlight beams inscribing a monumental 'V for Victory' into the night sky, exactly as it had towered above London's Buckingham Palace immediately after the war.

Since 1995, a 35 billion candlepower lightbeam has been sent vertically into the sky above Las Vegas' pyramid shaped Luxor Hotel, apparently as a vaguely symbolic reference to Egyptian beliefs about immortality. Around the world, the onset of the year 2000 inspired innumerable lighting projects, their vocabulary usually dependent on that developed during the first half of the century. In Berlin, for example, illumination artist Gert Hof was commissioned to develop fireworks and a searchlight display for the occasion. When he presented his concept, called *Art in Heaven* which included rows of 250 white xenon searchlights reaching 30 miles into the sky, thus creating a 'pyramid of light, a cathedral for the millennium' (Hasselhorst 1999) a storm of protest arose, voiced by prominent German writers such as Günter Grass and Peter Rühmkorf, historians such as Hans and Wolfgang Mommsen and many others, who saw similarities with Albert Speer's *Lichtdom* installations under National Socialism.

The ensuing debates demonstrated how closely the iconography of such an installation depended on its time and place and suggested that neither the artist nor his critics had sufficient knowledge about the medium's rich prehistory. The fact that Gert Hof had simply not associated Albert Speer with his lighting installation, could, at least partially, be explained by the fact that he had grown up in the East German city of Leipzig. Critical debates about the legacy of the Nazi era had been much more pronounced in West Germany than in the communist dictatorship in the East, which was also less hesitant to adopt cultural strategies that had worked well under Hitler. *Lichtdom* installations of searchlights pointing skywards around the edge of Leipzig's main stadium were a regular feature after major sporting events. Responding to public criticism, Gert Hof added more colour and movement to the choreography of his searchlight display (Haubrich 1999). Dense fog on 31 December 1999, however, greatly diminished the spectacle's visual impact.

This brings us back to our initial question: does it matter if New York City's *Tribute in Light* uses a visual language and technological installation reminiscent of Albert Speer's *Cathedral of Light*? The answer is complicated: it clearly seems to have mattered less in New York than when a comparable installation was proposed in Berlin in 1999. In both cases, however, the critics overlooked the fact that Speer's *Lichtdom* was only one of many similar installations that served a variety of different functions. The *Lichtdom* itself was, in all likelihood, inspired by the concerted light beams emerging vertically from the Ford Pavilion at the Chicago World's Fair of 1934. On the other hand, it needs to be acknowledged that many such installations had crucial political connotations, usually not too distant from the notion of warfare, where their particular technology had originated. What Leo Marx once termed the 'technological sublime' (Nye 1994: ix), could be used to foster a sense of technological supremacy, of resilience and readiness to fight. This iconographic history adds additional layers of meaning to an understanding of the *Tribute in Light* installation at the World Trade Center. The pure gesture of mourning the loss of thousands of innocent lives and of the twin towers is joined by notions of defiance, technological supremacy and a readiness to go to war.

While the creators of the *Tribute in Light*, in particular Julian LaVerdiere and Paul Myoda, were fully aware of, and welcomed, this richness of metaphorical meaning and the installation's iconographic undercurrent, the majority of the general public was not. LaVerdiere, a Yale trained artist in New York, has long been interested 'in the way history [is] remembered'. Both his art work and his commercial work (architectural sets and backdrops for fashion shoots and advertising) continuously weave complex and subtle layers of references, and thus usually complicate, sometimes undermine the intended message (Moshkovits 2000: 80–1; Tanguy, 2001). His collaborator Paul Myoda wrote that

> to analyze the material and social conditions in which a work of art functions is part of the artistic experience, and sometimes even the very point of art; to do so while ignoring art's aesthetic forms, and the effects of these forms on one's emotions and consciousness, is to miss out on the most important and unique quality of art. Art and politics are bound, not one and the same. To overemphasize politics over art is to be numb to beauty, to the subtleties of experience; to overemphasize art over politics is to be escapist and weak.
>
> (*The New York Times* 2002)

The ephemeral art of illumination leaves few traces and its history is little known. We may speculate, however, that subconscious residual memories of other contexts for floodlight installations might have helped the memorial's overwhelming success and acceptance. While the *Tribute in Light* is thus part of a long icono-graphic tradition, one important aspect of it is unique – the visual reference to the vanished twin towers. How close it comes to evoking their appearance is illustrated by an article that Paul Goldberger wrote for *The New York Times* in 1975 when the towers had just been finished:

> The World Trade Center remains largely lit for much of the night, and at night its vast towers undergo perhaps the most remarkable transformation of anything in the city. . . . The enormous metal shafts, which rise without setback or ornament, are always more like abstract forms than like buildings, and at night, they give up any pretense at all to being real. They stand, glowing, in an empty landscape, with silence all around, bigger than one had ever dreamed yet somehow, at night, able to be touched and perceived more clearly. It is an image at once terrifying and moving – an architectural experience of genuine power.
>
> (Goldberger 1975: 1, 10)

REFERENCES

Ames, R. W. (1946) 'Public Lighting for the Victory Celebrations in London as Designed and Executed by the Ministry of Works', *Light and Lighting* 39 (July): 117–30.

Bracker, M. (1956) 'Empire State Building Becomes Lighthouse as 4 Beacons Go On', *The New York Times*, 4 May: 27.

Brownlee, D., De Long, D. and Hiesinger, K.B. (2003) *Out of the Ordinary: Robert Venturi, Denise Scott Brown and Associates*, exhibition catalogue, Philadelphia: Philadelphia Museum of Art.

Candler, M. (1919) 'The Community House as a War Memorial', *American Architect*, 116 (13), August: 195–6.

Dunlap, D. W. (2004) 'Twin Beams to Return to City Skies, but Costs are Daunting', *The New York Times*, 9 July.

Eboy, D. (2001) 'Towers of Light for New York City', *Art in America*, November: 35.

Gamma, Dr (1934) 'Bau und Licht', *Deutsche Bauzeitung*: 1001–3.

Goldberger, P. (1975) 'At Night, City Comes Out of Hiding', *The New York Times*, 9 November.

Hasselhorst, C. (1999) 'Lichtbahnhof am Himmel' *Die Welt*, 9 November.

Haubrich, R. (1999) 'Kleine Taschenlampe brenn' *Die Welt*, 21 December.

Kelsey, A. (1930) 'Program and rules of the second competition for the selection of an architect for the monumental lighthouse, which the nations of the world will erect in the Dominican Republic to the memory of Christopher Columbus', Washington, DC: Pan American Union.

Kosfeld, C. (1997) *Das elektrische Licht im Nationalsozialismus*, Berlin: Abschlußarbeit Hochhschule der Künste.

Lelyveld, J. (1964) 'The Empire State To Glow at Night'. *The New York Times*, 23 February: 63.

Kostelanetz, R. (1970) *Moholy-Nagy*, New York: Praeger.

Moshkovits, B. (2000) 'Julian Laverdiere: Controlling Your Dreams', *Flash Art*, XXXIII (213) (Summer).

Neumann, D. (ed.) (2002) *Architecture of the Night*, Munich, New York: Prestel.

Neumann, D. (2004) 'Unbuilt Providence', exhibition leaflet published in conjunction with an eponymous exhibition at the Bell Gallery, Brown University, 14 April–31 May 2004.

The New York Times (1899) 'The Bridge Illuminated', 29 September.

—— (1912) 'Lighthouse Tower in Victims' Honor', 23 April.

—— (1913) 'Give Lighthouse for Titanic's Dead', 16 April.

—— (1929) 'New York Roofs Hold a Life of Their Own', 10 March.

—— (2002) 'Tribute in Light', online discussion forum containing 292 electronic mails sent between 7 March–14 May 2002 (now archived).

Nye, D. (1994) *The American Technological Sublime*, Cambridge, MA: MIT Press.

Schivelbusch, W. (1986) *Lichtblicke: Zur Geschichte der künstlichen Helligkeit*, Frankfurt: Fischer.

Shanken, A. M. (2002) 'Planning Memory: Living Memorials in the United States during World War II', *The Art Bulletin*, 1 March.

Speer, A. (1970) *Inside the Third Reich. Memoirs by Albert Speer*, New York: MacMillan.

Tanguy, S. (2001) 'Reconstructing History: A Conversation with Julian Laverdiere', *Sculpture*, December.

Venturi, R. (2003) Correspondence with the author.

Part III

**Reframing and
Reshaping the City**

Chapter 7: Out on a Limb?

Urban Traumas on the West Pacific Rim

Stephanie Hemelryk Donald

> I want a kiss from your lips, I want an eye for an eye
>
> Bruce Springsteen (2002)

In the wake of the attack on New York in 2001, the potency of mediated urban affect was painfully apparent. In choosing the sites of destruction that they did, the attackers also chose to make a resonant statement on the cinematic hierarchy of world cities. By attacking New York's skyline, they drew on a genealogy of images of disaster, where the central point of all disasters – whether caused by a flood, an ape or a marshmallow giant – is that it is happening in America, and is therefore happening everywhere in the so-called 'Western world'. In a post-2001 film, *The Day After Tomorrow* (2004), this point is made somewhat unsubtly as a man clutches the New York library's copy of the Gothenberg Bible, claiming that if Western civilization is now over, at least this will remain as a memory of its achievements. Given that the disaster at the centre of the film is that the northern hemisphere has suddenly plunged into a new Ice Age, this seemed both poignant and lop-sided. The northern hemisphere also includes China, Korea, and Japan, where the printed word and the idea of writing things down pre-dated the same inventions in Europe, let alone a transfer to the United States.

This chapter discusses the sustaining urban narratives of cities on either side of the Pacific Rim, arguing that the cinematic imaginaries and urban trajectories of the West Pacific cities have characters beyond the Hollywood imperative.[1] Taking the lead from Mike Davis's (1998) work on Los Angeles and urban trauma, it is proposed that the contradictory vortex of American domination and self-loathing attracts both cinematic narrative and critique, but that such universalism is not as global as might be supposed. While the imperial imagination of American film and academic writing is hard to resist given both the multitude and penetration of those cultural formations, nonetheless, neither should it be allowed to obscure other patterns which have emerged from different historical trajectories. Two cities, Sydney and Shanghai, have both experienced the processes of modernity through the lens of histories of colonial intervention. They are also iconic sites of cinema and regional (Austral-Asian) imaginaries of nostalgia, aspiration and global relevance. Neither, currently, have the level of international visibility of the American film industry. And the cities, while certainly 'on the map', do not possess the affective pull of the major cinematic cities of America: Los Angeles and New York, cities which even those who have never visited or will never visit in person feel that they 'know'. Yet, Sydney and Shanghai are also on the filmic map, as their international profile grows and consequently their distance from centres of global power shrinks. The argument of this chapter is that contemporary cinematic and architectural conversations and the histories of urban visualization in these places give insight into the political formation of the West Pacific and its own fears and loathing.

CONTENTION

In China in 2005, a television show, *Mengxiang Chengzhen* (*Dreams Come True*) on BTV (Beijing Television)[2] set one-child families up *against* each other to see which family had the most comprehensively developed (*quanfa*) and educated offspring. Games were played, quizzes contested, and cultural abilities exhibited. The winning family stood amazed on the stage at the end of the show, as they were presented with their prize: an all-expenses paid visit to . . . Sydney. The prize was represented on stage as a huge postcard of the Opera House. Tears rolled down the cheeks of mother, father and young son. These three Chinese dreamers, who hailed from the outskirts of Shanghai, the aspirational centre of commercialization with Chinese characteristics, were now about to visit another dream city on the West Pacific Rim, known for its Opera House, its Harbour, its Bridge and its city beaches. The media event encapsulated a perfectly achieved and anticipated modern urban pleasure, framed on a television set and a giant postcard, and realized entirely in the Asia-Pacific region.

Seeing that show, and particularly as I did so in the same week as re-reading the critical geographer Mike Davis's books on Los Angeles, was an odd experience. It was as though two entirely separate worlds had worked out, with no room for doubt, what it means, publicly, to be urban in the twenty-first century. The family on BTV knew that it involved self-cultivation, the maintenance of social 'quality' (*suzhi*) and the opportunity to travel to global cities as part of a project of internationalization. The keyword for the show and for the enunciation of the urban it demonstrates is 'dreaming', which is best glossed as 'aspirational'. In Davis's work (2002: 227–33), the city – and Los Angeles is the only city in which he is really interested – is already tired, frightened of its own potential for self-harm, and deeply corrupt. Whatever the actual problems, whether of governance or topography, in Shanghai and Sydney, these cities do not display their fragilities with such gusto, in both places there is a generally accepted, proairetic narrative of city development. It was the contrast between optimism, as displayed by the mediated urban imaginary on Chinese television, and the pessimistic fascination that Davis has with disaster, especially his allegorical historiography of the racialized traumas of LA, that formed the genesis for this argument.

The second impetus came, however, from my daughter, after another mediated experience. We were in the cinema, in Sydney, on a Saturday evening. Mayhem reigned on screen, but this was not especially unexpected. American cities maintain an iconic hold on the trans-global urban imagination, and their cinematic propensity to burn, implode, explode, and be trampled by monstrous others is common. As is patiently explained to Tom Cruise in Spielberg's *War of the Worlds* (2005) – as the street in which he lives rises up in a wave of malevolent asphalt to greet him and little Dakota Fanning – 'they've been waiting a million years (to . . .??. *I missed it in a crackle of flame?*)' . . . to do what? And who, really, are 'they'? But that was just the pre-release trailer. I was actually there to watch *Mr and Mrs Smith* (2005) do marriage counselling through sexualized domestic violence of quite impressively destructive proportions. At the closing credits, my ten-year-old daughter, noted – with the wisdom of a peripheral Australian pre-teen (and the anxiety that her mother would be thoroughly disapproving of the film that she had chosen) – 'the house fell down as usual, Mum, but at least they didn't blame the Koreans this time'. The previous film we had seen together had been *The Pacifier* (2005), where it does, and they do.

Mr and Mrs Smith live in a white suburb, in a big white house that is flattened, and later 'redecorated'; the destruction is wreaked by their criminal bosses because the parties decide that they prefer to fall in love than to kill each other. And the question arises: why does American film involve so much destruction, of suburban architecture, and of city landmarks? Undoubtedly the visceral pleasure afforded by such spectacular illusions of damage is one causal factor in these scenes and sequences. Another factor is surely the advanced skills and technological infrastructures available to American filmmakers, which encourage and enable spectacularization. Yet another generic factor might be the traditions of slapstick in American film comedy. But, despite these generic and industrial reasons, the problem remains. In Davis's (1998: 312 *passim*) work there is a strong suggestion that the recurring paradigm of destructive violence in American film (even in comedies) is open to an allegorical reading of urban character and despair. It is that contention that is the real starting point here.

Davis's books pore over real and imagined disasters in the LA region. Fictional catastrophes and the actual urban statistics and incidence of natural turmoil are laid out either in parallel chapters or within the same discussion. Davis tells us that the racialization of the urban quotidian, and – as Nichols (1996: 56–7) and others (Tomasulo 1996: 75–6; Naficy 2001: 188–214) have also shown – the structuring of historical memory, is rehearsed through cinematic fascination with catastrophe. Davis's argument, made not so much as an argument but, rather, as a cumulative, unstoppable certainty, is that everything imagined is already the case, and everything documented is embedded in the American allegorical imagination. There are moments where his own facts work against this technique of cumulation – as in *Ecology of Fear* when he compares the 70 dead in an LA quake with the tens of thousands who died in the Kobe earthquake (and we might add the 100,000 dead of the Boxing Day tsunami and the quarter of a million who died in the Tangshan Chinese earthquake in 1976) (Davis 1998: 31–8). Davis's implication seems to be that LA will catch up with these huge numbers, and that it deserves, despite the much worse catastrophes elsewhere, to nonetheless be understood as the universalist urban metonym for apocalypse.

Admittedly, Davis's essay at the end of *Dead Cities* (2002) is less appropriative, as he rolls out a truly global manuscript of ecological depredation, helped to ghastly fruition by the Bush alliance with non-sustainable fuel, and fuel wars. But, overall, his books do substantiate my daughter's comment. Why does the house fall down again? Not only is there a paradigm of destruction in the racialized imaginings of LA, but Davis's own work, itself, falls within that paradigm. For him, only disaster carries real historical weight and his prognoses of catastrophe are given as sufficient for political points to be carried. So, to be brutal about it, why does America take pleasure and set such store in 'falling down'? Or, to put it another way, why do my observations of West Pacific Rim cinemas, with the interesting exception of Japan – perhaps relevantly a post-imperial regime – suggest that they do not?

AN AMERICAN IMAGINARY

> Really pissed off now, the red Chinese decide to tunnel under the Pacific using a superlaser.
>
> (Davis 1998: 314)

In Davis's prurient (but in that case gloriously witty) discussion of race neurosis and disaster narrative in Los Angeles, the Chinese are the 'Red hordes under Malibu' and tsunamis whip through the city as though it were the only place on earth worth destroying, at least on camera. On the other side of the Pacific – out on the limb of a different, 'peripheral' regional identity – the themes of race and disaster are otherwise expressed and deployed. In particular, this argument notes that disaster is not necessarily crucial to the grammar of national cinemas, other than the American, and that within these cinemas it is certainly not assumed (as I am suggesting it certainly *is* presumed in Hollywood narrative of American cities) that disaster in a non-American city can immediately imply worldwide catastrophe. However, one also recognizes that Davis's central premise, that the cinematic idea of the city is sustained in part by the visualization of its fears and prejudice, is worth pursuing outside the American film context (Davis 1998). After all, Australian and Chinese imaginaries are not exempt from either fear or prejudice, but they are differently signified.

Besides a straightforward search for different cinematic formations, this position opens up two political motivations for a deployment of Davis's premise. First, the trope of destruction is so prevalent in the American cinematic imaginary that its reach needs to be questioned in an era of 'empire' and its attendant 'war on terror'. Second, the rising potency of the Asia Pacific region as an imagined centre of world affairs and the locus of new global cities, leads us to insist on defining how the idea of the city is driven and configured outside the United States. The idea of the city is a powerful thematic for film studies, one that brings cinemas into alignment, as much as it advises on their discrete aspirations and narrative parameters. It cannot be sequestered in one corner of an expanding and contracting world. What then is the urban character behind film on the Rim? How does it distinguish itself in relation to the dominance of American urban cinema? How does it deal with fear and (self-) loathing, if not through disaster?

There are, of course, links and echoes as much as there are differentiations across international cinematic ideas of the city: say, Chinese, American, Australian and European. These similarities of vision and imagination, often involve an acknowledgement of chaos and indeterminacy, which the urban provokes and allows. Taking classic examples from the early period of city films, for example *Sunrise* (1927), *The Lodger* (1927) and *Street Angel* (1937), one can see how urban themes, anxieties and aspirations wend discretely but in a tacit relationship one to another through the streets of cinema. Themes of female entrapment and mobility, of sexuality and youth in the ascendancy, of darkness lurking in the backstreets of the modern idyll, and of capitalism as a fledgling, necessary evil in the organization of metropolitan desire are systemic to all these texts. In *Street Angel* (*malu tianshi*), two sisters, one already working as a prostitute and the other still innocent and thus able to imagine happiness, represent the binary opposition between urban despair and degradation, and the opportunities that are open only to urban youth. In *Sunrise*, a couple are separated by the lure of the city, but finally reunited by its entrancing magic. In *The Lodger*, there is an ambivalence regarding the central character, who is assumed to be a killer (through the deliberate way that the film treats him as a malevolent, urban stranger) but is, nonetheless, revealed to be innocent. Ma Ning (1989: 24–8), a prominent Chinese film theorist, has noted in a now classic article, that *Street Angel* and *Sunrise* are clearly related films, with the first an echo of the other even as it moves Chinese film into its own plane of cinematic narrative and narration. Yet, the role of the urban imaginary as a localizing trope is still underplayed in the inscribing of Chinese cinematic history.

These tropes are, as the sociologist Michael Keith (2005: 26–8) has recently reminded us, both essential and essentialist aspects of how the city is imagined, aspects of a 'mirage' which allow us to easily identify the country and the city as antonymic structures of social life and human geography. These urban films have human weakness and emotional chaos at their narrative core, but the possibility of dénouement and resolution as their principle, even though it is clear that there is no such thing as a final happy ending in a city setting. The city neither closes nor rests, and the end of the film is a respite, not a final coming to rest. Order is thus perversely premised on doubt and uncertainty. Tony Kaes (2005) has argued in regards to Fritz Lang's *Metropolis*, seemingly a film about the fanatical order of the machine economy, that it is, in fact, the chaotic impulses of power, passion and degeneration, that organize the film's trajectory. Likewise, David Frisby (2001: 57–60) has pointed out that Victorian detective fiction developed in part to quell fears of the essentially chaotic nature of city life. Sherlock Holmes catches trains and uses the mail, says Frisby, so that we, creatures of modernity, may know that whatever the mayhem of the world we inhabit, there are nonetheless binding principles of an order which makes it, somehow, legible to the trained mind. The possibility of disaster is, then, already both latent and managed in literature and early cinema of the capitalist world (and in China's case the proto-capitalist).

The eruptions of disaster as a master narrative in the American imaginary today are somewhat different. The ordering principle of these explosions seems to be neither societal nor local infrastructure, but simply the knowledge of American pre-eminence in both suffering and surviving such catastrophe. Disturbingly for the West side of the Rim, the narrative of disaster is still likely to be premised on a repulsion of Asia and Asians. In his *Ecology of Fear*, Davis (1998: 338–9) traces a continuum from Kathryn Bigelow's *Strange Days* (1995) to Christian demagogue Pat Robertson's explicitly racist *The End of the Age* (1995). Davis suggests that characterizations of Vietnamese ferals in *Strange Days* lie on a slope to the mad rantings of Robertson's 'square jawed heroes' 'battling Satan . . . and his minions – a billion demonic Indians, Pakistanis, Persians and Arabs' (Davis 1998: 339). He thereby demonstrates the slip between quality film and fiction and ideological confusion and racist pornography in modern American Rim culture. The concern here is that Davis's own work is, nonetheless, premised on an American-centric version of disaster and apocalypse, wherein LA is metonymic of the world, and that for all his revelations he is complicit in minimizing the other side of the Rim as an alternative source of profound meaning. This leaves Asia, and indeed Australasia, as regional misfits, tunnelling their way into the global imaginaries of the United States. Provocatively, is Mike Davis's ecology of fear a compromised compounding of cultural power, which fuels his own writing as much as it underpins the violence of the symbolic systems that he so tellingly juxtaposes with natural threats and man-made catastrophes?

Davis is not alone in premising insightful critique on assumptions of the global acceptance of what we might call the American metonym. By 2003, the detective is impotent to bring order or even legibility to the streets of the city, but the global capitalist may do so, not by walking the streets and identifying the criminal, but by cruising in the comparative safety of a stretch limousine and identifying – at distance – *with* the elements of disorder. In *Cosmopolis* Don DeLillo's (2003) anti-hero, the hyper-capitalist billionaire Eric Packer, is faced briefly with his own complicity in destruction. He doesn't know how to react, partly we surmise, because he already knows 'this' (his part in destruction) to be the case, and because he recognizes as does DeLillo (2003: 91–2), how a reaction is going to be nothing more than a playing out of a scripted tic in the already anticipated event.

> Someone flung a trashcan at the rear window . . . All along there'd seemed a
> scheme, a destination. Police fired rubber bullets through the smoke, which began

to drift high above the billboards. Other police stood a few feet away, helping Eric's security detail protect the car. *He didn't know how he felt about this.*

'How will we know when the global era officially ends?'

He waited.

'When stretch limousines begin to disappear from the streets of Manhattan'

. . .

'They are working with you, these people. They are acting on your terms.' She said, 'And if they kill you, it's only because you permit it, in your sweet sufferance, as a way to re-emphasise the idea we all live under.'

'What idea?'

'Destruction' . . .

. . . There were many arrests, people from 40 countries, heads bloodied, ski-masks in hand.

Rather like Davis, DeLillo unpacks the problematic in this exchange, but he does not escape it himself. The end of the global 'world' will be read on the 'streets of Manhattan'. The idea 'we all' live under is a globally envisioned destruction, which – although recognized and fought off by protestors from '40 countries' – is, nonetheless, an American entity, created and contested on American terms.

The present argument is, therefore, partly provocation, but also a contribution to timely reconsiderations of the current regional organization of urban imaginaries of cultural power. The tacit correspondences of urban nightmares are, likely, still there to be found in the transnational streets of film, but certain dominances have become starkly obvious. The power to self-destruct and take the world along with you, or 'not quite', is one such dominance. The legibility or ordering principle of these American cinematic cities has become reliant on a narrative of realized chaos, in which the existence of the Other depends on the technology, military capabilities or lone heroes and anti-heroes of the United States.

REGIONAL CINEMA

Since the early days of film, the American cinema has established itself as the international standard for commercial genre films. These standards have done much to exalt and demonize American cities, metropolitan sprawls, and *unheimlich* suburbs (Merck 2005) in the global imagination. Unsurprisingly, therefore, received wisdom about cities in film is fixated on the United States (New York, LA) alongside certain European examples, usually Berlin, Paris and London, with momentary attention paid to Rome (Shiel 2006: 6 *passim*). The dominant imaginaries in cinema and in attendant academic regimes of truth are clearly situated in Western cinema and that of the Northern hemisphere. Speaking from another region to its particular interests, aesthetics and allegorical frames, entails therefore a certain amount of preliminary explanation. The following examples are explored to suggest other logics to urban narrative, not to contest that one or other is better or worse than that of Hollywood, but merely to note that it exists.

Early cinema on the West Pacific Rim stemmed from Shanghai and Guangzhou, and spread across the region through the work of entrepreneurs and film pioneers, such as Run Run Shaw and Lai Lei-man, its mobility cruelly assisted by warfare and political strife throughout the 1930s to the 1950s (Chu 2003; Fu 2003; Hu 2003). In recent years Shanghai has begun to regain a leading presence in the media industries, particularly with the establishment of the Oriental Pearl Shanghai Media Group, but it has yet to recapture the film eminence of the 1930s. Academically, Shanghai cinema is well served by Asian cinema experts and Chinese literary theorists both in China and in the US, including Leo fan-Lee (1999), Zhang Yingjin (1996, 2004), Shu-mei Shih (2001), Laikwan Pang (2002), and is an especially important site in discussing the emergence and nature of Chinese modernity. Writers tend to concentrate on Shanghai of the 1930s in exploring China's particular experience of internationalization, modernity and the place of visual culture in both processes. Nonetheless, Shanghai has not yet become paradigmatic as a global cinematic city. It has, however, achieved iconic status as a futuristic international zone emblematic of the rise of China.

Shanghai is characterized by both its rapid architectural and commercial energy, and by a reluctance to let go of a slim frame of nostalgia for the consumer chic of its first 'concession' period as an international trading zone. Chinese filmmakers from outside the city pursue and over-inscribe this nostalgia into contemporary film. The cityscape sequences in *Small Things in a Big City* (or *Leaving Me, Loving You; dacheng xiaoshi*, 2004) and *Baober in Love* (*Lian ai zhong de Baober*, 2004) are both examples of Shanghai narratives dependent on a nostalgic combination of place memory and romantic attraction. Shanghai serves as a vehicle for those traits of 'female entrapment and mobility', which are both exotic and intensely suggestive of the 'mirage' of the city, as noted in the London context by Keith (2005: 24–30). Shanghai films noticeably invoke the city itself as the eponymous hero(ine) of its own configuration in the past-as-present. Hou Hsiao-hsien's *Flowers of Shanghai* (1998), Zhang Yimou's *Shanghai Triad* (1995), are two such examples, where Shanghai encapsulates the emotional heat of modern people in urban intimacy through its own version of prurience, staring fixedly at the glamour of the high-class prostitute and her clients.

Romance, abandon and the dark spaces of the modern are paradigmatic of films set in Shanghai. Looking for destruction in Shanghai film is, however, a perverse task, both in terms of current developmental politics and in relation to historical experience. Destruction is not its *raison d'être*, it does not describe the city's aspirations or founding myths, nor would such a narrative support the city in either a regional or national agenda. Shanghai has had its share of disaster, of course. Historically, the Japanese occupation was an externally enforced catastrophe and is revisited in national epics or in occasional anti-Japanese demonstrations. Currently, forced relocation of long-term residents in older style accommodation, to make room for large developments, is destroying the historical and residential fabric of the city from within. There is a great deal of under-reported local anger, and some organized resistance to these traumatic relocations. That subject is certainly off limits for mainstream domestic films, but nor is it a story that appeals to overseas markets, at least to date. Thus, Shanghai's avoidance of disaster, if it is such, does not convey any particular or comparative moral rectitude on the city, but does produce an alternative imaginary for its account of urban pre-eminence.

Sydney poses a similar conundrum, but through a very different set of contingencies, some of which are economic and others of which are rooted in Australia's response to the encounter between unresolved racialized memory and the cosmopolitan city. The economic argument for Sydney's lack of spectacular destruction on film is straightforward. Sydney has an under-developed home film industry in part because of a long history of under-funding for film as a national project, and a small home market for commercial releases. Currently it operates as an offshore creative servicing centre for Hollywood and others in the United States (Goldsmith and O'Regan 2005: 45). More contentiously, Sydney's low cinematic profile is due to a prevailing Australian uncertainty about working through allegories of harm and trauma in the city. There is a culture of displacement, which keeps the streets clean and the buildings pretty much intact, but which mirrors a certain national disengagement with the soul.

For all these reasons, films in Australia tend to carry a great deal of significance, and this is particularly the case of those with an Indigenous storyline or a largely Indigenous creative team. *Rabbit Proof Fence* (2002) and *Beneath Clouds* (2002) were two recent films that lived up to the demands which Australian history makes on its chroniclers. The first deals with the Stolen Generations and Aboriginal removal in Western Australia, the second is a contemporary road movie that builds its drama around the chronic pain of being Aboriginal, and young, in a landscape of half remembered anguish. But, perhaps strangely, both films have grown from a British ancestor, Nic Roeg's *Walkabout* (1971). The film tells the story of two children who find themselves abandoned on the edges of bushland, following the suicide of their father. The bush in Australia is a general term for wilderness and non-urban, non-cultivated terrain. For these children it poses both a threat to survival and an escape from the failure of their parents' marriage. At another level, the wilderness underscores the failure of the White Australia policy[3] (that was still in place when the film was made), to occupy either the land or the region with much sensitivity or enlightenment. *Walkabout* is not a disaster movie, nor a predominantly urban film. It was directed by Nic Roeg, a British filmmaker, and could be dismissed as a fantasy image of Australia. But it is a remarkable and enduringly perceptive comment on the nation, on crises of masculinity, on landscape, and on the management of trauma through displacement (see Figure 7.1).

The city in *Walkabout* is always present in its absence, indicated at either end of the film by a sequence of telling, metonymic shots and glimpses. Disaster is present here, too, in the suicides of the white girl's (played by English actress, Jenny Agutter) father, and in the later suicide of her friend and unaccepted lover

Figure 7.1
Production still from
Walkabout, 1971.

(played by Australian Aboriginal actor, David Gulpilil). It is also present in the refusal of the girl to acknowledge the complexity of her present and presence in the Australian landscape. It is not, as one trailer documentary would have it, a 'film about two people 50,000 years apart' (*Walkabout* 1998). That would be much too convenient for Australian history for one thing, and disastrous for the narrative for another. The suicides, the sadness and the denial would be unnecessary, if there were nothing in the present that inextricably binds individual stories while also flinging them apart in uncompromising gestures of refusal. It is a film about people sharing a present without mutual acknowledgement. The film is premised on the unnatural disasters of colonialism, genocide and denial (see Figure 7.2 for an iconic rendition of an Australian 'unnatural disaster'). It is as much a story of a racially organized segregation, fear and loathing as anything to which Davis refers us to in LA. But here there are no explosions over the Harbour Bridge (the Opera House was not finished until 1973 so that was not an option).

The city is not imagined here as a seething hub of chaos – what a Sydney barrister recently and with telling inappropriateness termed through a reference to a client as 'a cultural timebomb'[4]. Rather, Sydney is already looking like that over-sized postcard on BTV. It occurs in the film as a place to hide from the fact of the presence of its Others, from the knowledge of the multiple Indigenous disasters that founded the city and the nation. Sydney in *Walkabout* is a city outside

Figure 7.2
One dozen unnatural disasters in the Australian landscape, #2,
Rosemary Laing, 2003.

its deeper history, perched on the rim of the ocean, built of blonde brick harbour views, red brick suburbia, and a tiny CBD – central business district – along George and Pit Streets (see Figure 7.3). The filmmaker and cultural critic Ross Gibson's (2002) also allegorical reflection on the Australian 'badlands' offers one way of deciphering the eerily quiet cities on the Australian end of the West Pacific.

In *Seven Versions of An Australian Badland*, Gibson suggests that Australian historical memory, named by the historian Henry Reynolds (1998: 4 and *passim*) as 'the whispering in our hearts', is corralled in the badlands; obscure and evil pockets of genocide and casualized murder crouching on the roads to the north and the trails to the west. Infamously, the badlands are the dead heart of the outback, but Gibson alerts us to another – the Horror Stretch on the road to Mackay, where

> the isolation of this landscape, its eeriness, its narratives of violence all set the Capricorn scrub apart from the rest of the Queensland coast. It is a place where evil can be banished so that goodness can be credited, by contrast, in the regions all around. It's our own local badland, a place set aside for a type of story that we still seem to need.
>
> (Gibson 2002: 17)

In another, much more recent film than Roeg's, Rachel Perkins'[5] *Radiance* (2000), three Indigenous sisters gather to bury and mourn their mother at her home by the sea. The film is a classic tale of truth spinning out at the end of a life – as the daughters exhume and confront one another with the truths and tragedies of the life and sexual exploitation of their mother. The youngest woman, Nona (Deborah Mailman), is pregnant, and has come home to escape the city and raise her child. She discovers that – far from being the love child of her mother and the 'Black prince', – she is the product of a rape of her 'sister' by one of her mother's casual lovers. What is more, the house, 'home', belongs not to her mother, but to a white ex-lover 'Harry', who wants it back now that she is dead. As the revelations accumulate, the sensible eldest sister breaks down and seeks a small

Figure 7.3
Sydney street, still from
Walkabout, 1971.

part of revenge. The three women torch the house, scatter their mother's ashes and drive off, – probably to the city, – liberated but somewhat hysterical. Perkins' film positions the city, where Nona falls pregnant and is seen only briefly in a night sequence, chaotic and out of control, as not the cause or locus of disaster but the receiving house of its casualties and escapees. In *Radiance*, catastrophe is not an urban prerogative, it is a specific, local (national) product of the badlands of racial and gendered violence across the country. The city neither contains, nor encompasses, nor allegorizes these tragedies. The seeds of disaster and the fruits of catastrophe lurk here under the pretty house by the sea, where the rape, and much else beside, occurred 20, 40 and 200 years before.[6]

Dispersing disaster to the landscape is thus both just and evasive in Australian film. In *Walkabout*, the city is a structured avoidance of country and peoples. The blonde brick apartment block where the girl lives with a dull husband, as did her mother, is not the dark, febrile city of Shanghai at night, nor does it share the pounding excitement of Berlin, New York or Paris in the 1920s and early 1930s. This city is preternaturally quiet, firmly determined not to talk about the catastrophe of its past, perched uncertainly on the Pacific Rim. In *Radiance* the city is more recognizably chaotic and receptive to disorder. The film suggests, instead, that human damage wreaked in the city is less terrible than the disasters lurking in the outback. Perkins' story takes the dénouement firmly back where it belongs.

CONCLUSIONS

Three months after the first discussion draft of this essay was written and delivered, Hurricane Katrina devastated New Orleans. Although the numbers of dead were far exceeded a few weeks later by the Pakistan earthquake, Hurricane Katrina signified an awful realization of both the prescience and self-delusion of American disaster film, and of Davis's hypotheses of racialized catastrophe. In *The Day after Tomorrow*, made a year earlier, the President of the United States evacuates half the country to Mexico and South America. In 2005, in an actual catastrophe, the President could not successfully manage the evacuation of a single state. The media coverage of the event, and the events that it triggered, depicted a society in collapse, where human value could not override racial difference, where systemic structures were not readily attuned to help people who could not help themselves, and where the Empire could neither save nor control its own people, let alone its assumptive dominions. Unlike the catastrophe of the 9/11 World Trade Center attacks when America looked horribly shaken but familiar, this natural calamity showed the surprised world a country with no clear sense of its responsibilities or its character.

In Davis's accounts, the metropolis is crippled by a cultural and historical addiction to racism. His perspective explains the disaster film, even if it does not make sense of the comparable addiction to universalizing the American experience. The Rodney King incident set off the riot in Los Angeles in 1992. It was sparked by white on black violence, but continued with attacks on the LA Korean community. The Koreans call it *sa-i-gu*, 29 April, when their houses burnt down around their ears. Discussing the Rodney King case, Frank Tomasulo (1996: 74) argues that the ontology of the event, rather than its motivations, is made visible on film. The inflicting of hurt displayed on that video clip of the LAPD officers beating King magnified its affect through the response from afflicted communities of colour, across the South Central district – and across the country. The video did not truly display the fears and prejudice of American race relations as they are conceived and nurtured in the quotidian of hurt and estrangement, but it provided a moment of recognition from which political action, physicalized anger and traumatic acknowledgement were derived. In 2005, with 9/11 now the assumed baseline of affect in America's horrified Oedipal imaginings, revisiting the riots of 4/29, in the wake of Katrina, makes one appreciate Davis's local understanding. The urban 'mirage' of race is still the real disaster, and it still rises up as a wave of fractured, suffocating asphalt in American cinema, as we watch the suburbanites driving home and away.

It is outside the eye of the storm that the force of natural fury is most terrifying, and when the damage wreaked is most complete. But in disaster cinema there is an elision between that dangerous stillness and the power of the attack. America imagines its own destruction as coming from an external enemy, but experiences it as an internal allegorically significant event: central, overwhelmingly focused on the local metaphor, and yet presumed globally significant. American disaster is essentially 'epi(c)-centric'. The imagined victim-self is saviour, interpreter and creator of the event in itself. It is a kind of national 'fort da'; a Freudian creation characterising a thing throwing itself away and picking itself up, in this case describing a nation making ontological claims for its survival while playing dead, throwing itself off the battlements like Batman, as Gotham City writhes below. As Freud illustrates:

This good little boy, however, had an occasional disturbing habit of taking any small objects he could get hold of and throwing them away from him into a corner, under the bed, and so on, so that hunting for his toys and picking them up was often quite a business. As he did this he gave vent to a loud, long-drawn-out 'o-o-o-o,' accompanied by an expression of interest and satisfaction. . . . The child had a wooden reel with a piece of string tied around it. It never occurred to him to pull it along the floor behind him, for instance, and play at its being a carriage. What he did was to hold the reel by the string and very skilfully throw it over the edge of his curtained cot, so that it disappeared into it, at the same time uttering his expressive 'o-o-o-o.' He then pulled the reel again by the string and hailed its reappearance with a joyful 'da' [there]. This, then, was the complete game of disappearance and return.

(Freud 1922: 14–15)

The little boy of Freud's pleasure principle finds comfort in his own game by which he confirms the worst, that his mother will leave, and insists on the best, that she will return. In American disaster films, the worst is confirmed, the loss of America, on the grounds that the best must still be possible, the continuation of America. It is the eye of the storm where the mote of putative empire gets stuck, a huge splinter spinning out of the maelstrom and going in deep.

Mike Davis's genealogies of the catastrophic imagination and descriptions of the most feral of these films are compelling, but his own prophecies of collapse also fascinate. As a roadside accident draws an audience, so Davis draws us towards the brink, which he both critiques and shares. 'The age of the edge city', he confirms

is the edge of a racial sorting out process . . . the semantic identity of race and urbanity within American political discourse is now virtually complete . . . Second . . . the increasing prevalence of strictly rim-to-rim commutes between job and home have given these bourgeois utopias unprecedented political autonomy from the crisis.

(Davis 2002: 255–6)

Does he also have the mote in his eye, and in which case is it a necessary blinding? Is it that the mote is symptomatic more of strength than of weakness? When the eye of the storm is both here and there, is there any doubt that the destruction is an allegorical riff on the state of the union? And, a restatement of the confidence that, notwithstanding all this mayhem, it is a big white house and it does not burn easily.

NOTES

1 This research was supported by the Australian Research Council, 2003–2005.
2 BTV's remake of the Japanese format *Happy Family Plan* (*Shiawase Kazoku Keikaku*). TBS *Happy Family Plan* was sold to more than 30 countries. In 2000, BTV bought the licence and presented it as *Dreams Come True* (*Mengxiang Chengzhen*), which was then on-sold to 43 stations throughout China. The terms of the collaboration between BTS

(Beijing) and TBS were three years in the making, according to a Chinese producer who had previously seen a version of the program screened on English television. As the English were unable to sell the licence, Beijing Television looked to the format owner, TBS. Licence fees were subsequently exchanged between BTV, TBS and the Beijing-based production company. The producers cited long-term goodwill with TBS as the reason why they paid fees rather than just copying like other Chinese stations. The original licence fee paid to TBS was equivalent to US$1500, but this was reduced over subsequent seasons as the local stations incorporated greater localisation. In particular, Beijing Television introduced a monthly version that allowed celebrities to participate (Keane interview with producer of Dreams Come True, June 2004). Endnote information courtesy of Michael Keane.

3   Immigration Restriction Act, 1901, or 'White Australia Policy' remained in place until 1966, and is a byword for resurgent racism at the level of politics.

4   The barrister was representing an Australian Pakistani young man on appeal for aggravated gang rape (October 2005). He was reprimanded by the judge for making a widespread racial insult in referring to his client as a 'cultural timebomb'. *Sydney Morning Herald*, 5 November 2005: 2.

5   Daughter of the late Charles Perkins, politician, rights activist and leader of the Freedom Ride in 1965.

6   For a detailed analysis of *Radiance* and other films of 'burning down the house' see Simpson, 2000.

REFERENCES

Chu, Y. (2003) *Hong Kong Cinema: Colonizer, Motherland and Self*, London: Routledge.

Cui, S. (2003) *Women Through the Lens: Gender and Nation in a Century of Chinese Cinema*, Honolulu: University of Hawai'i Press.

Davis, M. (1998) *Ecology of Fear: Los Angeles and the Imagination of Disaster*, New York: Vintage Books.

—— (2002) *Dead Cities: A Natural History*, New York: The New Press.

DeLillo, D. (2003) *Cosmopolis*, New York: Scribner.

Desser, D. and Fu, P. (2000) *The Cinema of Hong Kong: City, Arts, Identity*, Cambridge: Cambridge University Press.

Freud, S. (1922) *Beyond the Pleasure Principle*, New York: Boni and Liveright.

Frisby, D. (2001) *Cityscapes of Modernity: Critical Explorations*, London: Polity.

Fu, P. (2003) *Between Shanghai and Hong Kong: The Politics of Chinese Cinemas*, Stanford, CA: Stanford University Press.

Gibson, R. (2002) *Seven Versions of an Australian Badland*, Brisbane: University of Queensland Press.

Goldsmith, B. and O'Regan, T. (2005) 'The Policy Environment of the Contemporary Film Studio', in G. Elmer and M. Gasher (eds) *Contracting Out Hollywood: Runaway Productions and Foreign Location Shooting*, Lanham, MD: Rowman and Littlefield: 41–66.

Hu, J. (2003) *Projecting a Nation: Chinese National Cinema before 1949*, Hong Kong: Hong Kong University Press.

Kaes, T. (2005) 'Babel in Metropolis', Visualizing the City conference (unpublished keynote speech) Manchester: University of Manchester.

Keith, M. (2005) *After the Cosmopolitan? Multicultural Cities and the Future of Racism*, London: Routledge.

Lee, L. O.-F. (1999) *Shanghai Modern: The Flowering of Urban Culture in China, 1930–1945*, Cambridge, MA: Harvard University Press.

Ma, N. (1989) 'The Textual and Critical Difference in being radical: Reconstructing Chinese Leftist Films of the 1930s', *Wide Angle*, 11(2): 22–31.

Merck, M. (2005) 'American Gothic: Undermining the Uncanny', in K. Akass and J. McCabe (eds) *Reading Six Feet Under*, London: I.B. Tauris: 61–72.

Naficy, H. (2001) *An Accented Cinema: Exilic and Diasporic Film-making*, Princeton, NJ: Princeton University Press.

Nichols, B. (1996) 'Historical Consciousness and the Viewer: Who killed Vincent Chin?', in V. Sobchack (ed.) *The Persistence of History*, London: Routledge, pp. 55–68.

Pang, L. (2002) *Building a New China in Cinema: The Chinese Left-Wing Cinema Movement, 1932–1937*, Lanham, MD: Rowman and Littlefield.

Reynolds, H. (1998) *This Whispering in our Hearts*, Sydney: Allen and Unwin.

Robertson, P. (1995) *The End of the Age*, Dallas, TX: Word Publishing.

Shiel, M. (2006) *Italian Realism: Rebuilding the Cinematic City*, London: Wallflower Press.

Shih, S.-M. (2001) *The Lure of the Modern: Writing Colonialism in Semi-Colonial China, 1917–1937*, New York: Columbia University Press.

Simpson, C. (2000) 'Imagined geographies: gendering locale and locating subjectivity in contemporary Australian cinema', Murdoch University unpublished doctoral thesis.

Sobchack, V. (ed.) (1996) *The Persistence of History: Cinema, Television and the Modern Event*, London: Routledge.

Springsteen, B. (2002) *'Empty Sky'*, *The Rising*, New York: Sony Records.

Tomasulo, F. (1996) 'I'll See it When I Believe it; Rodney King and the Prison-house of Video', in V. Sobchack (ed.) *The Persistence of History*, London: Routledge, pp. 69–88.

Zhang, Y. (1996) *The City in Modern Chinese Literature and Film: Configurations of Space, Time, and Gender*, Stanford, CA: Stanford University Press.

—— (2004) *Chinese National Cinema*, London: Routledge.

FILMOGRAPHY

Baober in Love (*Lian ai zhong de Baober*) (2004) dir. Li Shaohong, Beijing Rosat FTV Production Co.

Beneath Clouds (2002) dir. Ivan Sen, AFFC, Autumn Films, Axiom Films.

Flowers of Shanghai (1998) dir. Hou Hsiao-Hsien, 3H Productions, Shochiku Co.

Mengxiang Chengzhen (2005) Beijing Television.

Metropolis (1927) dir. Fritz Lang, Universum Film AG (UFA).

Mr and Mrs Smith (2005) dir. Doug Liman, New Regency Pictures.

Rabbit Proof Fence (2002) dir. Philip Noyce, AFC, AFFC, Hanway Films.

Radiance (1998) dir. Rachel Perkins, AndyInc, AFC, Eclipse Films.

Shanghai Triad (1995) dir. Zhang Yimou, Alpha Films, La Sept Cinéma.

Small Things in a Big City (*Leaving Me, Loving You; dacheng xiaoshi*) (2004) dir. Wilson Yip, Paciwood Music and Entertainment Company, Tianjin Film Studio.

Strange Days (1995) dir. Kathryn Bigelow, Lightstorm Entertainment.

Street Angel (*malu tianshi*) (1937) dir. Yuan Muzhi, Mingxing Production.

Sunrise (1927) dir. F. W. Murnau, Fox Film Corporation.

The Day after Tomorrow (2004) dir. Roland Emmerich, 20th Century Fox.

The Lodger (1927) dir. Alfred Hitchcock, Gainsborough Pictures.

The Pacifier (2005) dir. Adam Shankman, Walt Disney Pictures.

Walkabout (1971) dir. Nicolas Roeg, 20th Century Fox.

Walkabout (1998 [1971]) dir. Nicolas Roeg, Film Trailer, Special edition DVD, Criterion Release.

War of the Worlds (2005) dir. Steven Spielberg, Paramount Pictures, Dreamworks SKG, Amblin Entertainment.

Chapter 8: The City Being Itself?

The Case of Paris in *La Haine*

François Penz

THE CITY BEING ITSELF

For over a century, cinema has been portraying the city in all shapes and forms, providing us with screen renditions of 'real cities' (shot on location), 'reconstructed cities' (shot in the studio) and now, of course, 'virtual cities' (created digitally). In this essay, we are solely concerned with 'city films' shot on location and attempts at finding *the city being itself*. In its purest form, the notion of *the city being itself* can be experienced in early cinema, such as in the scene of *La Place des Cordeliers* (1895) by Louis Lumière[1] (Figure 8.1; left). In this short scene, the still camera 'captures life as is'; the people are not actors, the traffic is not directed. The only directorial decision taken by Louis Lumière is the placement of the camera which dictates the location in the busy heart of the city – the framing and the angle in relation to the street. In this case capturing *La Place des Cordeliers* on the diagonal emphasizes the movement and the perspective.[2] In another example by Louis Lumière, a view from across the river in the heart of Lyon provides an astonishing composition (Figure 8.1; right). It is as if we were viewing, this time face on, a section across the city composed of three levels, each with their own narrative: the women washing below, the men in the middle and, finally, the street level above.

Subsequently, fiction films quickly became the dominant cinematic form and at that time, in the first half of the twentieth century, films were often shot in studios, particularly in the 1930s and 1940s. Rohmer, one of the original members of the *Nouvelle Vague* (New Wave), explains that before the 1950s 'the representation of Paris is scarce, apart from *Sous les Toits de Paris* and *Quatorze Juillet* by René Clair and the films of Marcel Carné, which in any case give very limited views of a reconstructed Paris' (Rohmer 2005: 22). With the advent of the Italian Neo-Realists and the New Wave in the 1950s, the lessons of the Lumière brothers and the City Symphonies were relearned and revisited. But in some ways it is the opening of Jules Dassin's *Naked City* (1948) that signals the return to

Figure 8.1
La Place des Cordeliers in Lyon (left). Scene from across the river (right). Lumière brothers, 1895.

location filming. Mark Hellinger, the producer, provided the memorable voice-over for the opening shot over Manhattan

> as you see we are flying over an island, a city a particular city, and this is the story of a number of people and the story also of the city itself, it was not photographed in a studio . . . quite the contrary Barry Fitzgerald, our star, Howard Duff . . . played out their roles on the streets . . . of NY itself and along with them a great many thousand of New Yorkers played out their roles also, this is the city as it is, hot summer pavements, the children at play, the buildings in their naked stone, the people, without make-up . . .

He famously concluded: 'There are 8 million stories in *The Naked City*, this has been one of them.' Significantly *Naked City* echoes the Italian neo-realist movement and anticipates the arrival of the French New Wave. The filmmakers of the New Wave took to filming in the streets of Paris as never before. Progress in technology (lightweight cameras, improved film stock, etc.) made this possible, and in allowing the filmmaking process to become much cheaper, it released a new generation of *auteurs* from the traditional studio culture. However, as Godard explained, it is not just the technological/economic argument that made filming in Paris attractive:

> What helps me to have ideas, is the décor. In fact often I start from that . . . I wonder how can one scout for locations after having done the script. We have to start with the location . . . One does not live in the same way in different settings. We live on *Les Champs Elysées*. But before *A Bout de Souffle (Breathless)* (1959) no film was showing what it looked like. In *A Bout de Souffle* my characters would have seen the *Champs Elysées* 60 times a day, so of course it had to be shown. We rarely see the Arc de Triomphe except in American films.
> (Godard 1962)

As a result, the emblematic *Champs Elysées* scene, with Belmondo and Seberg going about their flirtatious flânerie under the occasional gaze of a passer-by, captures the ordinary reality as had perhaps not been achieved since Louis Lumière 'caught life unawares' in Lyon in 1895 (see Figure 8.2). *A Bout de Souffle* (1960) was seen at the time as the manifesto of the New Wave (Marie 2005: 93), and caught the imagination of the public in France and abroad. Paris was back on the map . . . and on the screen!

A Bout de Souffle was, in Godard's (1961) own words, 'a fictional story but I tried to make it in a documentary style'. This documentary feel was common to other New Wave directors, such as Rivette and Rohmer. Its origin can be traced to the influence of Jean Rouch (1917–2004), in particular through his ethnographic films (Marie 2005: 70). As a result, the film historian Alain Bergala acknowledges in a recent encyclopaedia on *La Ville au Cinéma* (The City in the Cinema) that Godard's

> Parisian films of the time [the 1960s] are a precious and unique documentation on all which is changing in the city and the way it affects those living in it. He films almost at the same time the traditional and popular Paris used in *Vivre sa Vie* (1962), *Une Femme est une Femme* (1961), *Masculin-Féminin* (1966) as well as the new Paris which is emerging from the ground and modifying the way of life, the consciousness and the aesthetic views of its inhabitants. *Masculin-Féminin* and *Vivre sa Vie* are full of purely 'documentary' sequences with 'real passers-by' from which the actors are absent, sequences destined to record, as the Lumière cameramen did before, the state of Paris and its suburb at the time, which we would consider nowadays as archive material.
>
> (Bergala 2005: 713–14)

Figure 8.2
Belmondo and Seberg on Les Champs Elysées, still from *Breathless*, directed by Jean Luc Godard, 1960.

This appraisal is echoed by Rohmer, who, talking about his own film practice of working with real people and a real crowd (as opposed to extras), said that

> my main reason for doing so concurs with Lumière. I say that the passer-by in
> • the street being filmed is at the same time a spectator and as such he searches
> for the truth. If we show a very reconstituted Paris, he isn't happy, therefore he
> can't logically refuse in the street what he sees on the screen. He is keen to see
> the city as it is and that's a specificity of French cinema to avoid using the artifice
> of extras.
>
> (Rohmer 2005: 25)

This tradition of filming in the 'city as it is' is still acutely with us today. In this context, it is worth mentioning Robert Guédiguian (*Marius et Jeanette*, 1997/*La Ville est Tranquille*, 2001), who with 15 films staged in Marseille since 1980, has produced one of the most compelling and comprehensive portraits of a city, thus further exploring what Rohmer calls the tendency of French cinema to use real cities and real people. In so doing he has undertaken an 'oeuvre' where he patiently reveals Marseille to us. He states that 'Marseille is my language made of light and colours, architecture and costumes, sea and hills, body and gesture . . . I try to keep a balance between discourse and narration, between emotion and intelligence between pleasure and attention' (Guédiguian, 2000). Guédiguian also maintains a careful balance between the city and the fiction, thereby allowing Marseille to be an equal partner . . . and itself, in all its complexities.

To round off the idea of the *city being itself* we need to also briefly consider the notion of identity or identifiability. In other words, it would seem reasonable to assume that the audience can identify the location on the screen – not necessarily the exact location, but at least the city. This tends to be the case for most films shot on location whereby the city acts as an anchor for the narrative. Gardies coined the term 'referential space' (Gardies 1993: 78–9) whereby a film is geographically, socially and historically rooted. The city is often identified from the outset. Truffaut does it spectacularly in the opening sequence of *Les 400 Coups* (1959), in montage style, giving an 'Eiffel Tower-centric view' of Paris. Jarmusch does it at the beginning of each of the five city vignettes in *Night on Earth* (1991) and so on.

As discussed, Godard's *A Bout de Souffle* was the seminal film of the New Wave and, as such, was a powerful icon in shaping our collective imagination about what Paris and the French society was like in the 1950s and 1960s, as well as encapsulating the concept of the *city being itself* presented in the previous section. 40 years on, one could argue that *La Haine* (1995) became a repositioned icon of present-day Paris and similarly captures something of the essence of French society. There are striking parallels between the two films. Both were critically acclaimed and won major film festivals prizes although they generated debates and controversy. Both were first features for film directors of a similar age (Kassovitz was 28 and Godard 29). Beyond what could be conceived as trivia, there are further remarkable similarities. Both films are making overt references to American cinema, Godard to Bogart and Kassovitz to Scorsese with *Taxi Driver* (1976) and *Raging Bull* (1980). Most relevant here is the fact that both films are shot on location in Paris and reflect the evolution of the city over the second half of the twentieth century.

While Goddard's *Breathless* is essentially shot within Paris itself, *La Haine* is mainly a *banlieue*[3] (suburb) film. This location shift within the city echoes the evolution of Paris which, in the intervening period, has seen a significant growth in population taking place outside the confine of the 20 *arrondissements* (quarters). A vast public sector housing programme was developed, and was in part recorded by Godard in *2 ou 3 Choses que Je Sais d'Elle* (1966). Proportionally, and in real terms, Paris *intra muros* has lost population as business and offices expanded (Bullock 2003: 389). It has, therefore, been in keeping with social and economic trends to move individuals, such as those represented in *La Haine* to the outer city suburbs. In other words, Hubert, Said and Vinz are the modern day equivalent of Michel Poiccard (alias Laszlo Kovacs) and his friends, reflecting the increasing ethnic diversity of contemporary French society. In both films, the characters are streetwise small-time criminals motivated by a similar mix of greed and boredom. Police practices are portrayed in *La Haine* as having become more brutal, and in both films lead to untimely violent deaths on the streets of Paris. Despite the many similarities, the key distinction between the films is the urban environment, with the portrayal of the *banlieue*.

LA HAINE

The first half of *La Haine* takes place in a suburb of Paris, Chanteloup-les-Vignes, about 40 minutes to the west of the city. It belongs to a recently identified genre called *le film de cité*, which can be traced back to the early 1980s and which portrays the social problems traditionally associated with the *banlieues* stemming from racial and social tensions, drugs, unemployment and urban violence (Fourcaut 2005: 132). Undoubtedly *La Haine* captures aspects of all of those issues plus the evil twin of urban violence, police brutality. By the 1980s the modernity of the *banlieue*, the hope and excitement it generated in the 1950s and 1960s which was accurately captured by Marker in *Le Joli Mai* (1962), had been replaced by a deeply disturbing picture portrayed for the first time by Charef with *Le Thé au Harem d'Archimède* (1985), which announced the *film de cité* genre, and was followed in 1993 by *Hexagone* (1993). To this day the *films de cité* continue to be produced and are invariably staged on location, often around Paris. One of the most recent films of note in this genre is *L'Esquive* (2003).

La Haine tells the story in the life of three friends who live in Chanteloup-les-Vignes. It opens on stock images of urban riots from news reels, one of the characteristics of that period, and which unmistakably roots *La Haine* in its time and in the contemporary debate of that time, the first half of the 1990s. Eerily, those images over Bob Marley's haunting 'burnin'' and lootin'' lyrics could have just as easily applied to the autumn riots of 2005 in the same Parisian suburbs. It is as if *La Haine* had acquired a prophetic value, portraying in hindsight a near future repeating itself. The film has a 24 hours city symphony structure as the story begins the day after a riot in the *cité* where a policeman lost his gun which ends up in the hands of Vinz, who vows to even the score if a friend, critically injured by the police, dies. Vinz hangs out with friends Hubert and Said. They go to Paris for the evening where Said picks up some money that he is owed and, after a series of violent adventures, they make their way back to the *cité* after having heard of the death of their friend. As they separate at the RER station Vinz meets up with the police and is accidentally shot. Hubert who has taken over the revolver dies as he avenges Vinz's death while, horrified, Said looks on. Almost half of *La Haine* is staged in the centre of Paris, where the three protagonists arrive by using the suburban train. The centre of Paris is clearly identified through the presence of some unmistakable landmarks: the Eiffel Tower, the Forum des Halles and the Gare Saint Lazare (see Figure 8.3).

As for the anonymous street locations – the ubiquitous Paris – some of them are identified in *Paris vu au cinema* (Vincent and Saint-Exupéry 2003: 45). The balance at this point is tipped toward a world of interiors while the outdoor scenes are mainly constructed of anonymous streets, a generic metropolis where the characters wander aimlessly throughout the night. As Higbee (2001) remarked, 'Kassovitz . . . employ deep focus when shooting the characters within the *cité* so that they might be more closely integrated with their surroundings, whilst increasing focal length in Paris to detach the protagonists from their environment'. Indeed, the Paris sequence starts with an unusual compensated zoom which signals an alien environment as the city behind them becomes a blur. They do not belong to Paris and they do not know the city. There are no sequence or tracking shots, the shots are mainly from a static camera. This radically different cinematographic strategy further emphasizes the differences between the city centre and the *banlieue*. Similarly, the choice of interiors in Paris underlines this feeling of alienation and rejection: the Asterix bourgeois apartment, the art gallery and, of course, the *commissariat de police*.

More revealing for this study is the first part of the film which is shot on location in Chanteloup-les-Vignes, a *cité* built in the early 1970s by the architect Emile Aillaud, better known for the large housing project of *La Grande Borne* and his *tours nuages* (cloud towers) in Nanterre. Working closely with artist and

Figure 8.3
The portrayal of Paris – the Eiffel tower and an anonymous street, still from *La Haine*, directed by Mathieu Kassovitz, 1995.

colourist Fabio Rieti, Emile Aillaud's decorated his *grands ensembles* with gigantic murals and oversized sculptures in the spirit of bringing culture to the masses that was typical of the 1970s and Chanteloup-les-Vignes was no exception. But the colourful murals contrast with a harsh social reality: 25 per cent unemployment in 1994, a population badly hit by the closure of the Simca-Chrysler plant (the *cité* was originally built to house the workers) and 65 different nationalities in a population of 8,000 people. There has hardly been a month since the early 1990s when Chanteloup-les-Vignes was not in the news[4] for crime, violence and rioting. It was not just a local phenomenon but a widespread period of unrest in the French *banlieues* at the time.

Significantly Kassovitz chose to work in Chanteloup-les-Vignes partly because it was not as bleak as some of the other *cités* (Kassovitz 2005). He was then able to incorporate, to good effect, some of Chanteloup's unusual architectural features (see Figure 8.4), in particular some of the murals, portraits and sculptures. The part of the film shot in Chanteloup was essentially shot outdoors and there are very few indoor scenes, with some being shot in the studio, such as the famous *c'est à moi que tu parles* scene with Vinz.

Chanteloup-les-Vignes is not a very well known *cité* despite the relative celebrity of Aillaud in architectural circles. Most viewers would never have seen or heard of Chanteloup, and, in that sense, the issue here is more about its identification as the generic French suburb, or at least the idea the audience might have of the *banlieue*. Setting aside the larger issue regarding the suitability of Chanteloup as the generic suburb, it is obvious that in the context of film the *cité* itself is clearly identified and identifiable. Chanteloup is rather small and architecturally homogeneous and we get to know its topography rather well. The buildings are only four storeys high and are often a semi-circular shape with unusually shaped roofs. Although we do not get an establishing shot at the beginning of the film, at some point we discover the *cité* from a bird's-eye view

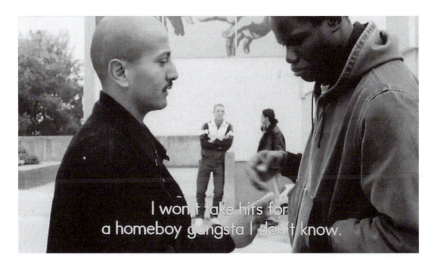

Figure 8.4
A mural in the background in Chanteloup-les-Vignes, still from *La Haine*, directed by Mathieu Kassovitz, 1995.

in a scene shot from a miniature helicopter swerving between and over the buildings.[5] This allows the audience to discover, among other features, that the end gables of the roofs are fake like on a Western set, something that one would normally not be aware of. Apart from the steadicam sequence shots, which are numerous, the *cité* is photographed in wide angle and long shot with great depth of field, giving the sense that the characters are part of the landscape, that they belong there. In using this strategy Kassovitz does justice to the *cité* landscape by allowing the audience's gaze to wander across the screen. Furthermore, he exploits the width and the breadth of the *cité* by showing the edges and the boundaries from one side to the other (Figure 8.5). One scene staged on a roof is also crucial in giving us a sense of the wider topography as we discover behind the *cité* a hill with the original village of Chanteloup-les-Vignes. At that point one gets a sense of the isolation of the youths – the roof is like a 'raft' lost in the middle of the countryside far away from Paris.

Filming in a *cité* in such a politically charged climate was not easy and only became possible through the decision by Kassovitz for all, the actors and the crew, to live in Chanteloup for over six weeks (Kassovitz 2005). This is an unusual move for such a film, but one which clearly paid off. Following from this the 'messengers', *les grands frères*, the elderly brothers of the local youths, helped greatly by providing the necessary link between the actors and the crew with the locals. As a result many of them were recruited to play out themselves and no extras were used. In that respect two scenes are worthy of note: the moment Hubert looks out of the window and we have his point of view observing the youths playing underneath his windows. This is very much a Godard moment as in *Vivre sa Vie* since nothing much happens except for the kids fooling around in the playground. The other moment to note is the barbecue roof scene which is entirely shot using people from Chanteloup-les-Vignes.

Kassovitz expertly uses the environment to support and set the stage for the narrative, as in the first scene when we discover the *cité* from Said's point of view in the dialogue *à trois* across the windows of facing buildings. In this first scene, we not only have an immediate sense of the racial mix and its potentially explosive intensity, but the topography of the *cité*, a given factor, is being revealed to us: its relatively human scale allowing this sort of interaction, with distinctive roofs and young trees in front of buildings. The *cité* is not revealed to us per se, as in a documentary, but through the careful staging of the dramatic action. And

Figure 8.5
Wide angle shot (left).
Barbecue roof scene
(right), stills from
La Haine, directed by
Mathieu Kassovitz, 1995.

150

Figure 8.6
Sequence shot and
soundscape, stills from
La Haine, directed by
Mathieu Kassovitz, 1995.

Figure 8.6
Sequence shot and
soundscape, stills from
La Haine, directed by
Mathieu Kassovitz, 1995.

yet there are sufficient elements to (re)present an architectural/urban coherence, to restore to the viewer a sense of 'being there'.

The rendition and creation of the screen environment is further enhanced and informed by the skilful exploitation of the notion of soundscape to characterize the space of the *cité*. Kassovitz took advantage of the Dolby stereo technology which was relatively new in 1994. For example, in the middle of the first steadicam sequence shot where the three characters first walk together in the *cité*, Said stops to pay attention to the sound of a motorbike which circles around them in the distance (see Figure 8.6). As he tries to identify its owner, Said stands with Vinz and Hubert in a pedestrian area in the middle of a group of buildings. They listen intensely to the sound of the motorbike on the outside of the buildings on a ring road. The rotating steadicam shot reinforces the circular nature of the sound as the camera is placed in the same direction as the sound source. It also gives the viewer a near 360-degree panorama shot of the courtyard. As a result, in the movie theatre the audience experiences this visual and audio looping effect through the surround sound while understanding, perhaps subconsciously, the relationship between the pedestrian area and the ring road without seeing it. Significantly, no film music comes between the viewer and the action; it is the sound of the *cité* which makes up the soundscape, apart from the diegetic music in the DJ and the rapper scene.

A large part of the cinematography in the *cité* consists of such sequence shots, some lasting two to three minutes, and reinforces this immersive feel. While this is a tough strategy for the actors, it allows the audience to experience the space in real time, to get a feel for the topology of the place, its levels, its thresholds, conveying a more realistic sense of time and distance and of the overall scale of the environment. This was part of Kassovitz's strategy, who tried to achieve a documentary feel, harder to get from the classic shot–reverse-shot continuity editing mode.

Paradoxically, Kassovitz was willing to sacrifice some realistic attributes by opting for a black and white aesthetic. Although he had always planned for a theatrical release in black and white, it is worth noting that the film was shot on colour film stock before being turned into black and white.[6] At the time this was due to the commercial imperatives of Canal Plus (the television channel sponsor). Regarding this issue Kassovitz (2005) stated that:

> I choose the b&w so that it would look good and I needed to achieve a certain uniformity . . . When you are on a limited budget the b&w is the best way to achieve something so-called artistic, something I wanted to achieve as I did not want it to be just a *film de cité*.

Similarly, Truffaut had stated that he preferred the black and white 'which operates a transformation which is what art is about . . . and that b&w unifies a film . . . Colour reveals aspects which are not necessarily useful and that in fact most people don't remember colour very well' (Truffaut 1978). In the case of *La Haine*, the black and white reinforces and accentuates the already homogenized environment of the *cité* but does not detract from it.

The resulting artistic 'look and feel' is more influenced by Scorsese's *Raging Bull* (1980) than inspired by the New Wave, and was widely praised: 'the filmmaker attempts to bring poetry to this sinister universe. The stunningly beautiful black and white, the panoramic view of the roofs [helicopter shot], or Vinz hallucination brings to the film a quasi fantastic feel' (Binh 2005: 204). In that sense Kassovitz moves one step away from a *cinema vérité* feel through the luscious black and white and more surrealist moments, something he readily confesses:

> This film cost 15 million francs. We could have done it for 300,000 francs, but it would have been a different film. I didn't want to do a film on a shoe-string budget . . . it's a heavily made-up fiction, not a documentary on the life of the *banlieues*.
>
> (Kassovitz 1995: 44)

Despite Kassovitz's obvious desire to create a portrait of Chanteloup as realistic as possible, he also recognizes the constraints that any filmmaking poses to a rendering of the 'city as being itself'.

THE IMPACT AND THE LEGACY OF *LA HAINE*

As the film became a success it put Chanteloup on the map, producing a temporary celebrity for an otherwise unknown place. It is a phenomenon that was remarked upon by Keiller (2003: 382), referring here to urban centres

> the representation of urban spaces in films does seem to be a factor in the current scenarios of urban regeneration . . . the sight of a familiar space in film can momentarily banish the sense of marginality that haunts even the most central urban locations.

In some ways this phenomenon was acknowledged by Kassovitz on 4 June 1995 as he organized a public projection of *La Haine* for the benefit of the youth population of Chanteloup-les-Vignes and fittingly screened in the prestigious Jean Vigo auditorium of 'La Grande Halle de La Villette'. 300 of them turned up brought in by a specially hired fleet of coaches. The screening was a great success and many of the young people there thought it would have an impact on their lives as reported by one of them: 'even if the film hadn't been a success it would have transformed my life' (Merigeau 1995). As they were milling around with 'Hubert, Said and Vinz', the youth of Chanteloup-les-Vignes enjoyed their 15 minutes of glory which temporarily 'banished their sense of marginality'.

La Haine won the Best Director award at Cannes that year and police guards at the screening at Cannes ostensibly turned their backs on Kassovitz, the cast, and crew as they came down the steps of the 'Palais des Festivals' in protest of its portrayal of police brutality (Merigeau 1995). The film started a polemic with the police and the government, as the newly nominated Prime Minister, Alain Juppé, arranged a special screening and ordered his entire cabinet to watch the film. Furthermore, an article in Le Monde on urban violence (Herzberg and Inciyan 1995), quotes a police report mentioning that 'this phenomenon [referring to violence] in 1995 has increased since June, possibly due to the local elections and the release of the film La Haine'. However, one must remember that 1995 had been a particularly difficult year in France with 6,000 incidents of violence as opposed to 4,000 in 1994. The article goes on to acknowledge that while increased violence may appear to have coincided with the release of the film La Haine, it is much more likely to have been in part caused by the anti-terrorist plan vigipirate which saw a vast increase in the police presence in the suburbs, thus exacerbating racial tension. But since La Haine was associated with a period of deep social unrest in France, there was a lot of political debate on social and racial integration and it became the object of deep resentment on the part of the French government, who accused Kassovitz of presenting a warped image of the banlieues. Two years later, Eric Raoult, the minister for integration at the time (Herzberg 1997), challenged filmmakers to make a more balanced portrait of the suburbs, and as a result Bertrand and Nils Tavernier took up the challenge and spent a year in the cité 'Les Grands-Pêchers' making the documentary 'de l'autre coté du periph' in 1997.

Ten years later, La Haine has achieved cult status and on the occasion of a special DVD release, a journalist acknowledged that 'La Haine has aged better than Chirac's promises' (Douhaire 2005).[7] Sadly, La Haine's portrayal of suburban violence has been vindicated by recent events in France in the autumn of 2005. Although Chanteloup-les-Vignes' sense of marginality that haunts all cités was momentarily banished at the time of the film's release, it carried on being in the news[8] – but for all the wrong reasons. As for Kassovitz he appears to have become an 'authority' on the banlieue. On his blog [www.mathieukassovitz.com/blog] of 25 November 2005, Kassovitz acknowledged that 'For sometime now I have been increasingly solicited by the media around the world to comment on the recent events in the French banlieues . . . However, I can't face so many demands which is why I have decided to express my views through my web site', and goes on to state that 'hate has fuelled hate for centuries and yet Nicolas Sarkozi [at the time minister in charge of the police and security] still believes that repression is the only means to prevent rebellion'. In an unprecedented move, Nicolas Sarkozi decided to respond to Kassovitz on his blog, thereby confirming Kassovitz in his status of *grands-frères des banlieues* (elder of the suburbs).

CONCLUSIONS

With its giant murals and oversized sculptures, Chanteloup-les-Vignes had elements of a utopian architectural vision which became the setting for a dystopia both on screen and in real life. In that sense *La Haine* does carry a certain form of realism of the type defended by Thomas Andersen who produced and directed *Los Angeles Plays Itself* (2003)[9] and who believes that cinema should have a direct, accurate relationship to reality (Andersen 2003). This is the tradition evoked previously with the New Wave and of which Truffaut reminded us:[10]

> Vigo was closer to realism than most . . . when we look at the programme that Langlois has put together about Lumière, one realises that as cinema became more refined, it had gradually lost touch with the reality . . . the Lumière brothers lessons were rediscovered by Vigo and subsequently by Godard.
>
> (Truffaut 1968)

With *La Haine*, Kassovitz has built on the legacy of the New Wave and achieved a portrayal that is true enough to the 'city being itself' notion to satisfy historians, sociologists and others as to its potential archival value. He has managed to straddle a difficult line between aesthetic and realism, between truth and illusion. This is certainly not an isolated case, but echoing Truffaut's words we can only observe that with the advent of digitality and advances in technology, cinema has become more refined but also, perhaps, less truthful and further away from the reality. The city is often being played with and tampered with as in Jeunet's portrayal of Montmartre, *Le Fabuleux Destin d'Amélie Poulain* (2001) where we move away from the notion of the 'city being itself' towards the concept of the 'city being played with'. Despite being shot on location, *Le Fabuleux Destin d'Amélie Poulain* has been perceived as a 'digital face lift of Paris' (Schmerkin 2005) which triggered Robert and Tsikounas to remark that:

> the Paris recreated in studio by Trauner and Meerson in the 30s, which takes us straight back to a nineteenth century iconography, is just as anachronistic as the Montmartre of *Le Fabuleux Destin d'Amélie Poulain*, new variation on an 'old Paris'.
>
> (Robert and Tsikounas 2004: 6)

With around 600 films made in the streets of Paris every year, there is certainly room for the 'city being itself' and the 'city being played with' notions to thrive side by side – and as for Paris itself, in the words of the Mayor Bertrand Delanoë 'every time we see Paris associated with a cinematographic enterprise it makes Paris proud' (Delanoë 2006). We are now in an era where city planners and decision makers can use the moving image to harness the power of cinema to promote an identity. This makes it crucial for designers, architects and planners to be able to understand better the mechanisms through which they, too, can convey their vision of a future city.

NOTES

1　In *La ville au Cinéma* (Jousse and Paquot 2005) there is a section by Thierry Frémaux on Louis Lumière (pp. 744–8), in the chapter devoted to '50 Urban Filmmakers'.

2　Those scenes are much admired by Tavernier in his commentary of the Lumière's work (Tavernier 1996).

3　The French word *banlieue* appears in the thirteenth century to designate the space comprised within one *lieue* (around four kilometres) all around a city and subjected to the *ban*, i.e. the city's jurisdiction. In its current meaning it defines the conurbation that is beyond the centre of a city. In the case of Paris it defines the area between the 20 *arrondissements* and the outer edge of the *Grand Paris*. It is where the vast majority of the population now resides (around 80 per cent).

4　Interestingly Chanteloup-les-Vignes was already the subject of a television documentary in 1991 when a TV crew came to live for three weeks in the *cité* (documentary directed by Francine Buchi and Michel Sallandre and shown on 29 March 1991 on TF1 channel, see: www.humanite.presse.fr/journal/1991–03–29/1991–03–29–640959).

5　This is one of the cult scenes of *La Haine* shot over DJ Cut Killer's song blasting out of his bedroom window followed by Edith Piaf's *rien de rien je ne regrette rien*. . . .

6　The lighting cinematographer, Pierre Aïm, used a particular colour film stock which he used previously and knew would produce the desired rich and lush black and white. In the event no colour version was ever released (*La Haine* DVD release 2005).

7　Chirac became president at the time of the release of the film.

8　A survey of *Le Monde* from 1987 has revealed that Chanteloup-les-Vignes has consistently made the headlines in relation to violent incidents but no significance can be attributed, one way or another, to the release of *La Haine* as 16 serious incidents were reported between 1987 and 1995 and 14 between 1995 and 2006.

9　The film traces the history of filmmaking in the city of Los Angeles with the help of film clips and a voice-over commentary by the director.

10　An interview by Rohmer dating from 1968 on French Television and part of the 'extras' in the DVD publication '*L'intégrale de Jean Vigo*' interview regarding Vigo's *L'Atalante*.

REFERENCES

Bergala, A. (2005) 'Jean-Luc Godard', in T. Jousse and T. Paquot (eds) *La Ville au Cinéma*, Paris: Cahiers du Cinéma.

Binh, N. T. (2005) *Paris au Cinéma: la vie révée de la Capitale de Méliès à Amélie Poulain*, Paris: Parigramme.

Bullock, N. (2003) 'Two Cinematic Readings of the Parisian Suburbs', *City: Analysis of Urban Trends, Culture, Theory, Policy, Action* 7(3): 386–99.

Delanoë, B. (2006) 'Signature d'une charte des tournages entre Paris et les professionnels du cinema', March. Online. Available: www.paris.fr/portail/Culture/Portal.lut?page_id=102&document_type_id=2&document_id=17693&portlet_id=818.

Douhaire, S. (2005) *Dix ans après sa sortie, le film de Kassovitz reste d'actualité. 'La Haine' est toujours là* Paris: Libération 3 June 2005. Online. Available: www.liberation.fr/migration_0/tentations_136/184206.FR.php.

Fourcant, A. (2005) 'La banlieue au cinéma', in T. Jousse and T. Paquot (eds) *La Ville au Cinéma*, Paris: Cahiers du Cinéma, pp. 124–33.

Frémaux, T. (2005) 'Louis Lumière', in T. Jousse and T. Paquot (eds) *La Ville au Cinéma*, Paris: Cahiers du Cinéma, pp. 744–8.

Gardies, A. (1993) *L'Espace au Cinéma*, Paris: Méridiens Klincksieck.

Godard, J.-L. (1961) *But 'Wave' adds Brightness*, London: Films and Filming, September: 35–6.

—— (1962) *Jean-Luc Godard Interview*, Paris: Cahiers du Cinéma, 23 (138): 21–39.

Guédiguian, R. (2000) *Tout Guédiguian*, Paris: DVD by Arte Vidéo.

Herzberg, N. (1997) '155 écrivains dénoncent à leur tour les lois sur l'immigration', *Le Monde* 14 February. Online. Available: www.lemonde.fr/web/recherche_breve/1,13–0,37–248815,0.html.

—— and Inciyan, E. (1995), 'L'année 1995 a été marquée par la montée des violences urbaines', *Le Monde* 30 December. Online. Available: www.lemonde.fr/web/recherche_breve/1,13–0,37–389403,0.html.

Higbee, W. (2001) 'Screening the 'Other' Paris: Cinematic Representations of the French Urban Periphery in La Haine and Ma 6-T Va Crack-er', *Modern & Contemporary France* 9 (2): 197–208.

Jousse, T. and Paquot, T. (2005) *La Ville au Cinéma*, Paris: Cahiers du Cinéma.

Kassovitz, M. (1995) 'C'est pas interdit', *Télérama* 31 May: 44.

—— (2005) *La Haine* DVD 2 'Interview', Paris: Studio Canal.

Keiller, P. (2003) 'The City of the Future', *City: Analysis of Urban Trends, Culture, Theory, Policy, Action*, 7(3): 375–86.

Marie, M. (2005) *La Nouvelle Vague*, Paris: Armand Colin.

McLuhan, M. (1964) *Understanding Media: The Extensions of Man*, New York: McGraw-Hill.

Merigeau, P. (1995) 'Les jeunes de Chanteloup ne se sentent pas trahis par "La Haine" de Mathieu Kassovitz', *Le Monde*, 6 June. Online. Available: www.lemonde.fr/cgi-bin/ACHATS/acheter.cgi?offre=ARCHIVES&type_item=ART_ARCH_30J&objet_id=367870.

Robert, J. L. and Tsikounas, M. (eds) (2004) *Imaginaires Parisiens*, Paris: CREDHESS.

Rohmer, É. (2005) 'Un cinéaste dans la ville-Entretien avec Éric Rohmer', in T. Jousse and T. Paquot (eds) *La Ville au Cinéma*, Paris: Cahiers du Cinéma, pp. 19–27.

Schmerkin, N. (2005) 'Numérique', in T. Jousse and T. Paquot (eds) *La Ville au Cinéma*, Paris: Cahiers du Cinéma, pp. 94–6.

Travernier, B. (1996) DVD voice-over in *The Lumière Brothers' First Film*, Association Frères Lumière, produced by Kino Video (US).

Truffaut, F. (1968) *Television Interview with Rohmer*, Paris: DVD: 'L'intégrale de Jean Vigo.

Truffaut, F. (1978) Quote from an interview (my own translation from French) on Radio-France 'Radioscopie', 17 March 1978. Online. Available at: www.ina.fr/archivespourtous/index.php?vue=notice&from=fulltext&full=truffaut&datedif_jour1=17&datedif_mois1=03&datedif_annee1=1978&mode_document=audio&num_notice=1&total_notices=1.

Vincent, M. C. and de Saint-Exupéry, F. (2003) *Paris Vu au Cinéma*, Paris: Éditions Movie Planet.

FILMOGRAPHY

De l'Autre Côté du Périph (1997) dir. Bertrand Tavenier, Little Bear.

2 ou 3 Choses Que Je Sais d'Elle (1966) dir. Jean-Luc Godard, Argos Films.

Le Fabuleux Destin d'Amélie Poulain (2001) dir. Jean-Pierre Jeunet, Claudie Ossard Productions.

La Haine (1995) dir. Mathieu Kassovitz, Canal.

Los Angeles Plays Itself (2003) dir. Thom Andersen, Thom Andersen Productions.

The Lumière Brothers' First Films (1996) Association Frères Lumière.

Marius et Jeannette (1997) dir. Robert Guédiguian, Agat Films & Cie.

Masculin-Féminin (1966) dir. Jean-Luc Godard, Anouchka Films.

Mon Oncle (1958) dir. JacquesTati, Alter Films.

Naked City, The (1948) dir. Jules Dassin, Hellinger Productions.

Night on Earth (1991) dir. Jim Jarmusch, Victor Company of Japan.

Quatorze Juillet (1932) dir. René Clair, France, Films Sonores Tobis.

Quatre Cents Coups, Les (1959) dir. François Truffaut, Les Films du Carrosse.

Raging Bull (1980) dir. Martin Scorsese, Chartoff-Winkler Productions.

Sous les Toits de Paris (1930) dir. René Clair, Films Sonores Tobis.

Taxi Driver (1976) dir. Martin Scorsese, Columbia Pictures.

Thé au Harem d'Archimède, Le (1985) dir. Mehdi Charef, K. G.

Une Femme est une Femme (1961) dir. Jean-Luc Godard, Euro International Film (EIA).

Ville Est Tranquille, La (2001) Robert Guédiguian, Agat Films & Cie.

Vivre sa Vie (1962) Jean-Luc Godard, Les Films de la Pléiade.

Chapter 9: Composing London Visually

Robert Tavernor

INTRODUCTION

In a global economy, city-image matters. It influences where international corporations choose to locate, which, in turn, affects inward investment and the infrastructure of daily life for the city's inhabitants. London, New York, Paris and Tokyo are the four 'Alpha' World Cities, pre-eminent cities that draw workers, visitors and huge wealth from around the globe (Beaverstock *et al*. 1999: 445–58, Table 7). Except for Tokyo, perhaps, they have highly recognizable urban images. Apart from New York they are also national capitals and, as such, are required to represent through their image the specifics of nationhood – history, national identity, language, culture. As a tangible means to transmitting an appropriately modern image for the future – technologically advanced and welcoming to innovation – modern architecture and tall buildings may literally figure large.

London has done its best to integrate old with new. It is consequently a city of considerable visual contrast, much more so than Paris, which has done its best to distance and group its tall buildings away from its historic centre in an exclusively modern business centre at La Defense. Canary Wharf is London's equivalent, but the ancient centre of London's commerce, the City of London – which includes St Paul's Cathedral, a monument of national and international significance, and the World Heritage Site of the Tower of London – incorporates a major cluster of modern tall buildings. The City is no stranger to change and has constantly renewed itself down the centuries, out of necessity – after the devastation wrought by the Great Fire it suffered in 1666, and Second World War bombing – or out of the desire to compete commercially at the highest level. To survive a new wave of competition, London has been reinventing itself again, while attempting to retain the visual and cultural link with the past with which it is identified internationally.

Although the City is of considerable importance for the wealth and identity of the nation, it is not afforded special licences to build as it wishes. The City of London sits alongside 32 London Boroughs, and its governance is subject to the same planning controls and regulations – national, regional and local – as any other local authority in England and Wales (Scotland and Northern Ireland having separate planning legislation). In addition, there is the more general European Union control of the environment which requires, for instance, an Environmental Impact Assessment (EIA) to be submitted in order to gauge the probable impact of large developments on their surroundings (Glasson 2005). Thus, the overall planning system necessitates that an assessment be made of the likely impact of any large development on the setting of its existing cityscape of buildings and spaces. Planning decisions about the positions, heights and clustering of large and tall buildings in London are determined by politicians, urban planners, architects and heritage groups. This includes assessing their visual impact on photographically recorded images of London taken from selected fixed viewing positions in and around the capital.

The intention behind this approach is to protect well-known views of the capital seen from surrounding hills and from the bridges crossing the River Thames. Initially, ten principal 'Strategic Views' were established across London in 1991, which were intended to safeguard the settings and silhouettes of St Paul's Cathedral and the Palace of Westminster. *The London Plan* (GLA 2004), produced for the Mayor of the Greater London Assembly, Ken Livingstone, refined, extended and linked these as a *London View Management Framework* (GLA, published in draft form in 2005) comprising 'Panoramas, Townscape and Linear Views'. In addition to the statutory strategic views, local planners invariably request incidental views to be assessed. A large building proposal, particularly one that is tall and can be seen from many different locations, might require between 30 and in excess of 100 views of the site to be assessed. To this end, a specialist Townscape Consultant acting on behalf of the developer will select precise viewing positions to be photographed, close-to and at increasing distances away from the project site. These positions are surveyed in relation to surrounding buildings so that realistic computer-generated images (CGIs) of the proposed development – accurate 3D computer models – can be montaged precisely into the photographs by a 'visualization' company, with varying degrees of realism, as required (Day 2002).

The notion that the future image of a city should be defined through a set of selected views is unique to London. It is an approach to urban planning borne out of a desire to find a way of balancing what is cherished of London's past with the demands of a high-quality, modern future. It has to succeed if London is to maintain its particular cultural essence and retain its own separate visual identity from just any other city. But it results in a slow and consequently costly planning process, and an extraordinary amount of negotiation between developers, their architects and consultants with the local planning authority and – when the process breaks down – regional and national government. This is not the place to discuss the merits and demerits of this complex process. Instead, I will focus on how this aspect of planning London, through views, came about, since few engaged in this process understand how this approach evolved and why it should be relevant to London and nowhere else. In fact, this approach is derived from traditional ways of viewing cities, particularly in Europe, which has its roots in 'view painting'.

I will review this development in order to consider the appropriateness and implications of visually composing a world capital through static views.

MEASURING QUALITY IN THE EUROPEAN CITY

For centuries, artists have created memorable images of cities through drawings and paintings. At their most prosaic, they were made in the form of simple plans that were intended to record – as simply as possible – the subdivision of property and land ownership: in antiquity these were inscribed on stone tablets (Rykwert 1976: 61). Less abstract, and more characteristic of a city's appearance, were the sketchy aerial pictograms-cum-maps of great cities that were drawn in the Middle Ages, often for the benefit of pilgrims. For great pilgrimage cities such as Rome, they showed the primary routes through the urban fabric that led to the principal churches (Tavernor 1998: 17, Fig. 14). In the fifteenth and sixteenth centuries, demand for more accurate maps of cities was related to acquiring control. Much as generals would obtain detailed maps of the field of battle, Pope Nicholas V sought to exert his authority on the disruptive, disparate ruling clans of Rome by commissioning the first physically accurate map of the city. This was created for him in the mid-fifteenth century by Leon Battista Alberti (1404–72), one of those brilliant universal men of the Italian Renaissance, by adapting standard astronomical techniques to land surveying (Tavernor 1998: 13–23). Leonardo da Vinci adopted Alberti's technique when he produced a wonderfully detailed map of Imola in northern Italy (Hayward Gallery 1989: 176, Fig. 98). Alberti is also linked with early view paintings of urban scenes using accurate one-point perspectival draughting to measure and represent space and form in proportion: a technique he was the first to codify (Tavernor 1998: 6–9, Fig. 72).

Italian urban view paintings – *vedute* – developed from two principal sources. They were used from the late fifteenth century by architects, to demonstrate urban ideals to their patrons and peers (how a well-ordered city should look, or would look if their designs were implemented); and, by the late sixteenth century, landscape painters working in Italy were developing them as souvenirs for European Grand Tourists: views of cities and archaeology were increasingly in demand. As an appropriate urban subject, Venice was soon to rival Rome, and the painter Antonio Canaletto (1697–1798) is a famous beneficiary of a lucrative market in view paintings. Canaletto took his lead from the established Roman *vedutista* Giovanni Paolo Pannini (1691–1765), and began developing his own instantly recognizable topographical style during the 1720s. An English merchant in Venice, Joseph Smith (who became British Consul in Venice in 1744), acted as his go-between with the English gentry, and business flourished for both men, until the War of the Austrian Succession reduced the number of English visitors to Venice. Canaletto was encouraged to move close to his market in London in 1746, where he remained for the next nine years.

Canaletto's *vedute* provide panoramas across water (the Venetian Lagoon and Grand Canal, or the River Thames in London), or local views of smaller groupings of buildings and places. They are static, perspectival compositions that represent physical relations precisely, having been produced by Canaletto using a portable *camera obscura*. Of course, they go beyond mere technique and he brought specific colour and lighting qualities to his views, rendering London with lucid skies and imbuing surfaces with the warmth of an eternal summer's evening. He was not interested – nor were his patrons – in depictions of the realities of overcast, watery skies, and the sometimes impenetrable smoke-laden atmosphere more familiar to Londoners. While accurately delineating buildings – their relationship to one another and surrounding spaces as well as their materials – the painted scenes were also lent a continental atmosphere, and populated with a staged society of people – ambling gentry and a few, non-threatening scallywags – to invigorate the view.

Unlike a sparsely populated landscape, in an urban scene there are many potential viable viewing positions. A joy of being in cities – compared to the countryside – is to see and be seen, and Canaletto captures this urban characteristic to perfection. Canaletto sometimes took views from private balconies, but very often they were from viewing positions that would be known to many of the gentle folk they depict. The art of Canaletto was to capture an urban theatricality for those who scrutinized his paintings, whereby they may be both dispassionate viewer and notional participants in the scenes that were so familiar to them. As in the theatre of the ancient Greeks, buildings provided the scenic backdrop, and views were stolen from balconies and windows of public life below as an integral part of the tragedy, comedy or satire being performed (Tavernor 1991: 100–5). As the writer Henry James (1843–1916) later observed of the relationship of Venetian water and buildings, when describing the church of Santa Maria della Salute at the mouth of the Grand Canal:

> The whole thing composes as if composition were the chief end of human institutions. . . . On the other side of the Canal [from the Salute] twinkles and glitters the long row of the happy palaces which are mainly expensive hotels. . . . They are almost as charming from other places as they are from their own balconies, and share fully in that universal privilege of Venetian objects which consists of being both the picture and the point of view.
>
> (James 1995: 34–5)

Certainly, cities are potent artefacts, and composing the city artfully as a brilliant backdrop for delight, human interaction and exchange provides civilized society with an enduring emblem of beauty; a heady combination of nature and artifice. One of Canaletto's more famous views of London is of a broad panorama of the River Thames from Old Somerset House, painted as diptych, two paintings set side by side (Tavernor 2004: 80). Old Somerset House (since replaced by William Chambers' eighteenth-century Somerset House) is situated at a major bend in the river, equidistant between the City of London and St Paul's Cathedral (to the east) and the City of Westminster and Westminster Abbey (to the west). Views were commanded of both 'cities' from there.

This is London depicted as 'Venice of the North', a mercantile city that had become rich through international trade, and which was seeking to reinforce its urban image through the Georgian era (an unbroken monarchical span of 116 years from Kings George I through to IV between 1714 and 1830), by reference to the architecture and arts of classical Italy. The great housing estates west of the City were laid out with a fairly regular geometry of Georgian architecture and planning, which is characterized by grand classical squares and palatial – Palladian style – terraces. The huge dome of Sir Christopher Wren's St Paul's Cathedral formed the spiritual and visual centrepiece of the commercial City and its tangle of ancient streets. Today, the dome of St Paul's and its west towers remain a prominent landmark. That it is possible to see the dome so clearly from key vantage points around London is the outcome of planning legislation that – uniquely for a British city, and perhaps for any city – has controlled where tall buildings that might affect its visibility and setting should be located.

LONDON'S SKYLINE AND THE SYMBOLIC IMPACT OF THE DOME OF ST PAUL'S

By the early seventeenth century, a primary west–east ceremonial and functional route had been established in central London, with the City of Westminster (including Parliament, Whitehall and St James's) at its western end; and the much smaller City of London, a district of about three square kilometres in area – known better as the 'square mile' – that includes St Paul's Cathedral and the commercial city as its eastern focus. The square mile is a legacy of the occupying Romans who established ancient *Londinium* there. Whitehall and Strand link to form a long street running roughly tangentially to the long curve of the River Thames, a route that connects these western and eastern poles. Whitehall was lined with royal palaces and governmental buildings, and Strand became the focus for several major private and public buildings. Westminster as the western pole of this axis had the space to develop and expand through grand squares and houses. The eastern pole, the City, was constrained by defensive walls (Roman, Norman and Medieval). It was, by comparison, a maze of densely inhabited and dangerously overcrowded streets.

The Great Fire of London thrived on this density and destroyed old St Paul's Cathedral and much of the City in 1666. Sir Christopher Wren's proposal (submitted with John Evelyn) was for a radically new replacement street layout, which was inspired by the long straight and radiating streets found in the Baroque seventeenth-century planning of Rome and Paris (Rykwert 1980: 146–7). They were to be focused on two main buildings, the Exchange and St Paul's. Wren proposed rebuilding the Exchange on its original site (close to the present site of the Stock Exchange), but as a freestanding structure surrounded by its own 'piazza', and at the centre of a new network of radiating streets. Indeed, he accorded the Exchange the most prestigious position in the City plan, and the geometry that orders its streets was to have emanated from that site. The new St Paul's Cathedral he positioned facing the Ludgate entrance into the City (as it does today), dividing the approach road from Westminster (Strand and Fleet Street): the uppermost branch was to connect St Paul's with the new Exchange and Aldgate, a major north-eastern gateway through the still intact medieval City walls. In Wren's master plan, commerce and religion had equal status. No matter, it was not adopted and the ad hoc flexibility of the City's medieval street pattern was reinstated so that London's traders could resume business with minimal further disruption, and the new St Paul's grew to dominate – physically and spiritually – the relatively chaotic street scene that surrounded it.

Wren's St Paul's is a magnificent architectural achievement (Keene *et al.* 2004). As the first purpose-built Protestant Cathedral, it was a symbol of the once supreme authority of the Anglican Church and the British Monarchy. The introduction of the 1667 London Building Act succeeded in limiting building heights to a maximum of four storeys (Summerson [1945] 2003), and well into the nineteenth century, non-public buildings were kept low, and buildings taller than 30 metres required special sanction. Consequently, it has remained a very visible icon of international significance for modern times too. During the twentieth century it provided a backdrop for the major state ceremonials that were broadcast around the world. The internationally famous photographs taken in the early stages of the Second World War show it rising phoenix-like through the fires and smoke of the Blitz (Keene *et al.* 2004: 461, Fig. 388), when large swathes of the City were destroyed once again. It has become a quiet centre for all faiths in the midst of the physical and economic changes that are continuously taking place around it.

DIFFERENT VIEWPOINTS OF THE CHANGING URBAN CONTEXT OF ST PAUL'S

The streets of the City are mostly narrow and winding, restricting views, and the best prospects of St Paul's are from high ground to the north and north-west (Highgate, Kenwood, Parliament Hill and Primrose Hill) and south-east (Greenwich and Blackheath). More locally, views from the south bank across the open space of the River Thames are important, and historically the most important panoramas of the City have always been those of the City viewed across the River Thames from the south and west, which have the river in the foreground. There are famous engraved views of London from the south bank in the sixteenth and seventeenth centuries of medieval, 'old' St Paul's, by Visscher (1616) and Hollar (1647), as well as easterly views of Wren's new St Paul's taken from Somerset House River Terrace. They include views by Antonio Canaletto in the 1750s, but also by Nicholson (1800), Parrott (1840) and O'Connor (1874). These scenes illustrate the changing setting of St Paul's down the centuries. Canaletto's view is from the River Terrace of Lord Protector Somerset's sixteenth-century former 'palace'. John O'Connor's is taken from the terrace of its eighteenth-century replacement designed by Sir William Chambers (1723–96) (Tavernor 2004: 81). Chambers' Somerset House (begun in 1776) has a riverside terrace raised on huge piers, which originally stood in the River Thames and provided a grand river frontage resembling a giant entrance portico. It was designed to impress: the River Terrace is set some 12 metres above the former sixteenth-century palace garden.

Canaletto's famous depiction from the former, lower set vantage point, is an idealized interpretation of life on the Thames and, as already mentioned, of London as the capital of a great maritime trading nation – a centre of European arts and culture, which rivalled perhaps the greatness of his native Venice. However, a changing national mood is evident when his view is compared with the later views. For instance, by 1874 John O'Connor was depicting St Paul's flanked by large smoke- and steam-belching cylindrical chimneystacks: two gasometers slightly obscure its elevation (Figure 9.1). A map of London, dated 1873, identifies these gasometers as part of the City of London Gas Works. The chimneys are probably spewing condensated air from steam engines used to drive machinery in the printing works and factories in the locality: *The Times* Printing Office was situated immediately east of Blackfriars Station, and there were other printers located nearby; there was even a mustard factory on Garlick Hill.

O'Connor's painting is no less emblematic than Canaletto's, but it has a different story to tell. When O'Connor painted this view, London was the capital of an empire of global proportions; its enormous wealth built on industrial might and military strength. He depicts traffic on Thames Embankment, which had been opened by the Prince of Wales on 13 July 1870, in relation to the modern and historic commercial core of the City of London beyond. Thames Embankment was constructed under the control of the chief engineer of the Metropolitan Board of Works, Sir Joseph Bazalgette, an admirer of Baron Haussmann and his modern restructuring of Paris. It was built to relieve surface traffic congestion along the Strand, and to provide a new link in the Circle Line for the Metropolitan District

Figure 9.1
View east from Somerset House river terrace, John O'Connor, 1874.

Railway. A major sewer also ran alongside the underground railway to prevent existing sewers from flowing directly into the Thames: another lesson learnt from Haussmann. With the construction of the Embankment, Chambers' eighteenth-century Somerset House lost its direct access to the river (Halliday 1999: *passim*).

O'Connor celebrated this major urban intervention and its new street life in the manner that French artists were presenting Haussmann's Parisian Boulevard. Beyond is the powerhouse of this wealth, represented by the gasometers and the smoke and steam of the industrial stacks and trains. They contrast with the powerful static image of St Paul's Cathedral. O'Connor makes no attempt to down-play the impact of recent industrialization. On the contrary, these new elements in the City are presented prominently as potent symbols of Britain's powerful industrial virility. It is curiously tendentious therefore that certain sectors of modern Britain continue to argue that the Canaletto view from Old Somerset Palace is somehow sacrosanct and still relevant to London today. For example, our current Prince of Wales, Prince Charles, was ill-advised when he claimed in *A Vision of Britain* that the skyline Canaletto painted was 'inviolate' and 'still substantially intact right up to 1960' (Prince of Wales 1989: 55). To make his point visually, Prince Charles overlaid a similar view taken photographically in the 1980s – in black and white – onto a colour print of Canaletto's painting. While this was effective propaganda for his vision of traditional urban values, it was a misrepresentation. As I have indicated, Canaletto's painting was not concerned with realism – it was painted to reflect and reinforce the cultural mores of its landed elite. O'Connor's image of smoking stacks around St Paul's marks another stage in its evolution and is a more relevant touchstone today than Canaletto's untarnished pre-industrial epitome of a harmonious Christian city. Time and necessity dictate that London constantly reinvents itself and responds to change, and its image evolves accordingly.

Prince Charles was right to point out the physical devastation that London suffered during and after the Second World War – through enemy action, and some poor post-war redevelopment as attempts were made to rekindle the British economy. But with the 'square mile' of the City again a thriving financial centre of global status with few equals, it is reasonable to suggest that the image of the City should demonstrate and be emblematic of the considerable power and authority of London now: not as we would like to imagine it might have been at some distant arbitrary moment in history. Certainly, this is what London's leading politicians and urban planners believe, and they regard modern architecture and tall buildings as desirable assets that London must have to meet the practical demands on the limited space available at London's core, and which project an image of an international, thriving metropolis of global significance. However, the push for height remains highly controversial among traditionalists and heritage lobbyists, who argue that tall buildings undermine the 'timeless' character of valued historic monuments, such as St Paul's Cathedral, when they appear together in the same view. Current debate is polarized by the pressure developers and some politicians exert to build more tall buildings, and by – what is essentially – artistic differences of opinion, issues of taste, which were informed during the long Georgian era. It is guided by the notion that urban planning should be regarded as an art.

URBAN DESIGN AS ART

The Viennese architect and planner, Camillo Sitte, was the first modern to describe urban planning as essentially an art. In *City Planning According to Artistic Principles* (Sitte [1889] 1965), he articulated his admiration for the civic and artistic character of pre-industrial European towns and cities rather than the relentless straight-edged, mid-nineteenth-century boulevards that Baron Haussmann sliced through medieval Paris. Sitte argued that the intuitive creative drives that underlay medieval examples of more varied urban spaces could be presented as artistic principles, while his contemporaries considered them to be no more than happy accidents. Sitte reasoned that city planning could, and should, be regarded as an art, and one based on the spatial and formal compositions that preceded the considerable population explosion of his century. He referred to the wisdom of the ancients as proof for his assertions, especially the architectural and urban accounts of the ancient Roman architect Vitruvius, and the Italian Renaissance architect and theorist Alberti. The basic premise of Sitte's (1965: 49) book, he wrote, 'is to go to school with Nature and the old masters . . . in matters of town planning'.

In London, the principles of classical design promulgated by these 'old masters' were filtered through Palladianism and the Hanoverians during the urban transformation and expansion of medieval London into a 'classical' city. The Victorians built to an even grander scale, retaining or extending the underlying spatial structure and urban character of London. Their larger buildings affected the grain of the existing built form by amalgamating several plots to create larger edifices that were usually bulkier than those they replaced. London's skyline, therefore, acquired a new silhouette. However, the changes brought by the nineteenth century were not as radical as those of the twentieth century, when commercial and residential towers were built increasingly tall.

There are no direct answers to the challenge that height presents to the image of a historic city such as London in the writings of Vitruvius, Alberti and Sitte: they were concerned with a human-scaled environment and five or six storeys was tall for them. Judging by recent planning proposals in London, the challenge of height is set to increase. Towers – residential and commercial – are being designed for London that will be the tallest in Europe. Planning consent was granted in 2002 for London's tallest building yet, the London Bridge Tower, a mixed residential and commercial tower designed to be 306 metres tall (66 storeys). In 2006, The Bishopsgate (DIFA) Tower for the City of London received planning consent at 288 metres tall (56 storeys). Not surprisingly, there is renewed interest in defining appropriate guiding principles that will enable tall buildings to sit well among the finest historic, architectural and urban successes that characterize London. Intriguingly, but without explicit acknowledgement, many of the traditional urban design principles advocated by Sitte have been absorbed into the official planning policy guidance of England and Wales in the last decade. This re-engagement with Sitte's urban ideals represents a curious volte-face. Tall buildings were earlier promoted by modernizers (and modernist architect-planners) as a powerful symbol of a new political and social ideology, which attempted to sweep away an attachment to the forms and spaces of the pre-industrial city of traditional streets and squares lined with buildings.

The consequence is that St Paul's Cathedral and its surroundings have become a battleground for modernists and traditionalists. Its physical and visual relation to the dynamically changing commercial centre of London continues to provide the focus for an extraordinary debate: one that is likely to have a dramatic effect on London's visual appearance during the early twenty-first century. Paradoxically, despite these differences there is a growing consensus regarding what constitutes the principles of good urban design.

MODERN LONDON: URBAN RENAISSANCE THROUGH GOOD DESIGN

Several publications produced between 1999 and 2002 give meaning to the art of urban design in England and Wales today. The government-sponsored think-tank, the Urban Taskforce, produced a report, *Towards an Urban Renaissance* (Urban Task Force 1999), which emphasizes the value of good design for the urban environment as a primary means of reversing the population exodus from English towns and cities. The report reasons that urban renaissance will be stimulated by re-establishing 'the quality of urban design and architecture as part of our everyday urban culture' by establishing 'a new vision for urban regeneration founded on the principles of design excellence, social well-being and environmental responsibility within a viable economic legislative framework' (Urban Task Force 1999: 1). They believe that the key to regeneration will be cities with densely populated, compact, well-connected cores, which will encourage people to travel by public transport and to cycle and walk. It goes on to sketch out ten key principles of urban design that will encourage the creation of '*more liveable places*' (Urban Task Force 1999: 70–1).

Another influential publication is *By Design, Urban Design in the Planning System: Towards Better Practice* (2000), produced by a now defunct government department (DETR) and a government quango, the Commission for Architecture and the Built Environment (CABE). Significantly, *By Design* defines urban design as the 'art of making places for people', and it describes a planning toolkit comprising seven key principles or objectives of urban design that need to be mastered by would-be urban designers (By Design 2000: 15). There is some overlap between the two reports: both are concerned to promote character in townscape by reinforcing locally distinctive patterns of development and culture, and by establishing a high-quality public realm where people are placed before traffic. Although never explicitly acknowledged as a primary source, there is a correlation between the ideas of Sitte and the planning toolkit of *By Design*. While

Sitte filtered the natural planning and design approach of Vitruvius and Alberti, Sitte's notion that urban planning is an art – that we should strive to create 'places' connected by a hierarchy of traditional squares and streets for the pleasure of people – has been accepted as 'natural' commonsense in *By Design*. The reversion to historic notions of place-making represents a considerable victory for traditional urbanists. Their success is due in part to the fact that there have been only a handful of modernist urban triumphs in the UK, while most were unmitigated physical and social disasters.

Similarly, *The Architectural Review* is also an unacknowledged influence on *By Design*. This monthly international journal had trumpeted the virtues of pre-industrial European place making, loud and long. It promoted a joint William Morris-Sittesque urban vision between 1947 and 1958 through a series of essays written by the English architect-planner Gordon Cullen and others, who articulated a humanist reinterpretation of modernism under the banner of Townscape. Cullen (1971: 7, 193) defined Townscape as the 'art of relationship' and the 'art of environment'. Like Sitte, he preferred the formal and spatial associations of form and space that appeared 'natural' to someone experiencing somewhere on foot: places that appeared to have been shaped by time and necessity, rather than the pragmatic dictates of urban regulators, especially traffic and lighting engineers.

Cullen was one of a powerful group at *The Architectural Review* at that time, which included notable historians and social commentators J. M. Richards, Nikolaus Pevsner and Osbert Lancaster. They retained a collective affinity for the art of place-making and largely opposed the French and German rationalism that had by then attained an intellectual and moral high ground in British schools of architecture. Cullen published *The Concise Townscape* (1961) on the back of his essays and the *Review*'s proprietor, Hubert de Cronin Hastings, wrote a parallel, but now less well-known volume, *The Italian Townscape*, under his pen name Ivor de Wolfe (1963). *The Concise Townscape* was the more popular success, partly because Cullen drew compelling images presented as elegant snapshot cartoons of familiar city scenery. Like Canaletto, he provided evocations, picture-postcard memories, of a vanishing, or already vanished, urban order. Townscape was inevitably dismissed by the modernist architectural elite for being reactionary and intellectually narrow in outlook, and its influence languished in Britain until the current Prince of Wales, Prince Charles, spurred on by the success of his own architectural and urban *Vision of Britain* (Prince of Wales 1989), engaged the talents of the architect-theorist Leon Krier to masterplan Poundbury as an 'historic' townscape extension of Dorchester in southern England.

TOWNSCAPE AND VISUAL ASSESSMENT

Modernists have generally deplored what they regard to be the mediocrity of the Prince's townscape vision, but this approach has strong intellectual roots of its own and has wide public appeal. Townscape has even entered the official planning lexicon: the effective implementation of these polices being judged through

'Townscape and Visual Assessments', a key chapter in an Environmental Impact Assessment (EIA). The EIA describes the use of materials, details, scale and massing in a proposed development, which is demonstrated through drawings, photographs and visualizations. These combine with professional judgement to provide an objective and subjective assessment of the proposals. Townscape and Visual Assessments are typically used to identify key views of the development site in relation to existing buildings and areas of historic and architectural importance. It contributes to a wide-ranging spatial masterplan of part of the town or city being developed, something that both *Towards an Urban Renaissance* and *By Design* consider essential to a positive urban design process.

Moreover, recent governmental planning policies provide the structure for traditional place-making. The government's Planning Policy Guidance Note 1 (PPG1 1997) was the first to emphasize 'good design' to help 'promote sustainable development; improve the quality of the existing environment; attract business and investment; and reinforce civic pride and a sense of place'. Its recent replacement, Planning Policy Statement 1: Delivering Sustainable Development (PPS1 2005) extends this concern, stating that a principal objective is that

(iii) A spatial planning approach should be at the heart of planning for sustainable development [and that]

(iv) Planning policies should promote high quality inclusive design in the layout of new developments and individual buildings in terms of function and impact, not just for the short term but over the lifetime of the development. Design which fails to take the opportunities available for improving the character and quality of an area should not be accepted.

(PPS1 2005: paragraph 13)

Places are created by time and PPG15 (1994) focuses on Planning and the Historic Environment. This planning policy guidance describes the general government commitment to preserving the historic environment, and it provides a full statement of policies for the identification and protection of historic buildings, conservation areas and other essential ingredients of the historic environment.

The relevance of a clearly presented three-dimensional framework of buildings and public spaces has been taken up with some vigour by the current Mayor of London, Ken Livingstone, in *The London Plan* (GLA 2004), a spatial development strategy for London. *The London Plan* has been developed to ensure an appropriate mix of buildings and land use for the capital. The policies of *The London Plan* reflect contemporary concerns: good design is central to all the objectives of this plan and it embodies 12 main policies designed to promote world-class architecture and design, and a fundamental objective – as with *Towards an Urban Renaissance* – is the compact city. The Mayor acknowledges that the desired compactness will inevitably lead to new buildings having greater height. Subsequent policies therefore focus on the size, scale and consequent impact of tall buildings on London's built heritage and skyline. The location of tall buildings and the relevant viewing positions from which to assess their likely impact will, therefore, be key issues for the future. It should not be assumed that tall buildings are an inevitable consequence of compactness. The government has concluded that their contribution to urban renaissance was 'very limited' and that the

> proposition that tall buildings are necessary to prevent suburban sprawl is impossible to sustain. They do not necessarily achieve higher densities than mid- or low-rise development and in some cases are a less efficient use of spaces than alternatives. They have, for the most part, the advantages and disadvantages of other high density buildings.
>
> (House of Commons 2002: 38, para. 98)

In fact, the Committee's research indicates that 'Tall buildings are more often about power, prestige, status and aesthetics than efficient development' (House of Commons 2002: 38, para. 98). Tall buildings might not be necessary, but the report recognizes that tall buildings are certainly objects of desire: 'There is one powerful and irrefutable argument in favour of tall buildings: some people find them very beautiful. The Mayor of London is delighted by the Manhattan skyline. His love of tall buildings is shared by many architects and others' (House of Commons 2002: 38, para. 102).

THE ART OF DESIGNING TALL BUILDINGS

It is not clear how numerous these 'others' are. It is probable that public dislike of tall buildings outweighs the enthusiasm of those who find them beautiful. However, the notion that they could be beautiful if well sited and designed – in contrast to the prosaic post-war residential slab blocks that sprang up seemingly randomly pepper-potted across London – was first mooted in the 1960s after the initial wave of commercial tall buildings were under construction in central London. The Royal Fine Art Commission (RFAC, the forerunner of the Commission for Architecture and the Built Environment, CABE) complained in its 18th Report of 1960–62 of the poor and inappropriate siting of tall buildings. But it noted that 'exceptionally high buildings look better in the form of towers rather than slabs and a carefully arranged cluster of towers may be preferable to a number of isolated ones' (cited in Catchpole 1987: 14). In 1969, a government-sponsored Public Inquiry, the Layfield Committee, recommended the creation of a High Buildings Map that would control where tall buildings would be permitted. A Skyline Protection Bill was introduced to Parliament in 1977 by Patrick Cormack MP, which recommended the protection of views by designation that would be similar to the status afforded to listed buildings and conservation areas. None of these recommendations passed to the statute books. However, the notion of 'clusters' of towers, combined with the protection from the intrusion of tall buildings of important views across London, have proved influential in relation to views of St Paul's Cathedral from the west. It was demonstrated at a major Public Inquiry in 1976 that a tall building proposed for Broadgate, next to Liverpool Street Station in the City of London – almost a mile north-east of the cathedral – would be seen in relation to the silhouette of the dome of St Paul's when viewed from Henry VIII's Mound in Richmond Park, some ten miles to the west. Planning permission was refused and a vast low-lying 'groundscraper' built instead, which consumes surface area on the ground, rather than being visible on the city's skyline.

The importance of distant views in this and other cases led to several follow-up studies through the 1980s. The government responded with its Strategic Guidance for London Planning Authorities (RPG3A 1991). This established a list of ten Strategic Views across London – eight of which focus on St Paul's Cathedral, and two on the Palace of Westminster (the seat of government and a World Heritage Site) – which was intended to prevent tall buildings from visually interfering with the settings and silhouettes of these internationally recognizable landmarks. It had been observed in the late 1970s, that tall buildings seen behind St Paul's can have two effects: they can either create an effective backcloth of building mass with which the character of the Cathedral can be compared, or spoil its distinctive silhouette by obscuring and diffusing its clear outlines (City of London 1978: 88). The 'backcloth' referred to is the group of tall buildings to the north-east of St Paul's. Known as the City or Eastern Cluster, it comprises a loose grouping of high-rise buildings which protrude above a general plateau of mid-height commercial buildings. For the last few decades it has included Tower 42 (the former National Westminster Bank tower) as its most prominent structure. Tower 42 is around 180 metres in height and surrounded by a lower tier – a plateau of buildings – mostly ranging between 80 and 120 metres in height. The financial boom of the late 1990s has seen City of London planners and property developers exploring the potential for expanding and consolidating the Eastern Cluster.

The most recent addition is the office tower at 30 St Mary Axe, also known more popularly as the 'Gherkin', which was designed by the architects Foster and Partners and completed in 2003: it has a similar height to Tower 42. The Heron Tower, designed by Kohn Pedersen Fox, was granted planning approval by the Secretary of State in 2002, and it will join Tower 42 and Swiss Re among an upper tier of office buildings in the Eastern Cluster, which is about to be supplanted by an even taller grouping at its centre led by the Bishopsgate (DIFA) Tower, referred to above. These are all tall, slender towers with narrow floor plates (compared to typical US plan dimensions for skyscrapers that have been adopted at Canary Wharf), because of the small plot sizes that characterize the City's ancient urban grain. As the RFAC predicted in the early 1960s, a grouping of tall slender towers has a pleasing appearance, and the overall effect here is to create a physical mass that appears hill-like in profile, and which provides a unified backdrop to St Paul's when viewed from the west.

The precise character of this particular assembly of tall buildings will not last for long. The dynamic of commercial change in the City is rapid, and many new towers have been planned for the Eastern Cluster in recent years. If built, they will stretch its boundaries and challenge its present maximum heights, as the existing and projected views in Figures 9.2 and 9.3 from the dome of St Paul's Cathedral demonstrate. The evolution of the Cluster's form requires careful – artistic – management, and a continuing three-dimensional appraisal will be essential of both the townscape experience at street level, and the skyscape in medium and long views. Meanwhile, the most useful attempt to reconcile the different attitude to tall buildings has appeared in a joint publication by English Heritage (EH) – the government's guardians of the nation's historic built heritage – and CABE, the principal overseers of design quality in the developing built environment. The EH/CABE *Guidance on Tall Buildings* (2003) recommends that any proposal for

Figure 9.2
View east from St Paul's
Cathedral Golden Gallery
– current view.

Figure 9.3
View east from St Paul's
Cathedral Golden Gallery
– projected view in 2012.

a tall building should be of the highest quality of design, aesthetically and environ-
mentally, and that proposals should be contextually considered in the round. In
particular, it recommends that these appraisals should identify

> those elements that create local character and other important features and
> constraints, including streetscape, scale, height, urban grain, natural topography,
> significant views of skylines, landmark buildings and areas and their settings,
> including backdrops, and important local views, prospects and panoramas.
> Opportunities where tall buildings might enhance the overall townscape, or where
> the removal of past mistakes might achieve a similar outcome, should be
> highlighted.
>
> (EH/CABE 2003: para 2.6)

The Mayor's spatial plan for London concerns itself with these urban
dimensions, and his office has published a *Draft London View Management
Framework SPG* (GLA 2005), to be formalized as an extension of *The London Plan*
(2004).

TOWARDS AN URBAN VIEW MANAGEMENT FRAMEWORK

While the RPG3A identifies ten Strategic Views in London, the *Draft London View
Management Framework* (*DLVMF*) includes these and more, providing 26 principal
viewing locations around London, which are subdivided where appropriate into
additional sub-views. A total of 34 views focus principally on the Houses of
Parliament, Westminster Cathedral and St Paul's Cathedral (Figure 9.4). The *DLVMF*
also updates the terminology and techniques used to assess the impact of new
buildings on London's historic townscape by adapting *Guidelines for Landscape
and Visual Impact Assessment* (2002) produced by the Institute of Environmental Assessment (now IEMA) and the Landscape Institute. As the name of the
latter organization suggests, the concern of this document is to establish a visual
approach to the rural landscape. It draws a distinction between landscape effects
(effects on the character or quality of the landscape, irrespective of whether there
are any views of the landscape, or viewers to see them) and visual effects (effects
on people's views of the landscape). Of course, London is experienced quite
differently from a rural landscape, and the EH/CABE *Guidance on Tall Buildings*
(2003) also makes the point that tall buildings should be assessed from viewing
positions that people can easily frequent, that is, they should be viewed from public
not private space.

The technical guidelines for determining the views are not without controversy. The Landscape and Visual Impact Assessment guidelines recommend the
use of a 50mm lens attached to a 35mm format camera, which gives rise to narrow
field of vision (a horizontal angle of about 40 degrees, and a vertical angle of
27 degrees). They consider that the effect of this lens suffers little distortion and
appears more natural. The *Draft London View Management Framework* sets out

Figure 9.4
Protected vistas and
assessment points
in central London, in
GLA, *Draft London View
Management Framework
SPG*, London: GLA, 2005,
pp. 202–3.

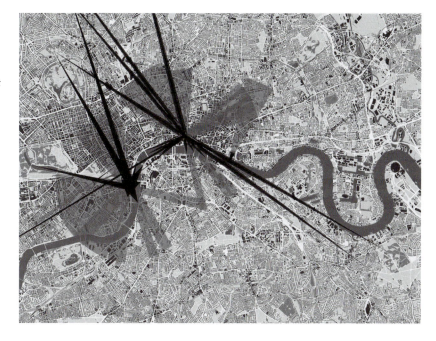

the limitations of this methodology – the point of view to a proposed building can be very close, limiting viewing angles, and reference may also need to be made to important townscape features outside such a narrowly defined field of view (GLA 2005: 208). In addition, the authors recommend creating panoramic views by combining multiple images taken from a common viewpoint, and also providing moving images using video or film-based conventions, or computer-based interaction (GLA 2005: 209).

Figure 9.5
View east from Waterloo
Bridge – current view.

Figure 9.6
View east from Waterloo
Bridge – projected view in
2012.

The potential for the future visual composition of London – indeed any city – surely lies in moving images. We experience cities kinetically, on the move by foot and by vehicle, and it is evident that the existing tall buildings of the Eastern Cluster appear to change in relation to one another when crossing bridges over the River Thames. Compare for example the existing and projected views in Figures 9.5 and 9.6 from Waterloo Bridge, to the view from St Paul's Cathedral. The technology already exists to explore London kinaesthetically using complex computer models, and what an extraordinarily democratic tool this could become if it were made available centrally for any interested body to use (Tavernor and Day 1996). It would be a logical step forward from static drawings, paintings and photographs of the city as landscape. And, as the development of cinema has demonstrated, it provides opportunities to relate image to emotion (Bruno 2002). We might then be able to plan the future city as more than a set of framed, fixed focal point pictures, with the confidence that the past has been preserved and that the future will be a desirable prospect from many points of view.

REFERENCES

Beaverstock, J. V., Smith, R. G. and Taylor, P. J. (1999) 'A Roster of World Cities', *Cities* 16(6): 445–58.

Bruno, G. (2002) *Atlas of Emotion: Journeys in Art, Architecture, and Film*, New York: Verso.

By Design (2000) *By Design. Urban Design in the Planning System: Towards Better Practice*, London: Department for Transport, Local Government and the Regions (DTLR – now DETR) and Commission for Architecture and the Built Environment (CABE).

Catchpole, T. (1987) *London Skylines: A Study of High Buildings and Views*, Reviews and Studies Series, no. 33, London: London Research Centre.

City of London (1978) *City of London Development Plan, Subject Study St Paul's Heights*, London: Corporation of London.

Cullen, C. (1971 [1961]) *The Concise Townscape*, London: The Architectural Press.

Day, A. (2002) 'Urban Visualization and Public Inquiries: The Case of the Heron Tower, London', *Arq: Architectural Research Quarterly* 6: 363–72.

EH/CABE (2003) *Guidance on Tall Buildings*, London: English Heritage and the Commission for Architecture and the Built Environment.

GLA (2004) *The London Plan, Spatial Development Strategy for Greater London*, London: Greater London Authority.

—— (2005) *Draft London View Management Framework SPG*, London: Greater London Authority.

Glasson, J. (2005) *Introduction to Environmental Impact Assessment*, London: Spon Press.

Halliday, S. (1999) *The Great Stink of London: Sir Joseph Bazalgette and the Cleansing of the Victorian Metropolis*, Stroud: Sutton Publishing.

Hayward Gallery (1989) *Leonardo da Vinci*, exhibition catalogue, London: Hayward Gallery.

House of Commons (2002) *Tall Buildings*, House of Commons Transport, Local Government and the Regions Committee, Sixteenth Report of Session 2001–02 (HC 482-I), September 2002.

James, H. (1995) 'Venice', *Italian Hours*, London: Penguin.

Keene, D., Burns, A. and Saint, A. (eds) (2004). *St Paul's. The Cathedral Church of London*, 604–2004, New Haven, CT: Yale University Press.

Landscape Institute and Institute of Environmental Management and Assessment (now IEMA). (2002) *Guidelines for Landscape and Visual Impact Assessment*, London: Spon Press.

PPG1 (1997) *Planning Policy Guidance Note 1: General Policy and Principles,* London: Department for Communities and Local Government, HM Government (www.communities. gov.uk).

PPG15 (1994) *Planning Policy Guidance Note 15: Planning and the Historic Environment*, London: Department for Communities and Local Government, HM Government (www. communities.gov.uk).

PPS1 (2005) *Planning Policy Statement 1: Delivering Sustainable Development*, London: Department for Communities and Local Government, HM Government (www.communities. gov.uk).

Prince of Wales, H.R.H. (1989) *A Vision of Britain*, London: Doubleday.

RPG3A (1991) *Regional Planning Guidance 3A: Supplementary Planning Guidance for London on the Protection of Strategic Views*, London: Department of the Environment, HM Government.

Rykwert, J. (1976) *The Idea of a Town*, London: Faber and Faber.

—— (1980) *The First Moderns. The Architects of the Eighteenth Century*, Cambridge, MA: MIT Press.

Sitte, C. (1965, first published in 1889) *Der Städtebau nach seinen künstlerischen Grundsätzen*, trans by G. R. and C. C. Collins, *Camillo Sitte and the Birth of Modern City Planning*, Columbia University, Studies in Art History, no. 3, New York: Phaidon and Random House.

Summerson, J. (2003 [1945]) *Georgian London*, New Haven, CT: Yale University Press.

Tavernor, R. (1991) *Palladio and Palladianism*, London: Thames & Hudson.

—— (1998) *On Alberti and the Art of Building*, New Haven, CT: Yale University Press.

—— (2004) 'From Townscape to Skyscape', *The Architectural Review*, March, 1285: 78–83.

—— and Day, A. (1996) 'Modelling the future city: a strategy for expert and community involvement', *Habitat 2, United Nations Center for Human Settlements, Rivitalizzazione dei centri storici. Atti preparatori/1*, Naples: Edizioni Graffiti: 40–3.

Urban Task Force (1999) 'Towards an Urban Renaissance', Final Report of the Urban Task Force chaired by Lord Rogers of Riverside, London: Spon Press.

Wolfe, I. de (1963) *The Italian Townscape*, London: The Architectural Press.

Part IV

Revisualizing the City

Chapter 10: The VJ of the Everyday

Remixing the Urban Visual

Scott Burnham

Every generation must build its own city.

Antonio Sant'Elia, 'Futurist Manifesto
On Architecture' (1973 [1914])

The humble 'Post-It' note is rarely publicly celebrated for playing a pivotal role in our lives. This diminutive object leads a thankless and unsung existence, carrying reminders of everyday key to-dos and occasionally serving as the bearer of revolutionary brainstorming notes. So, it is satisfying to have in my archive a photograph of one particular Post-It attached to a street sign in an urban back alley. Since the photograph was taken, this Post-It has arguably had enough visibility to make up for the anonymity of its discarded brethren. It has served as an introductory slide for lectures and talks, a one-image email communicating an entire body of work, and a computer screensaver functioning as a daily reminder of what is happening today in cities across the world.

This note covered the 'not permitted' circle and slash of a 'no parking at any time' sign. On it was written in bold letters: 'I Am Real'. The altered sign now read: 'I Am Real At any time' (Figure 10.1). The beauty of its positioning lay in the way it played with the language of the city – creating a dialogue with urban infrastructure in such a minute way, and yet, at the same time, communicating the heart of a movement active in urban landscapes around the world. A new relationship is beginning to emerge between individuals and the physical city, right at the centre of the impersonal urban landscape. This is a relationship of personal connections and contributions, most noticeably the remixing of the urban visual in order to transform the anonymous urban landscape into an arena which is 'real at any time'.

The exponential growth in urban areas and populations (recent estimates predict that by 2025, 75 per cent of the world's population will live in an urban environment) is arguably manifest in a sharp change of attitudes and collaborations between the city landscape and its inhabitants. As urban environments become denser, and their influence on our mental and physical selves increases, individuals

Figure 10.1
I am real at any time,
Manchester, UK, 2005.

are beginning to react in unique ways to shape the relationship that exists between the self and the physical city. The expanding urbanization at the heart of contemporary life has transformed the identity of home as *part* of the landscape, to the realization that 'home' *is* the landscape. This facet has given rise to an increased level of engagement with the aesthetics of public space, objects and surfaces of the city. These engagements articulate a desire to ingrain public objects and spaces with personal relevance for those who inhabit and use them – with or without authorization.

In a talk delivered to the Long Now Foundation in 2003, musician and creative innovator Brian Eno explored his relationship with the city. Eno described taking a cab to a singer friend's party in an unfamiliar part of the city soon after he had moved to New York:

> The cab driver started driving south and the street lights got darker and darker and the potholes got bigger and bigger. The steam was coming out of the streets and finally we ended up in a very dark gloomy medieval street at what appeared to be the address on the card, and I thought it's very strange that she should live down here: this must be a joke of some kind. I rang the bell and was buzzed in and got in the elevator and went up the stairs to see a glitteringly expensive loft. This was in itself a surprise – that someone had spent so much money in such a bad neighborhood, so I asked the hostess during the evening whether she liked living there, and she said 'oh yeah this is the best place I've ever lived', and I realized that what she meant was within these four walls. So this was very New York to describe the 'here' that you live in as the place within the walls, and not to include the neighborhood as part of the experience. So I had this

idea then that she lived in what I called a very small 'here' and I felt fairly confident that I wanted to live in a big 'here'.

(Eno 2003)

This desire for a connectedness to the bigger 'here' has generated a rapidly expanding area of urban expression – creative interventions which remix the urban visual to connect the individual to the city. These subversive processes and actions generate personal relevance within deeply impersonal urban landscapes and reawaken our relationship with urbanity. As the visual remix transforms the static visuals of the city into a continuum of expression, the city ceases to be a fixed terrain of commercial narratives and becomes a dynamic landscape, where expression is organic and ongoing storytelling is possible. The urban environment remains, as the 'I am real at any time' Post-It reminds us, forever in the present tense.

In his 1998 collection of essays *Relational Aesthetics*, the French art critic and curator Nicolas Bourriaud refers to mass communications as looped information – largely rhetorical, one-way communications that speak *at* the public. *Eye, The International Review of Graphic Design*, refers to visual communication in our cities as a medium that 'oscillates between the brand consultant's wet dream and the critic's worst nightmare'. For Bourriaud, 'spontaneous social relations are vanishing in the information age as communication becomes restricted to particular areas of consumption: coffee shops, pubs and bars, art galleries and so on' (Davies and Parrinder 2006: 21).

In five years of research, collaborations and working relationships with some of the world's most innovative urban interventionists and street artists I have come to recognize that it is precisely the challenge to this one-sided visual communication that inspires them. They consider that it is time to reverse the tide and weave personal dialogues into the urban visual, refusing to linger passively on the receiving end of commercial communications and static urban visuals. 'If you make an analogy between advertisements and noise', says Montreal's Peter Gibson (a.k.a. street artist Roadsworth), 'when you walk down the streets you would be hit by an insane cacophony of noise. Why should we be exposed to this and not have the right to respond?' (Cooper 2005: R3).

'CutUp' is a London collective of artists and graphic designers who formed through a shared desire to create original work by reworking the source material of urban commercial advertisements. The group's manifesto lays out their critique of the visual bombardment we are constantly exposed to:

Street adverts are a privileged form of address and the space they commandeer is disproportionate. Advertisements and the mass media depict life and how we should live it in a spectacular way. We find it increasingly difficult to know how to express our inner thoughts and feelings, which seem mundane in contrast to the emotional saturation in the plethora of advertising surrounding us.

(Kemistry Gallery 2005)

Working in the middle of the day, camouflaged in ubiquitous urban work-men's fluorescent vests, the CutUp team approach a billboard with ladders and razors, peel off large panels of print and retreat to their studio with rolls of adver-tisement. They proceed to clip the vast image into small squares, reducing it into hundreds of physical pixels, which they then reassemble – in a style inspired by Chuck Close – to form an entirely new billboard from the palette of colours and textures which comprised the original. Thus, the original aesthetic scheme of what was once a campaign for Britain's O_2 mobile phone company, was broken apart by CutUp and re-worked to create the image of a screaming child (Figure 10.2).

When observers first come across a CutUp work in a public space, there is a conspicuous sense of curiosity and delight. This random hacking into the visual system of the urban environment offers unexpected surprises, re-awakening the public's connection to the city. Just as our sensibilities have been drilled to consciously filter out television adverts or radio spots as we consume entertainment, our minds have been trained to filter out urban visuals as we move through the city in everyday life.

The all-consuming commercialization of public space as a vehicle for advertising and sales, has made us cynical about the visual landscape of the city. While CutUp clearly operate outside the law in their re-appropriation and subversion of public visuals, it could be argued that the impact of coming across one of their visual remixes refreshes the potential of other public visuals, salvaging public communications from being lost in the white noise of commercial messages and potentially transforming them into public dialogues.

Montreal's Roadsworth (a name adopted as an urban tribute to Andy Goldsworthy's poetic interventions into natural landscapes) is one of the boldest

Figure 10.2
CutUp London billboard,
London, UK, 2005.

artists re-working the visual topography of the city. Roadsworth's starting points are the most obvious and yet most anonymous icons of the city: demarcations of parking bays, pedestrian crossing areas, bike paths, and road merges. Roadsworth explains his choice of materials in this way:

> I guess I'm dealing with language, the nuts and bolts and foundation of the language of the street. The symbols on the street are a method of communication, but in a dry, utilitarian way, so I wanted to inject a little poetry, for lack of a better word. There's this banality and predictability to city life, and that's enhanced by urban planning and the way our movement is directed. I wanted to play with that.
>
> (Lejtenyi 2005)

While street markings exist on one level as the final statement from the Montreal municipality on legitimate movement and behaviour in the city, for Roadsworth they are the basis for playing with the notion, as he jokingly phrases it, of: 'What would happen if the guys who are hired by the city to paint the lines on the street decided to drop acid?' (Flannery 2005). Roadsworth plays with urban iconography by perfectly mimicking the colours, materials and aesthetics of Montreal's metropolitan street markings: suddenly, two streets seem to be joined as he paints the image of a zipper at the merging point of street lines. The 'L' at the border of a parking space becomes a floral pole with stencilled vines and flowers wrapped around it. A pedestrian crossing becomes a row of oversized birthday candles (Figure 10.3). The controlling grids of the city no longer function

Figure 10.3
Roadsworth, Montreal,
Canada, 2004.

as controlling signage, but as catalysts for expression. Roadsworth explains, 'I am turning the city's language around on its head. I take something and re-appropriate it, parodying it. And by doing this, I can bring out the nature of the old meaning, exposing it' (Cooper 2005: R3). His ludic intent is understood by residents of the city. As one of them, Tibor Van Roy, told *The Globe and Mail* newspaper: 'It is like someone is playing a game' (ibid.).

The most iconic of urban navigational systems, The London Underground map, has also found itself party to a visual remix. In 2003, Birmingham, UK designer Matt Jones, a.k.a. 'Lunartik' designed a series of stickers that appropriated the icons, lines and fonts of the Northern Line section of the map. These stickers were placed on sections of the map in between existing station stops, advising passengers of locations where a 'Loop the Loop' could be found on the line, the risk of a Pac-Man themed ambush, or a space alien abduction – to say nothing of the warning indicating Space Invader characters who were actively shooting at and disintegrating the lines (Figure 10.4). One observer described the day after the stunt:

> A little rain (sic) of terror for a bit of cheeky fun, Lunartik and his posse went on a night time mission . . . distributing ammo among unsuspecting commuters on the London Underground. The Northern Line was the ideal target for the small scale offensive that went down that night.
>
> (Schiller 2003)

The night the stickers appeared I was riding on one of the altered trains and witnessed first hand the London Underground map coming alive in a new way. As late-night passengers began to notice subtle changes, people began moving

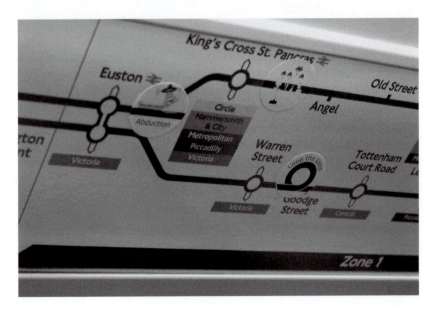

Figure 10.4
Lunartik's London Underground stickers, London, UK, 2003.

from carriage to carriage looking for new stickers. At one moment, as the train travelled from Warren Street to Goodge Street station where a sticker advised us that a Loop the Loop awaited between the stations, one passenger who had clearly spent a respectable amount of time in the pub that night exclaimed: 'Everyone! Hold on!' Unfortunately, given what some might term the 'selective efficiency' of London Underground, the stickers were removed the next day.

The appropriation and remix of urban imagery has, of course, a long cultural lineage, from Robert Rauschenberg's collages to Piet Mondrian's urban-inspired grids. Yet it is the actual remixing of the existing urban visual, not only at street level but *on* the street itself, that makes this an activity of contemporary significance. Urban underground culture has always had an affinity for authentic creations conceived from the appropriation of existing material. Increasing urban density has recently fuelled a remix sensibility with roots in the remix culture of the rave and club scene of the 1980s. A striking characteristic of the early years of the club scene was that architecture itself formed part of the visual remix on club nights. City walls served as notice boards for underground parties and warehouses, and disused factories were transformed by nothing more than a PA system and a bank of lights into weekend-long raves. More mainstream clubbing nights converted abandoned churches and moth-balled dance halls into realms of contemporary play.

Just as physical spaces were remixed, so too resident VJs (Visual Jockey, a variant on DJ), remixed an arsenal of stock imagery and footage from the Golden Age of cinema to create the visual identity of the club scene. Famous scenes from classic films were mixed into the rhythms of the DJ's customized tunes – they sped them up, stopped them, clipped and re-coloured them – and made these clips fresh all over again. As these visual remixes were fashioned every night, clubbers perceived familiar imagery in an altered way, re-appropriating it in this new cultural context. The VJs of the city work in the same way – remixing familiar imagery, public signage, road markings, navigational systems and advertisements in order to stir up and invigorate the everyday so that we can own it afresh. Innovative remixes of urban visuals make the city seem malleable, mortal.

Lunartik's stickers may have been removed after a day on the London Underground map, but those of us on the train that night became members of a communal experience. New dialogues and new collectives emerge from new visuals, as Davies and Parrinder (2006: 24) have observed in an article in *Eye*: 'Scenarios that foster spontaneous human relations in the way that Bourriaud describes them, are what he would call "microtopias" . . . [interactions] embedded within the everyday to make the now more pleasurable.' Making the everyday more pleasurable is arguably the effect of The Bubble Project (www.thebubble project.com). The designer, Ji Lee, initiated the sticking of thousands of blank 'speech bubbles' on public posters and advertisements, inviting people to write their own dialogue for the characters in the ads. Lee printed 15,000 of these bubble stickers and stuck them on top of ads all over New York City. He explained, 'Passers-by fill them in. I go back and photograph the results . . . [then print] 15,000 more' (cited in McKee 2005). The Bubble Project manifesto explains their use of the visual infrastructure of the city to offer people an opportunity to engage with their surroundings:

> Once placed on ads, these stickers transform the corporate monologue into an open dialogue. They encourage anyone to fill them in with any form of self expression, free from censorship. More bubbles mean more freed spaces, more sharing of personal thoughts, more reactions to current events, and most importantly, more imagination and fun.
>
> (Lee 2005)

The Bubble Project represents an interesting frontline in a growing trend – street projects that have tapped into the public imagination and continued organically. After its initial launch, people began printing off their own stickers and placing them on advertisements in their own cities. The project web site now hosts a gallery which is updated daily with photos submitted by participants across the world, and dedicated web sites have been set up in Italy and Argentina. This phenomenon is a prime example of a specific genre of urban activity known as 'culture jamming'. Culture jamming has become synonymous with high-profile campaigns by anti-consumerism organizations, such as the Canadian magazine *Adbusters*, known as 'the flagship publication of the culture jamming movement' (Heath and Potter 2004). The Billboard Liberation Front – probably the original culture jammers – state proudly on their web site that it has been 'Improving Outdoor Advertising Since 1977', while 'Establishing a New Paradigm in Street Marketing'.

Culture Jams performed by Adbusters and The Billboard Liberation Front bring the remix of the urban visual into the activist realm, reversing the intended messages of billboards and public advertisements in order to communicate slogans directly opposed to the original intention. The Billboard Liberation Front takes particular pride in remixing the text and imagery of existing signage for subversive purposes – taking the phrase 'the medium is the message' to a new level of meaning. One of the group's most celebrated 'jams' was when members selectively disconnected neon lights in a Joe Camel advertisement, leaving the main character smoking and relaxed with a saxophone in hand, next to an illuminated message which now read 'AM I DEAD YET?'.

Another legendary jam involved an advertisement announcing the opening of the Hillsdale shopping mall. The original billboard announced, 'HILLSDALE: something new is happening'. After The BLF's remix in which the first and last three letters of the name were darkened and a new banner was pasted below in the same typeface, motorists were treated to a decidedly more intriguing advertisement for: 'LSD: The Beginning of Something Wonderful'. While the visual iconography and commercial signage of the city has long been fodder for subverting existing messages and aesthetics, a recent trend has begun to alter the urban landscape itself in tactile and sculptural ways.

The definitive online resource for street-level creativity is The Wooster Collective (www.woostercollective.com), a web site that receives over 100,000 visits a day from people looking for updates of new work on the streets of the world's cities. A new term recently appeared on Wooster: '3D' – physical expressions woven into the city. 3D Graffiti is the visual remix of the urban taken to another level, using the physical infrastructure of the city as source material, transforming the concrete jungle into potter's clay.

Among the most prolific practitioners of the 3D remix genre, is the duo Darius (Leon Reid) and Downey (Brad Downey). They have taken the art of re-working the visuals of the city into a new area of tactile intervention, inserting their work into the physical fabric of the city and challenging people to re-imagine and re-interpret the most prosaic objects (Figure 10.5). In their five-year partnership, Darius and Downey have installed more than 200 pieces in over ten cities – of which dozens still remain. 'Street signs, cement bricks and public telephones in unexpected places are manipulated to create personal relationships with each other and with passers-by', explain the Jen Bekman Gallery (2005): 'These temporary disruptions – persisting as little as minutes and as long as months – toy with interrelations between individuals as they inhabit public and private space'. They are compared to 'modern day alchemists' – principally because 'they have the talent to not only bring inanimate objects to life, but to also infuse them with a heart and a soul' (ibid.).

Figure 10.5
'Walkin' by Leon Reid IV (Darius Jones), London, UK, 2004.

Darius and Downey infuse the streets with a sense of play, engaging in a physical call-and-response with the objects of the metropolis. One of their early interventions in New York City was a One Way sign bent over at the top to look as if it was kissing a Public Telephone sign high above the pavement. Stop signs were mimicked with 'baby' stop signs positioned next to them – a motif continued when they expanded to London, with speed limit signs acquiring mini partners announcing half the speed limit. Darius and Downey share the same playful outlook as Roadsworth, with his comedic remixing of city markings, but they play a more physical game, inviting people to – in a crass paraphrase of TS Eliot – arrive at the object they once knew, and know it again for the first time.

The work of Darius and Downey creates a parody that hovers between the ridiculous and entirely plausible. In one of their more daring stunts, they reworked a London Underground station sign above a bench to read: 'Sit your arse down and wait (just like everyone else).' It is either a comment on the stoic attitude of Londoners to public transport, or on the successful integration of Darius and Downey's subversion into the existing visuals of the station, that the sign drew little attention as people read it and obediently took a seat beneath it. Downey explains how they choose locations for their work:

> I have heard people say 'Why would you put art in that neighbourhood – they're not gonna care about it'. But I believe everyone needs and benefits from creative acts. And everyone needs to question his or her surroundings and reality. Construction workers are invisible because they are a diversion of the normal flow of traffic; they are not questioned because they are working for the city. I feel the same about the street objects and control devices, they are never questioned because they are the normal flow of traffic. They are not questioned because they are working for the city.
>
> (Tingulstad 2006)

Downey's reference to the construction worker introduces another layer of appropriation. A common denominator among a great number of practitioners is that they will hit the streets to do their most ambitious and visible projects dressed as the city's metropolitan work crews. This approach is clarified by one of Wooster's periodical 'How To' columns to introduce street artists to techniques and methods developed by others. Downey's (2006) instructions given in 'Brad Downey's How To Become Invisible' are a virtual clarion call for intervention:

> City workers get paid to maintain the order of the outside space, that space, which functions for the public. If you live or work in a city you will probably ignore a few of these guys or girls every day on your way from home to work. Dig into your memory . . . Can you remember any of their faces or what they were doing (unless they were 'cat calling' you)? . . . The construction vest is a tool to fool the ages. Especially if you're installing city property. cheeky. hocus-pocus. presto chango. So get our there and touch your city . . . – Civil Servant, Brad Downey.

Existing definitions of private and public, legal and illegal activity are beginning to blur as never before in urban culture, possibly as a result of increasing urban density combined with an increasing desire for personal connectivity. As the longing grows for individual relevance and freedom of expression, previously immutable lines between public and private spaces and the activities allowed within them, are questioned, and occasionally overruled, by public action. In one of the most renowned cases of unsanctioned urban creativity being endorsed by the public, a mural by the British street artist Banksy (the celebrity of the graffiti world) became a cause célèbre in his hometown of Bristol, UK. The image appeared in Banksy's trademark stencil style, showing a woman in her underwear standing behind a man in a suit. It appears that the man has come home from work earlier than expected, as he looks out of the window, oblivious to a naked man hanging onto the ledge below him.

Spontaneous petitioning from the public the morning after the mural appeared, provoked Bristol City Council to take the unprecedented step of opening a public debate about whether the painting should stay or be removed. 'We have to decide if it's public art or graffiti', a spokeswoman said to the BBC (2006). 'We are encouraging debate among residents and would like to hear people's views and comments about this latest addition to the Banksy collection'. Soon after, the BBC reported that following 'overwhelming support' from the public, the piece was to remain. 'An internet discussion forum showed 97 per cent of submitters supported the work. Many people who logged on highlighted the fact that Banksy is a Bristolian, and that his work 'brightened up' the urban environment' (ibid.). An online note from one respondent, 'Goeshi', explains: 'In a monochromatic world sculpted by the very few I think we need to relax the laws on street art and graffiti. Freedom of expression gives life to a city and this is a classic example!' (ibid.). The philosophy of street artists and interventionists, that the city is the shared property of its inhabitants, rather than a collection of discrete zones, appears to be making its way into the public sphere.

A scene often cited by street artists as inspiration for this philosophy comes from the 1979 Walter Hill film, *The Warriors*. The scene opens with Cyrus, the leader of New York's largest and most powerful gang, addressing a gathering of representatives from every gang in New York:

> I say the future is ours . . . You're standing right now with 9 delegates from 100 gangs. And there's 100 more. That's 20,000 hardcore members! 40,000 counting affiliates, and 20,000 more not organized, but ready to fight. 60,000 soldiers. Now there ain't but 20,000 police in the whole town. Can you dig it? . . . One gang could run this city. One gang. Nothing would move, without us allowing it to happen . . . because we've got the street, suckers! . . . The problem in the past has been the man turning us against one another. We have been unable to see the truth, because we have been fighting for 10 square feet of ground. Our turf. Our little piece of turf. That's crap brothers! The turf is ours by right, because it's our turn . . . We take over one borough at a time. Secure our territory. Secure our turf. Because it's all our turf.
>
> (*The Warriors* 1979)

The growth in sentiment that the urban landscape is 'all our turf' can be observed in the popularity of some recent visual remix projects. An innovative sub-genre has sprung up – projects where intervention is no longer the end result, but merely the beginning. These projects are made as catalysts for continuing intervention, open invitations for people to become directly involved in the visual narrative of their city.

The Chicago-based You Are Beautiful group (www.you-are-beautiful.com) has created an array of public involvement projects. Their most accessible and interactive one to date was spelling their signature phrase 'you are beautiful' into a long chain link fence by placing Styrofoam cups into the fence's holes, transforming a mundane barrier into a tactile LED panel for public use. As documented on their web site, over the course of several months after its original installation, members of the public began to re-work the cups to create an ongoing conversation: 'You are Bad. You Are Beat. You Are Beat (never). You Are Forever. You Are A Fever. You Are a Lover. You Are Over. You Are Loved. Disappointed . . . Rejuvenated!' The project ended its documentation with 'Rejuvenated'. 'The cups are now quite dirty and covered with snow', the group writes, but 'this conversation continues' (You Are Beautiful 2004).

Like the organic spirit of the piece that propelled The Bubble Project onto the global stage, You Are Beautiful taps into the spirit of another cornerstone of contemporary culture – the open source movement. Just as open source developers release a source code into the public domain to be modified and developed by others, these projects release version 1.0 of the project and hand it over to the public to develop and remix. Yet, municipalities may spend considerable time and resources contesting these interventions in the public realm and ignoring their potential. In contrast to the prescribed commercial narratives that rule the shared spaces of the city, these projects are vehicles for dialogue, windows into one potential future model for the relationship between the city and its citizens.

The remixed billboards of CutUp, the re-imagined street markings of Roadsworth and the reconfigured street objects of Darius and Downey, present moments of connectedness, in what can be an alienating public realm. In this context, London pedestrian crossing beacons are just as likely to feel as lonely a place as a random pedestrian, so Darius and Downey take it upon themselves to give the lamp post a mate with a fondness for public displays of affection (Figure 10.6).

Although urban interventionists are often stereotyped as marginal characters working on the fringes of society, the artists and collectives referenced here have advanced degrees in visual art and design. They have made conscious decisions to take the shared surfaces of the city as their canvas and use the infrastructure of the urban visual as their source material. As with any innovation in contemporary culture, it is only a matter of time before advertising companies embark on harnessing the energy and piggybacking on the ethos of street-level activity in order to gain credibility in urban markets. The recent explosion of guerrilla advertising and marketing campaigns is an obvious attempt to import this energy into the

Figure 10.6
'The Kiss' by Leon Reid IV
(Darius Jones) London,
UK, 2004. Photograph
by Ed Zipco.

establishment for commercial purposes. Interestingly, the commercial world has found itself subject to a system of checks and balances when it plays the visual remix game. The same creative force that gave birth to the movement can also police activity when it crosses the line from creativity to blatant commercialization. There is an unwritten code when a commercial guerrilla campaign hits the street – if it is clever and well executed, it is given its space. If it steps on too many toes, those who created the genre will step back into the mix and intervene.

In 2005, Sony launched its portable PlayStation PSP with a series of spraypainted images throughout New York. Done in an over-the-top spraypainted graffiti style, word quickly spread that these icons were not works by new artists, but advertisements copying the street style. In the days following their appearance the ads were defaced, humorously altered and painted over by dozens of street artists out for revenge. As Schiller (2005) explained:

> The issue with the Sony ads is not that they blasted cities with their cute characters. Rather, it's that they made it look like it was done by artists on the street illegally and un-commissioned. They faked it. They made it seem that they had illegally taken the walls, when what they actually did was to purchase them . . . But what was interesting is that they picked walls that made it seem like the ads didn't belong there as ads, and this appeared to be, at least at first, as real graffiti done illegally. It wasn't. If they had done all of these characters on billboards and bus shelters then it wouldn't have been so divisive. But because

they faked it, and made it seem like the ads were done illegally, it smacks of corporate invasion of a space that they shouldn't be in.

A regular Wooster contributor, Brazilian street artist 'Renato' (2005) offered a more textured and ambivalent analysis:

Companies have been capitalizing on street art and culture for a while now, and there have been no major complaints up to now. It was as if every side was benefiting from the 'mutual appropriation' (or 'my money for a bit of your style'). What seems to me is that with this, Sony has crossed some sort of line, messing with other issues by not explicitly mentioning itself on the pieces, like pretending to be someone else. However in the end, what we are seeing in my humble opinion . . . is the shift of direction, where instead of artists appropriating from brands and industries, companies are finding it profitable to appropriate back. From what I understand, it is their right as a participating part of our society to experiment with it, as well as deal with the possible reactions and consequences, just like we all do.

This ambiguously symbiotic relationship between the world of commercial advertising and that of street interventions was intriguingly unpacked in a recent campaign by Adidas, given the accolade of a Wooster headline: 'Adidas gets it right with adicolor.' Wooster noted that although they had previously taken Sony PSP to task for a fraudulent campaign they were now wanting to praise a company which had showed how to 'get it right':

First, Adidas put up a series of mostly white flyerposters – branded with the adidas logo – that subtly encouraged people to tag the billboard and basically fuck it up. But then, days later, they came back to those same ads and placed another poster over it. The new poster features the Adidas adicolor show, now with the original tags from the previous poster incorporated into the show design. Of all the recent street campaigns we've seen lately, this is our favourite one by far. It's extremely clever, but most importantly *it fits the brand perfectly* [my emphasis]. It takes advantage of the street to the fullest. And most of all, it turns the tables in an absolutely brilliant way that is extremely impressive.

(Schiller 2006)

The Wooster article is unstinting in its praise of the heights of invention reached by a corporate campaign (to sell more sports apparel) and perhaps surprisingly it even celebrates the effectiveness of its commercial appeal. The key goal here is to 'get it right', to engage in a dialogue. From remixing the visuals of existing commercial advertisements to playing with the infrastructure of the city itself, urbanity is moving progressively to a state of more adventurous visual and physical flux to match its parallel societal flux. The remix continues to work towards (paraphrasing Sant'Elia) helping us build *our own* city. Each day we are faced with new urban realities and the VJs of the urban visual are rising to the challenge in their own way. As Jackson Pollock stated:

> New needs need new techniques. And the modern artists have found new ways and new means of making their statements . . . the modern painter cannot express this age, the airplane, the atom bomb, the radio, in the old forms of the Renaissance or of any other past culture.
>
> (cited in Johnson 1982)

We are now two decades on from the seismic battles waged over the sampling and remixing of existing commercial works in hip hop music – and the musical landscape has changed. All kinds of music are now open to entirely new forms of mix culture, which were originally inspired by outsider and underground activity. In the visual remix revolution, city authorities are beginning to pay attention as the momentum grows. Early one morning in 2005, Roadsworth was arrested, caught in the act of making one of his street marking remixes in downtown Montreal. The authorities recognized his distinctive style and quickly linked him to a back-catalogue of warrants for each of his street markings. He was charged with 53 counts of public malfeasance and faced fines totalling CAN$265,000. This arrest threw both Roadsworth, and the entire issue of what he called 'cultural exchange' in the city, into the media spotlight. On reflection, Richard Coté, political adviser to the mayor of Montreal's Plateau Mont-Royal borough, declared, 'Roadsworth's work makes people smile' (Cooper 2005: R3).

In an interview following his arrest, Roadsworth admitted that his predicament 'has brought these issues and my thoughts on them into concrete form'. He then added, 'I just hope it does not get too concrete, as in four cement walls' (ibid.). In 2006, all charges against Roadsworth were dropped, and he is now working on a series of commissions to augment parking areas, bike paths and pavements. His growing client list holds some impressive names, but a recent sponsor draws the most attention: The city of Montreal.

REFERENCES

BBC Online (2006) *Artist's saucy stencil for city.* Online. Available: http://news.bbc.co.uk/2/hi/uk_news/england/bristol/somerset/5103306.stm (accessed 15 November 2006).

Billboard Liberation Front (2006) *Manifesto.* Online. Available: www.billboardliberation.com/ (accessed 15 November 2006).

Cooper, R. (2005) 'When the stencil hits the road', *The Globe and Mail*, January, R3.

Davies, C. and Parrinder, M. (2006) 'Part of the Process', *Eye* 59 (Spring): 18–25.

Downey, B. (2006) *'Wooster How To. . .' #5 – Brad Downey's How To Become Invisible.* Online. Available: www.woostercollective.com/2006/02/wooster_how_to_5-_brad_downeys_how_to_become_invisible.html (accessed 12 September 2005).

Eno, B. (2003) *The Long Now.* Online. Available: www.longnow.org/projects/seminars/ (accessed 16 April 2006).

Flannery, C. (2005) *Art on the road fails to appeal to Montreal officialdom*. Online. Available: www.recirca.com/artnews/396.shtml (accessed 16 April 2006).

Goeshi (2006) *BBC Online forum*. Online. Available: www.bbc.co.uk/bristol/content/articles/2006/06/23/banksy_art_feature.shtml (accessed 15 November 2006).

Heath, J. and Potter, A. (2004) *The Rebel Sell*, Toronto: Harper Collins Canada.

Jen Bekman Gallery (2005) *Darius + Downey: we're on it press release*. Online. Available: www.jenbekman.com/dariusdowney/press.html (accessed 12 September 2005).

Johnson, E. H. (ed.) (1982) *American Artists on Art from 1940 to 1980*, New York: HarperCollins. Online. Available: www.constable.net/arthistory/glo-pollock.html (accessed 15 November 2006).

Kemistry Gallery (2005) *CutUp Exhibition Press Release*. Online. Available: www.artshole.co.uk/exhibitions/feb%2025%2005/CutUp%20Show.html (accessed 5 April 2005).

Lee, J. (2005) *Bubble Project Manifesto*. Online. Available: www.thebubbleproject.com/02.Manifesto/ManifestoFrameset.html (accessed 15 November 2006).

Lejtenyi, P. (2005) 'Roadsworth R.I.P', *Montreal Mirror* 20 (3) (20–26 January). Online. Available: www.montrealmirror.com/2005/012005/news2.html (accessed 14 March 2006).

McKee, I. (2005) *The Bubble Project*. Online. Available: http://thepowerofinfluence.typepad.com/the_power_of_influence/2005/12/the_bubble_proj.html (accessed 15 November 2006).

Renato (2005) *The Dialogue Continues*. Online. Available: www.woostercollective.com/2005/12/the_dialogue_continues.html (accessed 15 November 2006).

Sant'Elia, A. (1973 [1914]) 'Manifesto of Futurist Architecture', in U. Apollonio (ed.) *Futurist Manifestos*, London: Thames and Hudson.

Schiller, M. (2003) *Northern Line Stickers from Old*. Online. Available: www.woostercollective.com/2003/07/northern_line_stickers_from_ol.html (accessed 4 October 2005).

—— (2005) *The Dialogue Continues*. Online. Available: www.woostercollective.com/2005/12/the_dialogue_continues.html (accessed 15 November 2006).

—— (2006) *Adidas gets it right with adicolor.* Online. Available: www.woostercollective.com/2006/03/adidas_gets_it_right_with_adicolor.html (accessed 15 November 2006).

The Bubble Project (2006) www.thebubbleproject.com.

The Wooster Collective (2006) www.woostercollective.com.

Tingulstad, J. (2006) 'Interview with Brad Downey'. Online. Available: www.woostercollective.com/2006/05/julia_tingulstad_interviews_brad_downey.html (accessed 12 September 2005).

You Are Beautiful (2004) *Installation Overview*. Online. Available: www.you-are-beautiful.com/INSTALLATIONS.html (accessed 5 December 2005).

FILMOGRAPHY

The Warriors (1979) dir. Walter Hill. Paramount Pictures.

Chapter 11: Employee Entrances and Emergency Exits

Exposing the Invisible Imagery of Consumption

David Michalski

In the corner of a shopping centre there is a small red-lettered sign, a disturbance in one's field of vision. It is the only indication of the existence of an often over-looked, but powerful aesthetic system at work in the contemporary city (Figure 11.1). It represents a visual language operating just beyond the phantasmagoria of consumption. While advertising imagery and the visual displays of consumer spaces attract intense investigations, less critical attention has been spent analysing the visual culture of consumption's social and technical support networks. But the deconstruction of the consumer imaginary requires one to look beyond marketing images, to investigate meanings produced by this other visual culture. The fantasy-inducing images and packaged desires of consumer society are not independent of the amenities which support consumer spaces. Instead, the visual signs of these amenities work to inform and frame the greater spectacle of consumption. Beneath, alongside and in-between the images and spaces most associated with consumerism: commodities, their models, advertisements and displays, lie the indicators of service industry infrastructure, such as employee entrances, emergency exit signs, waste disposal systems, security equipment and warnings. In this project, I have used photography to highlight these urban design details, first to show how municipal and corporate networks use a coherent visual language to distinguish and regulate different social spaces, and then to argue that this visual system must be subjected to aesthetic criticism if one is to appreciate the nature of experience in consumer society.

This widely understood but often unexamined public visual language is a fitting candidate for an aesthetic critique. Although the primary meaning assigned to these visual elements is related to their function as signs in the support of commercial enterprise, their ability to create meaning does not stop there. They participate in the visual world of all the people passing through the shopping centre – the stockroom worker and the customer alike enter into juxtaposition with consumer society's other visual languages. While a social historical or etymological analysis of this visual language of infrastructure elements can produce

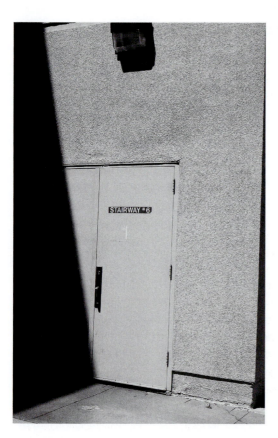

Figure 11.1
*Stairway #6 at Arden
Faire*, 2002.

insight into the development of their form, this essay theorizes their synchronic meaning within the contemporary consumer imaginary.

What appears at first to be the antithesis of consumer spectacle is, itself, spectacular, in that it is saturated with *significata* far beyond its indexical meaning. If one is to study how the everyday psycho-adaptive rhythms of shopping contribute to the hegemony of consumer society, the universal pretensions and presumed neutrality of this omnipresent visual language merit interrogation. Despite the lack of traditional ornamentation and the use of strategic camouflage in the design of infrastructure elements, this visual language not only helps regulate spatial behaviour, but it contributes to our understanding of the relation between consumption and production. As a formal system, it influences the performance of work and leisure, it informs contemporary notions of safety and authority, and it helps to place and frame the commodity. Understanding this visual culture can help us to reconnect the tenuous separations in the internal relations of consumer society.

DOCUMENTING A VISUAL CULTURE

Is it possible to conceptualize a visual culture of service industry and emergency system infrastructure – one which encompasses such diverse functional sites as employee entrances, maintenance closets, plumbing, security and emergency equipment? What might be the outward or inward limit of such a visual culture? Would worker uniforms and job application forms be included? What about electrical boxes and posted employee notices? And how about construction sites, waste disposal equipment, and the very bodies of employees themselves? These are all necessary support mechanisms for consumption. We might also include restrooms, parking lots, and maybe even streets and traffic signs, for these too comprise the built environment through which consumer society replicates itself. A comprehensive account would have to include nearly everything supporting the consumer landscape. The assemblage of such a heterogeneous and nebulous grouping potentially defies structural analysis.

On the other hand, a well-defined collection of visual signs, or a set of particular exits or entrances, also presents a challenge to a critical examination of the phenomena that surround consumer spectacle. A narrow focus on the history of particular designs or the use of particular doors obscures the macro-aesthetic analysis needed to ultimately bring this visual culture into relation with the broader visual world of shopping spaces. We have, it seems, an elusive subject, one that appears both everywhere and nowhere. Yet, its formation as an object of inquiry is necessary if we are to understand how the visual culture of the service industry infrastructure shapes consumer society.

In the summer of 2002, I began a study of shopping malls in Sacramento, California to discover how people negotiate public and private space. I travelled east of the city centre to the Arden Arcade district, a large commercial shopping area which contains several contiguous shopping malls, busy multi-lane boulevards, big box retail stores, factory outlets, chain restaurants, and smaller strip malls. (An historical overview of Arden Arcade can be found in Westover 1978.) The homogeneous effect of the architecture and signage in this district produces a *mallscape* similar to other retail commercial districts across California and the United States.

Scholars of urban culture and consumer spaces (Certeau 1984; Miller 1995; Underhill 2004) have applied empirical methods to demonstrate that despite the prevailing uniformity of designs and messages, the expectations of retail developers can differ dramatically from the actual use of social space. Their research has convincingly documented how both the policies regulating mall behaviour and the packaged meanings of commodity marketing can be creatively interpreted by people using spaces or products for 'unintended' uses. However, as Jon Goss (2004) explains in his recent review of the literature on the geography of consumption, the prevalence of empirically oriented studies describing the nuances of mall behaviour has inadvertently overshadowed the theoretical implications of how designers employ visual cues to facilitate consumption. Despite observable local differentiation at Arden Arcade, what repeatedly struck me as interesting and worth further exploration was the formidable visual dynamic that served as a cohesive platform upon which the social relations of the district were performed. Local negotiation with space and mass consumer culture was bracketed and influenced by a quieter and more durable substrate of visual elements which functioned as a stage upon which these negotiations were performed. If one were to conduct an anthropological study of consumer spaces, such as this *mallscape*, one would have to account for the effect this visual culture has on everyday meanings. As illustrated in the selection of figures presented throughout this essay, I began using photography to document the visual culture of consumer infrastructure so that the significance of these images might be unfolded within the context of consumption – framing and isolating both employee entrances and emergency exits signs from the kaleidoscope of advertising images and commodities surrounding them.

Traffic patterns in a mall problematize strict distinctions between public/private or customer/worker spaces. A mallscape is interwoven with different degrees of authority and control and different power relations. Its multi-layered networks require a complex sign system to communicate spatial differentiation. Workers often travel through customer spaces to and from work, and customers inevitably see the signposts of employee areas. In the Arden Faire district, I found work and consumption spaces to be interlaced. Service areas exist as islands within seas of customer areas. There were also vast work zones with only small out croppings of commercial signs. I attempted to identify the intended use of space by reading its aesthetic qualities. I looked for markers of employee spaces and emergency systems that were visible from customer areas in order to identify the signs that interacted with commodity displays. I repeated this activity at other locations in the Sacramento area and found that the signs of employee entrances and emergency exits bore visual similarities across locales, and shared representational techniques with other parts of the consumer support infrastructure (see Michalski 2004).

OBSTACLES TO AESTHETIC CRITIQUE

The signs rendered in these photographs serve as microborders, drawing upon a common visual aesthetic, which is used to denote spatial differences. They cue shifts in performance and mark points of change between different normative patterns. They operate as 'actants', Bruno Latour's concept for images, machines, or signs that participate in the creation of social space as actors do, and thus complicate the subject–object distinction (see Latour 1987; Law and Hassard 1999). Like the colour or style of a worker's uniform, consumer infrastructure design is enacted to elicit specific reactions within particular social cultural contexts (Fussell 2002). In this essay, I wish to consider the role these actants play in the constitution of consumer culture, not only the message they communicate to those trained to understand their primary coded meaning, but also to theorize how they are experienced by the uninitiated, the passer-by.

It is difficult to find theoretical architectural literature that critically engages with the aesthetics of employee entrances and emergency exits. Discussion of the design of these infrastructure details is often deferred to the more practical field of engineering, where it is handled in a rational and functional manner. When consumer infrastructure is applied in planning documents, such as in the circuitry of floor plans, it is often done mechanically, based on the internal logic of the building. In these models, the signifier designed for particular doors rests on its *indexicality* and is understood to broadcast a clear and precise signification. The effectiveness of graphic design as an indicator of public or private space, or as a warning of danger, is measured by the design's ability to strike an unambiguous meaning. This perceived neutrality and clarity leads to the replication of a dominant style, and forestalls any understanding of the meaning and effect of this style when read outside the functional practices of engineering and architecture.

For planners and designers, a critical engagement in the design details of consumer infrastructure is further deterred by a reliance on ready-made building codes. Once municipal building codes are adopted in the United States they enter into the public domain and are free to copy. Companies such as the Municipal Code Corporation have formed to distribute these codes nationwide (Ward 2001: 48). The choice to use ready-made codes is largely based on economic expediency. Designing creative codes for service areas and other infrastructure elements is seen as too expensive for local contractors, and too restricted by owner/operator demands, municipal rules, and insurance regulations. There are also systemic economic challenges in play. Mass production of architectural components, global commerce, and the increased power of remote, national and international developers over local projects have led to increased standardization. Rather than rethinking these aspects of building design, local designers, planners and architects either turn to the vast collection of commercially and publicly available building codes or cede the authority to distant developers. Consequently, a building can share building codes and architectural components with other same-use buildings across the United States. This practice has resulted in a striking homogeneity across shopping centre developments in diverse locales, and makes employee entrance and emergency exit imagery appear to lack authorship.

Another reason for the widespread adaptation of similar employee entrances and emergency exits designs can be found in the discourse of organizational behaviour and environmental psychology, which has a long tradition of manipulating spatial design to communicate specific, functional, and normative values in the development of service industry infrastructures (see Lang *et al.* 1974; Lym 1980; Starkey *et al.* 1996). Much of the literature portrays the field as a science of psychological adjustment (Schermerhorn *et al.* 1982: 9). Organizational behaviour often begins with the premise that behaviour can be diagnosed and managed through spatial representation. First, environmental psychologists seek the alleged universal indices that prompt the behaviours desired by managements, and then graphic artists dutifully apply these visual signs and tropes in service industry infrastructure. Phenomenologists and semioticians, however, have argued against this approach of reading only the response-sequences of the objects observed (see Bachelard 1964; Eco 1980). In the case of employee entrances and emergency exits, this behavioural method ignores the deeper connotative effects that this increasingly global visual system has in relation to consumer culture.

Employee entrances and emergency exits have escaped critical analysis by visual cultural studies for similar reasons. As actants, they possess seemingly disembodied and asocial features and are literally relegated to the backstage of consumption. They are viewed as mere apparatus, purely rational, devoid of personal signature, emotion or art. This designation places the visual culture of infrastructure outside the tradition of visual criticism and interpretation. Visual cultural critiques of consumer society have focused instead on the meaning of advertising media and the veil of commodities rather than the spectacle of infrastructure signage. The former is seen as cultural, while the latter is taken for granted as reflective of the material base. This essay serves to highlight and deconstruct this base as one that is fashioned to represent structural relations of consumer society.

THE EMERGENCE OF A CRITICAL AESTHETIC

A sub-field of organizational behaviour, called organizational aesthetics, has positioned a critique of the aesthetics of instrumental rationality (Strati 1996, 1999; Guillén 1997; Cairns 2002). In a study of the corporate office, for example, Sewell and Wilkinson (1992) found that the application of Taylorist design practices, such as *Just-in-Time Manufacturing* and *Total-Quality-Control* systems, coupled with anti-theft measures, have conspired to dominate the aesthetic practices of today's workplaces. This new awareness of the cultural implications of infrastructure design draws from both anthropology and semiotics. In a recent essay, Philip Hancock (2005) called for an interpretation of the 'technologies of enchantment' operating in the contemporary office, arguing that stylized coding endows technologies with the capacity to charm (Gell 1992: 43). The actant is said to reach beyond and beneath intellectual cognition to secure the acquiescence of individuals. Hancock's work builds on earlier critical organizational studies (Burrell 1997; Baldry 1997) which have also looked at the aesthetics of office layout and organizational ephemera to address the 'darker, hidden recesses of organizational life' (Hancock 2005: 30).

Artists and art theorists are beginning to meet the discursive movement made by organizational aesthetics (see Muschamp 1998; Fortino 2005; Ise 2005; Meier 2005). Jem Cohen's video *Chain* (2004) can be seen as an attempt to reintegrate infrastructure design practices into a wider critique of the visual culture of consumption. He de-centres the media image of shopping spaces and focuses on the framework of consumer space to draw attention to the overlooked, but omnipresent, aspects of urban sprawl. The video's mise-en-scène, an anonymous American suburb, was composed in 11 different states from across the United States. In his *Village Voice* review Ed Halter (2005) writes:

> *Chain*'s formidable power rests on the notion that these unlovely incrustations
> of worldwide anti-regionalism bespeak a fundamentally dehumanizing global
> economy, a concept that is immanent rather than argued. As such, the film verges
> on a kind of negative sentimentality, albeit of a radical bent, and offers only

the merest glimmers of hope. In one segment, a bird nests incongruously within the oversized B of a store's name. Elsewhere, Amanda imagines a drowned world that would take it all away.

The dialectical logic of safety and disaster played out in *Chain* underlies and conditions today's consumer society. Cohen's video represents the aesthetic style of consumer support networks as a positive, politically strategic, geographical intervention which is increasing prevalent and aggressive in its application.

Other visual artists, such as Scott Fortino, Carsten Meier and Daniel Mirer, also resist the deflection of vision these sites induce. They choose, instead, to focus on the allegedly acultural symbols which populate arenas of consumption. In their images, as in mine, it is easy to see a cityscape stripped of pathos and sensuality, victimized by mechanical agency, but they are far from dispassionate. In writing about Mirer's work in the exhibit catalogue, *Vanishing Point*, Claudine Ise (2005: 13) describes his photographs as representative of 'non-spaces' – Marc Augé's (1995: 87) term for spaces that cannot be defined as relational, historical, or concerned with identity. Ise (2005: 14) sees the visual culture of mundane consumer infrastructure as 'symptomatic of the diminishing relevance of the human built environment'. However, Hal Foster (2005: 27) in the same exhibition catalogue, argues that Mirer captures a 'simulacral resemblance', which developed out of specific human relations surrounding a post-Fordist economy. It is not that the references Mirer captures on film have no referent in the human world, instead Foster (2005: 27) insists the referential system in Mirer's photographs actively and materially 'derealizes' these connections. By presenting images of employee entrances and emergency exits, I want to reinforce a humanist reading of these signs. This cannot be done by simply reversing the derealization of the simulacra and returning an anachronistic authenticity to space. The intent is, rather, to focus on the authenticity and omnipresence of what might be called a *derealist* style and explore how it is constitutive of current political, economic and social modes of existence.

Concentration on profane and commonplace visual systems, such as those that are complicit in the postmodern aesthetic, can work against a visual system's techno-naturalization. The first step is to bring into focus what was overlooked or neglected, the next is to expose the ways this previously hidden apparatus constructs both sight and knowledge. Walter Benjamin (1968: 236) acknowledged the power of photography to spark dialectical thinking: 'the enlargement of a snapshot does not simply render more precise what in any case was visible, though unclear: it reveals entirely new structural formations of the subject'. I hope that my photographs can help place these doors in the social context of which they are a part, the *lebenswelt* of consumer society, and allow some reflection on the cultural and aesthetic contributions their imagery makes to that context. These contributions include sensory alienation, an image of the relation between production and consumption, and conceptions of power, authority and safety.

THE STRATEGIC USE OF SENSORY ALIENATION

Many of the architectural details I photographed in (Figure 11.2) use camouflage and other aversion strategies, such as negative ornamentation, to deflect the consumer's gaze from networks operating beneath or behind them. They are intentionally decorated with dull flat colours in order to fragment and blur operational circuits (Figure 11.3). This strategy allows employee entrances and emergency exits to redirect attention toward other signs, such as advertising and product displays. This bland design distinguishes the infrastructure from commodities which appear, by contrast, to take on a vivacious aura. The design style serves as a frame. It becomes the supplement of consumption, performing as its parergon. Consumer culture, like all culture, is constituted by its differences as well as its essential qualities, and the visual culture of consumer infrastructure plays a contextual role in constituting the focus of the mall.

In its neutrality and obscurity, the infrastructure takes on an a priori status and its design functions as the stage of consumer desire. But the visual culture of employee areas and emergency exits also trains and conditions that desire by enforcing limits on consumer fantasy. These sites mark the termination of leisure and playfulness. Unchecked fantasies are restrained and the wandering eye is returned to marketing narratives. Attention is refocused onto the commodities for sale. Consumer society shapes and tempers its stories by juxtaposing them to the anti-story of infrastructural aesthetics. More than the shadow of consumption, this system of signs has become the necessary optic through which mass media culture and commodities become visible.

The articulated language of this visual aesthetic even lends legitimacy to establishments by adorning them with the mark of corporate professionalism. Ali Madanipour, in his book *Public and Private Spaces of the City* (2003: 64), theorizes

Figure 11.2
Beige with intercom,
2002.

Figure 11.3
*Purple shield and beige
HVAC,* 2002.

that nuanced distinctions between public and private space corresponds to a level of perceived civilization, arguing that signs of spatial distinctions are used as status symbols. Consumer spaces cite the visual imagery of employment, emergency or safety to help embellish and showcase their products. People might, in fact, look for the visual culture of safety mechanisms when picking places to shop and eat. For instance, *Masque Ristorante* an upscale restaurant in the *La Borgata at Serrano* shopping centre in El Dorado Hills, California decorates its exterior with an ersatz 'Tuscan' motif. However, it might not be the appearance of provincial authenticity that ultimately attracts the out-of-town customer. When driving into an unknown area, a customer might be just as attracted to a restaurant's conspicuous adherence to standards and codes. Some corporations recognize this aspect of human behaviour. Early national television advertising campaigns for McDonald's restaurants did not show off cheeseburgers, fries, or shakes, but employees mopping the floor (McDonald's Corporation 1971). Actants written to control worker behaviour enforce safety measures or illuminate emergency procedures, also function as a kind of regalia, which communicate that an establishment belongs to an international community of consumer environments. They therefore announce a tacit agreement to engage in a universal standard of exchange. Customers understand these regulatory signs as evidence that an establishment has acquired a cosmopolitan authenticity.

LABOUR VALUE AS OBSCENITY

There is another dimension of citationality at work in these images of employee exits and entrances (Figure 11.4). As the antithesis of consumption, these doors denote officiousness and alertness, but careful reflection might allow one to unfold such commonplace significations. By focusing attention on the contextual frame, the imposed a priori stage of consumption may disintegrate. If the opaque neutral coloured doors (Figure 11.5) could give way to a transparency, they would reveal the structural networks running through these deflective devices. Behind these signs is inventory. Boxes of products appear piled to ceilings, disconnected from the marketer's narratives. If one were to see the boxes in this form (perhaps labelled by another geographic deflection, 'Made in the Northern Mariana Islands') one might reconnect the theatre of consumption with the processes of labour power. This vision could help one re-imagine the commodity chain, its circulation of material and people and its effect on ecosystems and politics. Beyond the stockroom doors, commodities are divorced from mythology. In unseen shipping containers set apart from contrived desires, the manufactured commodity lies in state. The labour worked into them has become converted to exchange value, but beyond this abstraction it is possible to imagine the work of an individual's hands, hands conditioned by the distribution and exchange of global labour power. Whole systems which support transnational patterns of corporate accumulation lie concealed in commodity form, just beyond these plainly hued doors.

Figure 11.4
Twice labeled in worker grey, 2002.

Figure 11.5
White on white with peephole, 2002.

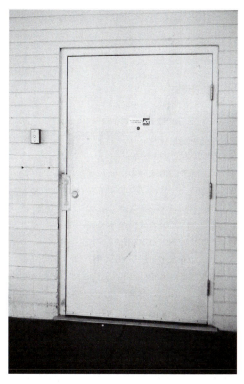

To see the commodity in this dormant state is to witness the symbolic entombment of homogeneous labour.

Employee entrances evoke this dematerialization of work through a specific mimetic display. They cannot, however, dematerialize themselves. While the design of employee entrances appears to protect the consumer from the obscenity of 'dead labor-value' (Trenkle 1998), the doors are more than veils. Employee entrance designs are active, positive markers of the real abstraction necessitated by modern capital (Postone 1993). They do not render labour invisible; instead they stand in for abstract economic processes that are displaced through a feigned misrecognition – a misrecognition provoked by the deflective aesthetics of service entrances. The sign of employee entrances communicates the logic that influences both immediate exchanges as well as global economic relations. When confronted with this sign, the viewer rehearses a habitual distance between consumption and production. The design of employee entrances both guards and adorns labour power with symbolic conceptions of value and control. Employee entrances teach displacement and alienation every day by enacting performances of both denial and transformation. In the process of shielding labour, these actants stage its naked presentation.

Drawing on Baudrillard's concept of the 'ob-scene', as the not scene or the not seen, David Clarke (2003) refers to this geography of displacement as *pornogeography*. The ob-scene is said to arouse and curb anxiety by scrambling and dislocating cause and effect (Clark 2003: 168). It is said to confuse and distort relations (such as the relations between production and consumption) by removing critical distance. The ob-scene presents conditions in their raw proximity, and disorients viewers by the lack of illusion. As a veil, the enchantment and efface-ment of labour at the employee entrance ultimately fails. Instead, the rational and brutal design of employee entrances reveals labour's manifestation in capitalist society. It becomes an interchangeable and abstract commodity. However, the 'act of disavowal' performed by the ob-scene 'has merely resulted in a kind of excrescence' (Clark 2003: 170). If one concentrates on the semiotics of the doors' visuality, one may see them as representative of the circuits that reconnect global economic and social relations. They become symbolic not of place, but of remote systems, of transnational capitalist enterprise. Through them, labour and consump-tion become coextensive, leisure and work flicker to and fro. These actants connote processes of accumulation and the ephemeral of exploitation. As regulatory signs they are endowed with spirit and force. This allows them to become the root fetish of consumer culture: the enshrinement of abstract value.

DISCIPLINE AND SUBJECTIFICATION

Because theft, workplace violence and the destruction of private property often occur at these 'back' doors, the managerial and behavioural design literature is predominantly concerned with the disciplinary function of this visual culture. All doors to retail spaces are considered vulnerable and surveillance and policing is recommended. Sometimes surveillance equipment is made inconspicuous, other times it is blatant, but it is always recognizable. Surveillance equipment and other design tropes demonstrate authority and power and reinforce rules about property, social class and social conduct. In *The Politics of Collective Violence*, Charles Tilly (2003: 84–5) characterizes violent rituals as those that: activate boundaries, create a polarization or widening of social space between groups, engage in monitoring actions within a site, and validate and invalidate participants in their space. The space of employee entrances exercises these symptoms as they protect the state of inequality in consumer society.

In this light, the heavily secured spaces of employee entrances and emergency exits suggest a kind of violence at work. This violence, however, is distributed dif-ferently according to the processes of interpellation, which occur selectively as different people travel through these spaces in different situations. One Sunday morning when I was called upon to identify myself while taking pictures in these sensitive spaces, I named myself as an aspiring architect. This identity worked to distinguish me from a vagrant, terrorist or thief. In other circumstances, one can imagine different possible outcomes to this interaction.

Through the collision of these two poles of activity, consumption and production, this visual system has opened a third space – a border region, where the control and meaning of space develops. The different processes of subjectifi-cation in this border zone provide insight into larger social forces. It is here where race, class, gender and other identity tags are made visible. Just as international borders are sites of inspection, the concentration of economic, political and cultural forces at these *microborders* has made employee entrances and emergency exits the arena where social forces collide and identities take shape.

CONTESTING THE SIGN

The places where this aesthetic system is deployed most robustly often become the site of heightened contestation. Employee entrances and emergency exits can even become zones of ritual transgression. The parking lots and alleys of consumer retail structures, partially shielded from view, are places where homeless people can rest, skateboarders can congregate, and graffiti or poster artists can express themselves and mark territory (Figure 11.6). The anti-ornamentation of these spaces invites reclamation and reinvention. They also attract litter and human waste. As the symbolic antithesis of consumption, they have become sites of ritual expenditure or revolt against the processes of micro-regulation. They operate as a kind of sacred space, positioned between the public and private realm. It is in these highly trafficked, yet highly protected sites, that social taboos are enforced and broken. Employee entrances and emergency exits, through their publicly understood visual culture, have become sites where alternative ideas of progress and the use of space clash, where the human geography of consumer culture is both imposed and resisted.

A person performing as a service industry worker experiences this sign system quite differently from one performing as a customer. A worker might see the employee entrance as a passage to the theatrical backstage of consumption – since service work is also a dramaturgical occupation (Hall 1993). He or she

Figure 11.6
Blue with torn poster,
2002.

might view these doors as a transformative space between his or her other social roles. One day the worker might be a customer, but another he or she will be a 'team member' and, therefore, the employee entrance figures as point of transition. It engenders a kind of self-governance, teaching one to be a good worker, or a good customer.

The employee entrance, as an ideal, extends beyond its perceptual reach. It becomes a conceptual space that travels with the worker when she or he takes her or his job home. It becomes an organizer of tasks and memories. As a mental image, it might become a subconscious cue. An employer might conjure the door's image to remind an employee of the importance of following rules about work-space demeanour, dress, language and behaviour once the employee has passed through the portal. Alternatively, an employee might envision the door as a pathway to success or at least another pay-cheque. Employee entrances can also represent opportunities to acquire specialized knowledge. A produce purveyor was happy to tell me about all the strange and secret entrances he knew. The catacombs of the city were revealed to him as he went through his delivery route. A custodial worker in the city concurred. To him, the buildings in which he worked were like a massive organic machine. He knew their visceral innards, and through his labour saw the city in its brilliant complexity. Through the employee entrance these outsiders were turned insiders, in more ways than one. They were welcomed into a system of expertise.

These spaces can also mark where workers prepare and unwind from their roles as corporate caricatures. They are a threshold between physical/mental/emotional labour, and a non-work identity – the worker's home life or the worker as shopper. Here, workers can speak together, get into character, or debrief each other about their day. These austere images might even connote a zone free from the stress and obligations of the consumer world or home life: worlds that can become more stressful and repressive than the workday. It may represent an escape or a place of independence, a place in between societal demands. Indeed, around the flatly coloured and heavily secured doors we often see chairs, for employees on a break (Figure 11.7). These places are not only representative of the exit or close of the workday; they serve therapeutically as decompression chambers for workers in need. The employee entrance is a place to chat, smoke or rest, outside the gaze of the emotionally demanding and often annoying customer. Under-standing the diverse symbolism of employee entrances as well as the performances and transgressions around them requires that one be alert to the multiple senses these images can create. Employee entrances are inextricable from the dialectic of work and consumption because they are positioned at the crux of global markets. Their images influence the performances of workers consuming, and consumers working, in multifaceted ways. The concentration of forces that produce the sign of employee entrances undoubtedly complicates simplistic allegories of the universal subject and makes difficult the equation of freedom with leisure, as well as romantic ideas of work and selfhood.

Figure 11.7
*Two chairs for cigarette
break*, 2002.

SOVEREIGNTY AND THE SAFETY REGIME

Alongside the naming of labour, another kind of power is enacted through the visual culture of service industry infrastructure, one that is exercised most stridently by the communication of safety and emergency insignia. Fire exits, hydrants, warnings signs, and fire suppression equipment, all employ signals recognized by emergency teams assigned to rescue people and property in times of disaster (Figure 11.8). But just as one found that the visual culture of employee entrance spaces symbolize more than its denotative messages, these emergency spaces also contribute to, and are informed by, wider connotative associations. Within the mallscape, safety and emergency actants remind the consumer of architecture's biosystemic qualities. Through the sight of sprinkler systems and fire alarms, a visitor to a shopping mall is made cognizant of the law of safety. Emergency exits call to mind a specific kind of mental concentration, one that is different from both leisure and work. They reflect an unquestionable sovereign authority, a martial law that waits in the wings for disaster to strike. Through their ever-present reminder of crisis, the certainty of our constructed individuality is made less sure.

Figure 11.8
Blue with sprinkler room sign, 2002.

Subjective and hetero-chronic notions of time, the time of consumption and leisure, are braced and contained by the visual culture of emergency emblems, such as fire lanes, exit lights and the bold red-lettered words that dot shopping malls. They recall the constant threat of disaster overshadowing free time. They warn of a looming emergency time, a present without past or future, where the modern subject disintegrates and individuals are transformed into bodies. Emergency time destroys subjective independence; in its wake the technological networks that monitor buildings envelop the consumer and worker. People become part of a system based on actuarial statistics. With the onslaught of disaster, the interpellation of consumption disintegrates, and the shopper becomes the function of a grisly bottom line.

Emergency exits become sovereign symbols of the disaster regime. They convey an underlying equality at the base of a highly competitive consumer society, one that neutralizes consumption's Hobbesian war of individual gain. In this narrative, the foreboding of calamity becomes an effervescent social ritual around which a shared culture can be formed. This perverse form of social cohesion rests on a narrative of equality that can ameliorate the hardships of an uneven society. The prolific exit beacons shining in the corners of shopping malls, advertise a constant state of emergency, one that erases status differentiation while transforming shopping into a dangerous and even heroic activity. By engaging in it, consumers develop a form of social solidarity predicated on the equality of potential victimization. In the United States, the new fear of terrorism and the exaltation of its opposite image, the firefighter, buttress and support the play of consumerism.

The sovereign power of the emergency sign, in its endless repetition, has come to operate as a contemporary symbol of charismatic unity and nationhood in the global spaces of consumption. However, this narrative of equality in times of disaster is illusionary and unsubstantiated by events. Real instances of risk differentiate along lines of social class and status group. The markers of safety are, to the disenfranchised, no more than the harbingers of disaster itself.

CONCLUSION

Art theorist Rosalind Krauss (1979) in her essay 'Sculpture in an Expanded Field', mapped minimalist sculpture and earth-art works as a first step towards seeking an explanation for the logical and systemic dynamics at work in the creation of postmodern sculpture. She built a structure of comparisons based on oppositional categories (i.e. Architecture/Landscape, Not-Architecture/Not-Landscape). In this essay, I have also tried to expand the field of critical aesthetics to encompass a visual culture that is just beginning to attract attention. I have not attempted to plot examples of individual infrastructural details on a conceptual grid but certain oppositional tensions can still be discerned in this visual culture. Under the sign of this mundane visual aesthetic, I have argued that the spaces of employee entrances and emergency exits influence more than behaviour, producing both normative and moral values. This visual culture conveys disciplinary, governmental and sovereign power (see Foucault 1977). The system demarcates spaces to either attract or deflect attention, and it nurtures both an investment in social structures and a divestment from them. Finally, I have argued that these consecrated sites become places where social roles are either adopted, resisted or transformed.

In each case, the design of employee entrances and emergency exits creates spaces where subjects are called into being. To understand these spaces of interpellation it is important to consider the oppositional logic at work in the formation of this aesthetic system. As Krauss (1979: 44) underscores, it is pertinent that one address the 'cultural determinants of the opposition through which a given field is structured'. I hope that these photographs and arguments can add to such a discussion by putting these images in the context of the consumer environment. A critical look at this visual culture's aesthetic system, one which is attuned to multifarious signification, must guide the fieldwork necessary to unravel the frequency, potency and signature these sites transmit in order to further unfold the constitution of these ubiquitous social spaces.

All around the city, just past the effervescent images of commercial displays, the visual culture of employee entrances and emergency exits is called upon to define the most sensitive spaces in society. It is a tool used by developers to prompt and guide the daily rhythms of social interaction in their establishments. But this visual system connotes far more. The visual culture of consumer amenities has become the front guard in the accumulation of new consumer space. If one can induce these visual elements to answer for their form – to understand the internal logic of their composition, as well as their significance to the project of consumer society, one might be able to reconnect global economic processes to local patterns and intimately held beliefs. These signs of the consumer infrastructure are neither the sole purvey of planners nor anonymous anti-signs forever outside our grasp; they represent us. They are the reflections of contemporary folkways, forged in the cauldron of both global and local social forces. One need only stray and linger in their midst to coax out the power relations that fabricate their surface.

REFERENCES

Adams, P. C., Hoelscher, S. and Till, K. E. (eds) (2001) *Textures of Place: Exploring Humanist Geographies*, Minneapolis, MN: University of Minnesota Press.

Adkins, L. and Lury, C. (1999) 'The Labour of Identity: Performing Identities, Performing Economies', *Economy and Society* 28(4): 598–614.

Auge, M. (1995) *Non-places: Introduction to an Anthropology of Supermodernity*, London: Verso.

Bachelard, G. (1964) *The Poetics of Space*, New York: Orion Press.

Baldry, C. (1997) 'The Social Construction of Office Space', *International Labour Review* 136 (3): 365–78.

Benjamin, W. (1968) 'The Work of Art in the Age of Mechanical Reproduction', in A. Hannah (ed.) *Illuminations*, New York: Harcourt, Brace & World.

Burrell, G. (1997) *Pandemonium*, Thousand Oaks, CA: Sage Publications.

Cairns, G. (2002) 'Aesthetics, Morality and Power: Design as Espoused Freedom and Implicit Control', *Human Relations* 55 (7): 799–820.

Certeau, M. de (1984) *The Practice of Everyday Life*, Berkeley, CA: University of California Press.

Clarke, D. B. (2003) *Consumer Society and the Postmodern City*, New York: Routledge.

Eco, U. (1980) 'Function and Sign: Semiotics of Architecture', in G. Broadbent, R. Bunt and C. Jencks (eds) *Signs, Symbols, and Architecture*, New York: Wiley.

Fortino, S. (2005) *Institutional: Photographs of Jails, Schools and Other Chicago Buildings*, Chicago, IL: Columbia College.

Foster, H. (2005) 'Six Notes on Vanishing', in C. Ise (ed) *Vanishing Point*, Columbus, OH: Wexner Center for the Arts, pp. 27–34.

Foucault, M. (1977) *Discipline and Punish: the Birth of the Prison*, New York: Pantheon Books.

Fussell, P. (2002) *Uniforms: Why We Are What We Wear*, Boston, MA: Houghton Mifflin Company.

Gell, A. (1992) 'Technology of Enchantment and the Enchantment of Technology', in J. Coote and A. Shelton (eds) *Anthropology, Art, and Aesthetics*, Oxford: Oxford University Press.

Goss, J. (2004) 'Geography of Consumption I', *Progress in Human Geography* 28 (3): 369–80.

Guillén, M. F. (1997) 'Scientific Management's Lost Aesthetic: Architecture, Organization, and the Taylorized Beauty of the Mechanical', *Administrative Science Quarterly* 42: 687–715.

Hall, E. J. (1993) 'Waitering/Waitressing: Engendering the Work of Table Servers', *Gender & Society* 7 (3): 329–46.

Halter, E. (2005) 'Memories of Overdevelopment', *Village Voice*. 13 September. Online. Available: www.villagevoice.com/film/0537,halter,67750,20.html (accessed 28 September 2006).

Hancock, P. (2005) 'Uncovering the Semiotic in Organizational Aesthetics', *Organization* 12(1): 29–50.

Ise, C. (2005) *Vanishing Point*, Columbus, OH: Wexner Center for the Arts.

Krauss, R. (1979) 'Sculpture in the Expanded Field', *October* 8: 30–44.

Lang, J., Burnette, C., Moleski, W. and Vachon, D. (eds) (1974) *Designing for Human Behaviour: Architecture and the Behavioral Science*, Stroudsburg, PA: Dowden, Hutchinson and Ross.

Latour, B. (1987) *Science in Action: How to Follow Scientists and Engineers through Society*, Milton Keynes: Open University Press.

Law, J. and Hassard, J. (eds) (1999) *Actor Network Theory and After*, Malden, MA: Blackwell Publishers/Sociological Review.

Lethaby, W. R. (1956) *Architecture, Nature & Magic*, New York: G. Braziller.

Lym, G. R. (1980) *A Psychology of Building: How We Shape and Experience Our Structured Spaces*, Englewood Cliffs, NJ: Prentice-Hall, Inc.

Madanipour, A. (2003) *Public and Private Spaces of the City*, New York: Routledge.

Meier, C. (2005) *Carsten Meier: Public Parking*, Bielefeld: Kerber.

Michalski, D. (2004) *Employee Entrances and Emergency Exit Photography*. University Library, University of California, Davis. Online. Available: http://people.lib.ucdavis.edu/dem/ee/EE.html (accessed 29 September 2006).

Miller, D. (ed.) (1995) *Acknowledging Consumption: a Review of New Studies*, New York: Routledge.

Muschamp, H. (1998) 'The Office's Subconscious', *New York Times Magazine*, 18 January: 30–5.

Postone, M. (1993) *Time, Labor, and Social Domination: a Reinterpretation of Marx's Critical Theory*, New York: Cambridge University Press.

Schermerhorn, J. R. Jr, Hunt, J. G. and Osborn, R. N. (1982) *Managing Behavior*, New York: John Wiley & Sons.

Sewell, G. and Wilkinson, B. (1992) 'Someone to Watch Over Me': Surveillance, Discipline and the Just-In-Time Labour Process', *Sociology* 26(2): 271–89.

Starkey, K., Tempest, S. and McKinlay, A. (eds) (1996) *How Organizations Learn*, Boston, MA: International Thomson Business Press.

Strati, A. (1996) 'Organizations Viewed Through the Lens of Aesthetics, *Organization* 3 (2): 209–18.

—— (1999) *Organization and Aesthetics*, Thousand Oaks, CA: Sage.

Tilly, C. (2003) *Politics of Collective Violence*, New York: Cambridge University Press.

Trenkle, N. (1998) 'Terror of Labor', *Krisis*. March. Online. Available: http://members.blackbox.net/oebgdk/trenkle_terror-of-labour.html (accessed 29 September 2006).

Underhill, P. (2004) *The Call of the Mall*, New York: Simon & Schuster.

Ward, J. (2001) 'Everywhere People', *Architecture* 90(11): 48–51.

Westover, T. N. (1978) *The Suburban Shopping Mall as a Leisure Environment*, unpublished thesis, University of California at Davis.

FILMOGRAPHY

Chain (2004) dir. Jem Cohen, Antidote Films.

You Deserve a Break Today (1971) McDonald's Corporation, YouTube. Online. Available: www.youtube.com/watch?v=MP8D8AzvBtE (accessed 29 September 2006).

Chapter 12: Rain in the City

Jill Stoner

> Fantasy is a place where it rains.
>
> Italo Calvino (1988: 81)

This chapter is, perhaps, a rogue current running through the deep waters that comprise a book on the cinematic city. It is offered not as film criticism but, rather, as a critique of the filmic and cinematic aspects of the city itself, and a speculation on the architectural potentials of transparency (film) and motion (cinema) which challenge the static weight and opacity of contemporary urban form. I begin with the assertion that the metropolis is the only meaningful province left for architecture, and, at that, as a context not for building but for un-building. I claim that if architecture is to continue to be a fruitful voice of culture and aspiration, it must put itself into reverse, and that this action will result not in projects, but in empty space.

What follows is a call for fantasy, for a conjuring forth of fantastic images and bidding them to enter our urban life. But fantasy is a slippery substance which, once captured, becomes that 'real' stuff that is fantasy's opposite. The point of fantasies is not to construct them – for, sadly, the built once built loses its fantastic quality, being no longer behind the eye but in front of it. So fantasy serves another purpose – to alert us to what is missing in our cities, without necessarily suggesting its form.

Architecture has always had, and will continue to have, human purpose, but the definition of that purpose needs constantly to be challenged. Past purposes have included: shelter (the house), significance (the cathedral), performance (the theatre), remembrance (the memorial) and assembly (the hall). Now (I claim) architecture's *purpose* is none of these things, which are attended to adequately in other ways. I assert that the task of architecture today is to remove weight from cities through the sheer force of imagination. Writers such as Italo Calvino and John Updike can assist us in opening up gaps within the conventional literature of urbanism – spaces for us to fill with imaginative possibilities.

Ours is a culture in motion, not just the motion of physical bodies and digital bits, but also the motion of concepts. This is a liberating time, in which the imagination can once again (as it has at some of the less rational moments in history) subvert pure reason. The incessant movement that drives contemporary culture suggests a dominance of verbs over nouns, and it is with the verb form of 'rain' that we will begin. The epigraph to this chapter refers, Calvino explains, to the following line from Dante's *Commedia*: '*poi piove dentro a l'alta fantasia*', which Calvino translates as: 'then rained down into the high fantasy'. Here is Calvino's (1988: 82) further paraphrase of Dante's allusion:

> Oh imagination, you who have the power to impose yourself on our faculties and wills, stealing us away from the outer world and carrying us off into an inner one, so that even if a thousand trumpets were to sound we would not hear them, what is the source of the visual messages that you receive, if they are not formed from sensations deposited in the memory?

The etymology of 'fantasy' takes us back to the Indo-European root *BHA*, a root that it shares with the verb 'beckon' and the noun 'beacon'. Its more historically immediate ancestor is the Greek verb *phantazein*, meaning 'to make visible', and the corresponding noun *phantasia*, which translates as 'appearance, image, perception, imagination'. Another form, *phantazesthai* means 'to picture to oneself', from *phantos* 'visible', and in late Greek – 'to imagine, to have visions', which is related to *phos* meaning 'light'. Thus, the title of Calvino's lecture 'Visibility', from which the introductory epigraph is taken, aptly refers to the internal light of the mind's eye.

There are many reasons to look to the contemporary city as a source of images that 'rain down into the high fantasy'. The thoughts that follow are not verbal blueprints for built projects; in the spirit of fantasy, they are a 'bringing to light' of imaginings that might or might not inspire physical acts. Though some are grand in size, they are not grand projects. In fact, this essay is intended as a counterpoint to, and a critique of, 'grand narratives' such as new urbanism and critical regionalism – intellectually codified practices that suggest solutions to our current crises of place and space.[1] In this essay, I suggest that we replace the project with the fantasy, and the building with the empty field, as one way to apply levity to the debate on the future of cities.

Calvino's imaginative writings began with the pure lightheartedness of his first work of fiction *Cosmicomics* (1976); his final novel *Mr. Palomar* (1982) shows a literary restraint that reduces the language of imagination to a series of acute and detailed observations of everyday events. The three sections of the latter book devote themselves, respectively, to recreation, urban life and contemplation. The last chapter is titled 'Learning to be Dead', and within three years Calvino had completed this lesson – he died en route to Harvard, where he was to deliver the 1985 Charles Elliot Norton Lectures. He·had at that point written only five of the six lectures, of which 'Visibility' is the fourth.

In that lecture, he speaks of the cerebral immediacy of the imagination: 'it is better to place the visions directly in the mind without making them pass through the senses' (Calvino 1988: 93). His invocation of Dante, and the metaphor of the 'rain into high fantasy', asserts the unpredictability of the imagination, its weather-like capriciousness. It is just such rains of images that haunt the sensibility of Mr Palomar:

> Mr. Palomar sees a wave rise in the distance, grow, approach, change form and color, fold over itself, break, vanish, and flow again. At this point he could convince himself that he has concluded the operation he had set out to achieve, and he could go away. But isolating one wave is not easy, separating it from the wave immediately following, which seems to push it and at times overtakes it and sweeps it away; and it is no easier to separate that one wave from the preceding wave, which seems to drag it toward the shore, unless it turns against the following wave, as if to arrest it. Then, if you consider the breadth of the wave, parallel to the shore, it is hard to decide where the advancing front extends regularly and where it is separated and segmented into independent waves, distinguished by their speed, shape, force, direction.
>
> (Calvino 1985: 3)

Like Mr Palomar's wave, rain also is blurry and imprecise. Even in the context of the city, its formlessness suggests an absence of architecture. But perhaps it holds clues to architecture's redefinition; it acts both literally and metaphorically as an agent of chaos, of emptiness and of chance, and these three qualities offer liberating alternatives to the current conventions of urban design.

RAIN IN LOS ANGELES

Calvino describes the imagination as a sort of movie inside our head: 'This mental cinema is always at work in each one of us, and it always has been, even before the invention of the (technology of the) cinema' (Calvino 1988: 83). He goes on to differentiate two modes of the imaginative process – one which begins with words and ends with images, and the other which reverses that order. He places himself, particularly in his later work, in the second category of imaginative composition – that in which the image precedes the story. In speaking of the attributes of visibility, he alludes to film and cinema interchangeably. But I find it useful to reflect upon the difference between these two words as a means to differentiate between two forms of urban imagination. *Cinema* (sharing its etymology with *kinetic*) is the medium in motion, while *film* refers to its transparency. Both words oppose the solidity of buildings – the first challenges the stasis of architecture, the second its opacity. The first of these concepts makes way for the second; it is not its busyness that will give the city a continued relevance to daily life, but its leisure.

Ridley Scott's *Blade Runner* (1982) reveals a future Los Angeles that is more filmic than cinematic. In fact, when the movie first came out, one of the main criticisms was that it did not have enough action. The film opens not with the torrential downpours that occur in California's 'rainy season', but with a steady acid drizzle (Figure 12.1). This Los Angeles has left behind Disney images and earthquakes, Hollywood scandals and landslides, drought, sunshine and over-population. It is a city of tremendous loss and pervasive distrust. The entire film is shot in a darkness made still more obscure by the incessant rain. The infamous city has become its opposite: from arid desert to poisoned wetness, from a glut of humanity to the leftovers that have not escaped to the outlands.

But, like the Los Angeles we know, it is still a city of simulations. At the futuristic bazaar, extraordinary replicas of exotic animals are produced and sold – their value a fraction of that of the real thing, which has become impossibly scarce. Says one exotic dancer: 'Think I'd be working in a place like this if I could afford a real snake?' In a laboratory, an ancient Chinese man fabricates 'only the eyes' of the replicants that are the ultimate simulation in this city of simulations. At the headquarters of the Tyrell Corporation, the raptor in the vast atrium is a replica of a raptor; and the replicants themselves have replicated the ultimate emotion – the will to live. While the originally released version of the movie ends with images of a recognizable and romantic landscape that suggests an escape from all the replications and simulations that precede it, the 'director's cut' resists such capitulations. In this version, the film closes on an elevator door, with the ambiguous suggestion that Decker and Rachel are, themselves, the fifth and sixth replicants alluded to at the beginning of the film.

Figure 12.1
'Rain in Los Angeles', still from *Blade Runner*, directed by Ridley Scott, 1982.

This dark representation of Los Angeles emerged in 1982, only ten years after Reyner Banham (1973) published his optimistic vision of LA as a landscape of 'four ecologies'. Banham's Los Angeles is the antithesis of Scott's; like Venturi's Las Vegas, it is a seminal reckoning with the American landscape of the 1960s, a light-hearted and un-sentimental celebration of the non-European urbanism that flourished in the American post-war euphoria. In *The Architecture of Four Ecologies*, LA is acknowledged as a metropolis unapologetically devoted to the pleasures of entertainment and acquisition. Banham suggests that Los Angeles lacks only rain to complete its biblical perfection: 'It remains one of the ecological wonders of the habitable world. Given water to pour on its light and otherwise almost desert soil, it can be made to produce a reasonable facsimile of Eden' (Banham 1973: 13). At a time when the notion of ecology as a discipline was just coming into common use, Banham uses the word to apply equally to natural and man-made forms. The science (*logos*) of habitats (*oikos*) is literally what ecology refers to, and he makes no distinction between habitats constructed by us – the freeway and suburb – and those that preceded us – the plains and foothills.

John Updike, best known for novels that capture the culture of the American suburbs of the north-east, where he lived, wrote poems about cities far away. Here is what he says about Los Angeles:

> Lo, at its center one can find oneself
> Atop a paved and windy hill, with weeds
> Taller than men on one side and on the other
> A freeway thundering a canyon's depth below
>
> Its bell of blue a promise that lured too many
> To this waste of angels, of ever-widening gaps

(Updike 1993: 175)

In Updike's poem Banham's three ecologies of hill, freeway and plain are blurred. Suburbia, so present in all of Updike's novels, is absent from the poem. The 'waste of angels, of ever-widening gaps' is the subject of much of this essay, in which emptiness achieves the virtue of urban rooms for the imagination, rather than the body, to inhabit. The Indo-European root of room is *REUh*, meaning 'to open, to enlarge', and these gaps can act as catalysts for the enlargement of the city from within. Their roominess is conditioned not by size but by paradoxes and ambiguities of the built and the natural, of the interior and the exterior, of the 'empty, too full view' of the contemporary metropolis.

THE IMAGINED INTERIOR: BENJAMIN'S SOCK

Putting architecture into reverse is not the equivalent of running a film backwards, but more like turning a sock inside out. Walter Benjamin (2006: 28) describes the phenomenological wonder of this seemingly simple act in *Berlin Childhood*:

Among the nightshirts, aprons and undershirts which were kept there in the back was the thing that turned the wardrobe into an adventure for me. I had to clear a way for myself to its farthest corner. There I would come upon my socks, which lay piled in traditional fashion – that is to say, rolled up and turned inside out. Every pair had the appearance of a little pocket. For me, nothing surpassed the pleasure of thrusting my hand as deeply as possible into its interior. I did not do this for the sake of the pocket's warmth . . . but when I had brought out 'the present', 'the pocket' in which it had lain was no longer there. I could not repeat the experiment on this phenomenon often enough. It taught me that form and content, veil and what is veiled, are the same.

While Benjamin drew on this naive experience as a way to entertain the complexities of literature, we might now take his sock as a direct metaphor for the investigation of habitable space. This suggests an interior that is mysteriously hidden in the seemingly exterior fabric of the contemporary city. In fact, Benjamin himself discovered in Naples, Italy a similar paradox of the urban interior. He writes: 'Just as the living room reappears on the street, with chairs, hearth and altar, so, only much more loudly, the street migrates into the living room' (Benjamin 1986: 221). Much like the maddeningly ambiguous sock of his childhood, the streets of Naples refuse to be codified into spaces of privacy and publicity, of interior and exterior. The porosity that he describes operates at a different scale from the classical urban figure-ground. The idea of public space in the tradition of the piazza gives way in Naples to the informal honeycomb of smaller interstices – staircases, doorways, halls and narrow streets that blur the distinction between urban and domestic territories.

Adjacent and analogous to this distinction between public and private space is the distinction between the man-made and the natural – the one (like private space) contained and surrounded by the other. But which is the interior? Historically, it is the natural world within which and against which the city imposed itself. I suggest that the postmodern city reverses this order of contained and container, potentially supporting elements of wilderness within itself.

This new relationship reflects both the shrinking of the wilderness and the growth of the world population. Each of these perpetually current events is chronicled, respectively, in a pair of clocks at the Bronx Zoo in New York. At the exit to the exhibit called 'Jungle World', a display informs visitors: 'Each minute, 100 more acres are cut and burned . . . and lost forever. Tropical forest acres remaining at this moment: 1,825,233,024'. Even as one watches, the number races downward, seemingly toward an inevitable zero. A second clock provides the population count-up, telling us that we are reproducing at the rate of '180 people every minute, 260,000 every day . . . each person requiring more space, more food and more raw material. Human population at this moment: 5,691,872,559 . . . We are crowding out nature'.

Our unease with these escalating events is relatively recent. The modernist project sought to establish an absolute and rational order, celebrating urban growth and excluding from its programme both the nostalgia for cultural pasts and the romance of nature. While claiming on the one hand to abandon the traditions of past centuries, it continued to tame the wilderness, in fact did this more emphatically than past periods. It was a project that self-destructed in the wake of its own ambitions, but not before completing its agenda to near-perfection. 'Wilderness' is a concept not present in any of the CIAM manifestos, and the 'radiant city' as proposed by le Corbusier, though not constructed exactly according to his plan, is in fact the sought-after plan of the contemporary megalopolis everywhere. It is precisely one of the grand narratives that Lyotard's postmodern theory sets itself up against.

Interiority fundamentally defines the city – it is the refuge, the retreat from the external, non-human elements of the world. It can also be either the space of the event itself, or a space that excludes time. In either case, interiority guards against dangers that include both the physical manifestations of exterior, such as rain, and the social ones, such as human threat. The city was the invention that orchestrated protection from both. Thus, 'rain in the city' is a paradox, a paradox that is suddenly relevant because the ethos of interiority has finally played out its full trajectory, from the Paris arcades to the hermetically sealed office buildings of the post-war metropolis. A truly new urbanism will emphasize an ambiguity that defies these historic distinctions. Like Leibniz's monad and like Benjamin's sock, such an urban space contains its exterior inside itself. When turned inside-out, the inside and the outside overlap and merge in a new spatial harmonic that defies Cartesian description.

Fantasy encourages us to redefine the city's physical presence to include aspects of wilderness, and hence to begin to tame it. By this means we might begin to acknowledge chaos as a new kind of order, emptiness as a new kind of presence, and chance as a new kind of opportunity. While architecture has traditionally claimed the values of solidity, permanence and groundedness, the urban visions that follow capitalize on the qualities of porosity, temporality and lightness already present in both the fabric and the mythology of São Paulo, Detroit and Houston. These speculations, involving both visual and verbal imagery, are equivalent to Benjamin's search for the interior of his sock: propelled by curiosity and seeking that which cannot be found, there rains down into the urban imagination spaces insupportable by either substance or event, spaces to be valued simply as provocation. The resulting fantasies quite literally turn the city and its buildings inside out.

CITY OF CHAOS: SÃO PAULO

São Paulo, with the highest per-capita ownership of helicopters in the world, is a city expanding at a dizzying rate in the same country in which the world's largest rain forest is so rapidly disappearing (the count-down and count-up clocks of the Bronx Zoo are both highly relevant to Brazil). It is an assemblage of tiny pockets of wealth insulated by high walls from vast blankets of poverty. It is the city of which Teresa Caldiera (2000) isolates and analyses a culture of crime and fear, and the city about which John Updike, in 1984, wrote the following poem:

SÃO PAULO
Buildings to the horizon, an accretion
big beyond structure: no glass downtown shimmering
with peacock power, just the elephantine
color of poured concrete repeated in clusters,
into the haze that foots the horizon of hills,
a human muchness encountering no bounds.

From the hotel window, ridged roofs of ruddy tile,
the black of corrugated iron, the green
and yellow of shopfronts, a triangular hut
revealed survival's piecemeal, patchwork logic.
All afternoon, the view sulked beneath my room
in silence – a city without a city's outcry.

And then a pronouncement – thunder? – overruled
the air conditioner's steady whir, and a tapping
asked me to look. The empty, too-full view
held thousands of foreshortened arrows: rain,
seen from above, a raying angelic substance.
I felt lifted up, to God's altitude.

If the rain was angelic, what of the men and their works?
Their colorless habitations, like a drenched
honeycomb: men come in from the country
to the town's crowded hope, the town grown
to a chaos but still open to the arrows
of Heaven, transparently, all life a veil.

(Updike 1993: 250)

The omniscient narrator of the first stanza, who acts with his vision upon the scene before him, becomes in the final lines the one who is acted upon; he acknowledges that he is the unwitting victim of his own imagination. The rain operates literally here, together with the thunder, as an awakening, as an agent of urban radiance in an otherwise glum and grey metropolis. The 'men come in from the country' suggest a city growing not outward from a centre but, rather, one that accumulates density, and hence seemingly shortens the distance between things. It is in the vertical dimension that the city expands and becomes roomy; the rain from above inserts transparency into the elephantine weight of the buildings, and a deluge of tiny voids into the human muchness.

Teresa Caldiera (2000) presents the same metropolis, in *City of Walls*, as a space of escalated violence. She portrays São Paulo (as Mike Davis does Los Angeles in *City of Quartz*) in terms of discipline and power, walls and enclaves, a city whose chaos is both modified and exacerbated by increasingly condensed hierarchies of control.[2] She describes a simple trip across town as a tribulation of endless thresholds, where

> the physical distances that used to separate different social groups may have shrunk, but the walls around properties are higher and the systems of surveillance more obvious. It is a city of walls in which the quality of public space is changing immensely . . . where a visit to a sister involves dealing with private guards, identification, classification, iron gates, intercoms, domestic servants, electronic gates, dogs – and a lot of suspicion.
>
> (Caldiera 2000: 157)

Caldiera's picture of São Paulo, as befits a social scientist's work, is painted through the analysis of objective interviews with its inhabitants. Updike's, on the other hand, transforms the ordinary with the sensibility of the poet, finding in the thunderstorm a filter through which the reality of the banal is magically overlaid with 'the arrows of Heaven' (Figure 12.2).[3] Like Benjamin in his wardrobe, he invests the everyday view with personal vision, suggesting that the subjective and intuitive can play an important role in architecture and urban design.

John Berger, stopped in his car at a railroad crossing to let a train pass by, reflects similarly upon the surrendering of an objective viewpoint to become a participant in a spatial phenomenology. The short essay is titled 'Field', referring literally to a green grazing pasture within his frame of vision. But this title has also metaphorical importance, as a description of a transformative event: 'Suddenly

Figure 12.2
Rain in São Paulo – for John Updike, J. Stoner and A. Chang, 2004.

an experience of disinterested observation opens at its center and gives birth to a happiness that is entirely your own. The field you are standing before appears to have the same proportions as your own life' (Berger 1980: 197). Though admittedly a non-urban example, Berger's epiphany describes the nature of being drawn into a space, rather than considering it objectively from the outside. He defines by example the means by which we take possession of space simply by abdicating the intention to do so – surrendering, as it were, to the rain (and perhaps reign) of the imagination.

THE EMPTY CITY: DETROIT

In *The Poetics of Space*, Gaston Bachelard (1969: xxxiii) tells us that 'an empty drawer is *unimaginable*'. His phenomenology of place could be superficially read as a domestic parallel of the rhetoric of new urbanism – that is, he identifies transcendent and nostalgic qualities of space to which he suggests we should continue to aspire. According to his metaphysics, drawers, cupboards, chests, nests and attics are always full – that is, full of images latent in our poetic sensibility. Thus, the word 'unimaginable' takes on a literal rather than a colloquial meaning – these containers are the repository not of things but of imagination, and thus are never empty.

Etymologically, the root of 'empty' has temporal rather than spatial connotations. It derives from the Old English, *æmettig*, meaning 'at leisure, not occupied', (and also, 'not married'). Later, the Greek word specifically referred to 'absence of fear'. (Ironically, it is the empty city that is today considered dangerous, whereas the suburb has acquired the reputation of safety.) In any case, the word suggests a lack, a missing something. Being full, like being busy, is considered a condition to be proud of. We fear emptiness as we once feared flying – as an opposition to our secure attachment to the ground and to history. But this is a time of drift, and I wish to make a case for emptiness in the city, with rain as its agent. Empty time as well as empty space – not voids to accommodate public events, but reconciliation with the absence of events, an uncoupling of the concept of busyness (and hence the reality of business) with the definition of urban health.[4]

In *Architecture and Utopia*, Manfredo Tafuri (1988: 88) quotes George Simmel's description of the modern city as a construct in which: 'all things float with equal specific gravity in the constantly moving stream of money. All things lie on the same level and differ from one another only in the size of the area which they cover'. This state of flux marks the achievement of late-capitalism – the economy of flexible accumulation as a weightless, product-less, groundless order. And in this event-space of the modern city, other elements can begin to replace capital in the postmodern equation of shifting weights and precarious balance.

Capitalism has as its parallel a physical condition of container and contained, of figure and ground. Late capitalism, according to Fredrick Jameson (1991: xvii–xx), renders this condition obsolete. Detroit is a singular location in which to contemplate this shift, being the city of Fordism *par excellence*.[5] Its former downtown is awash in empty blocks, vacant now for almost 40 years, largely as a result of the riots of 1967. When I visited Detroit in 1991, the violence had scarcely diminished, the city's population had shrunk from three million in the 1960s to 900,000, and the wasted acreage suggested the scale of an agrarian landscape.[6] This shrinking of cities is one of the phenomena of the old 'Fordist' centres of industry, while the city of flexible accumulation has no need of population, as its economy operates independently of the working body. Thus the potential for Detroit's future is embedded in the congruence between its recent economic and physical conditions, and the respective periods of modernism and postmodernism of which Jameson speaks.

By a paradox that is difficult to apprehend, it is the very opacity of Bachelard's drawer that makes it resistant to emptiness. In Detroit, this opacity has been subverted by historical events. Ruins are transparent, and within them emptiness can flourish without purpose. In her essay on the mall, Joan Didion (1979: 180) says of the architects of the post-war suburban landscape: 'They made something of nothing.' Today it is, rather, the task of architecture to make nothing of something; it is to clear away some of the debris of the past 50 years or, in a city such as Detroit, to allow nature, agriculture and leisure to celebrate the clearing that has already taken place (Figure 12.3).

CITY OF CHANCE: HOUSTON

Houston is the 'significant other' to Detroit – its growth was spurred by the oil so necessary to the auto industry. Just as the territories of ground were rendered empty in Detroit in the late 1960s, the office buildings in Houston suffered similarly in the early 1980s, when oil wells began to dry up and office vacancies reached

Figure 12.3
The Empty City: Detroit 1991, J. Stoner, 1991.

85 per cent. Because of the un-zoned nature of this particular metropolis, the emptiness is not expressed as continuous acreage but, rather, as a dispersed landscape of voids, what Lars Lerup (2001: 47–63) calls a 'holey plain'. Lerup describes Houston as a quintessential non-city – a suburb without the 'urb'. In his seminal essay 'Stim and Dross', he explains that the landscape of contemporary Houston is defined not by its physical form (hardware) but by its mode of life (software). He asserts the presence of the *stimms*, heightened moments in mostly private contexts that form a constellation of brightness in the otherwise dull *dross* of the suburban metropolis (ibid.).

The French Symbolist poet Stephan Mallarmé initiated a poetic revolution that replaced the romantic celebration of nature with an increasingly obsessive search for absolute abstraction. In this he was a pioneer modernist, inventing a poetics of minimalism decades before architects such as Loos and le Corbusier stripped their buildings of ornament. His late poems in particular take this form, but their content describe the postmodern preoccupation with contingency. According to Mallarmé (1945: 457–77), chance cannot be abolished, even by a throw of the dice. Merging form and content, his final and most hermetic poem 'Un Coup de Des' prefigures the space of Houston, operating not only as a narrative but also as a formal construction. The white spaces of the page establish territories of the imagination that, like the in-between and vast *dross* of the Texas metropolis, make the words that float in its whiteness more intense. An excerpt from the poem reads:

EXISTAT-IL

autrement qu'hallucination eparse d'agonie

COMMENCAT-IT ET CESSAT-IL

sourdant que nie et clos quand apparu

enfin

par quelque profusion repandue en rarete

SE CHIFFRAT-IL

evidence de la somme pour peu qu'une

ILLUMINAT-IL

LE HASARD

Choit

La plume

Rythmique suspens du sinister

S'ensevelir

Aux ecumes originelles

Nagueres d'ou fursauta son delire jusqu'a une cime

Fletrie

Par la neutralite identique du gouffre[7]

(Mallarmé 1945: 473)

Walter Benjamin had this poem on his desk in 1919. It was bound in a special quarto edition that included various typographies and different colours of ink. He professed not to understand the content, but according to Gershom Scholem (1981: 85) was fascinated by the form. In it he recognized a keen intelligence attempting to dispel order, and to establish a facsimile of chance. The white space of the poem explicates in its form the content of his theory – that meaning is a condition of betweenness, and that what matters is the articulation of the voids rather than the solids. This suggests that the essence of Houston's urbanism might lie more in the *dross* of Lerup's analysis than in the *stimms*.

Houston's fabric is, after all, the result of a most authentic chance – a chance not evident in any other American city, possible only because of the absence of zoning laws. In this case, the emptiness of these vast in-between territories may precipitate a true wilderness, one supported by the steamy climate and occasional hurricane forces of south-east Texas (see Figure 12.4).

THE FALCON'S RETURN

Some cities, more than others, lend themselves to these kinds of experiments in the nearer future – Houston, with its lack of zoning restrictions; Detroit, with its vast acreages of empty burned-out blocks; São Paulo with its density of 20 Chicagos. The white spaces of Mallarmé's poem and his symbolic throw of the dice resonate in the spaces of the postmodern city, where rogue events in the animal and vegetable kingdoms continue to subvert the classical assumptions that exclude

Figure 12.4
Houston Wilderness: projection c. 2050,
J. Stoner and
A. Chang, 2004.

nature from civilized space. The recovery of the peregrine falcon from the brink of extinction serves as one illustration of this kind of urban phenomenon.

In 1972, only a few falcon pairs existed east of the Mississippi, and none in the west. The pervasive use of the chemical DDT had seeped into the soil of the birds' habitats, causing eggshells to thin and crack before hatching. When wildlife biologists proposed transplanting the birds to high-rise buildings in urban centres, where the food supply would be free of DDT, their plan was greeted with scepticism. Yet, over 50 cities in the United States and Canada eventually participated in the programme, depositing pairs of birds on such cliff-like promontories as the Brooklyn Bridge in New York and the Fisher Building in Detroit.[8] In 1992, with over 900 pairs counted, the species was removed from the endangered list.

The example of the falcon introduces porosity into the city – not the shadowy porosity of Benjamin's Naples but, instead, a city shot through with wildness, a city reducing its mass by introducing small pockets of decidedly non-human use. Animals operate according to their own timeframe, and the nesting box on the roof of the P G & E building in San Francisco sat empty for 17 seasons before being discovered and claimed by a falcon pair in 2003. Since then, a web-cam entertains humans with the daily urban life of the two falcon parents and their offspring George and Gracie.[9]

The financial district of San Francisco, as with many world cities of commerce, is formed by a cluster of tall and densely packed buildings, a built topography that echoes the natural topography of the city's hills. Like Calvino's Baron Cosimo, who takes to the treetops in an adolescent fit of rebellion and spends the rest of his days without ever again touching the ground, the urban imagination of these financial centres can embrace the falcon and all that it represents – a delight in the nature of the aerial realm. One dictionary defines nature as 'the features and products of the earth itself, as contrasted with those of human civilization' (Brown 1993: 1890). I propose that this definition is obsolete, that it is precisely the features and products of human civilizations that are the 'nature', or beginning, of a new language of urban space (Figure 12.5).

It might or might not be significant that the year the falcon recovery project began in 1973 is the same year credited as the beginning of the postmodern era (Jameson 1991: xx–xxi). Both these events acknowledge elements of conjecture and contingency in the fabric of knowledge; both also claim an audacity that challenges conventions and assumptions that have formed cornerstones of Western development.[10] In the case of the falcons, the anthropomorphic interests that have historically defined the function of the city itself are partly let go; the intellect of urbanism embraces its sensual other half.

THE MATHEMATICS OF THE CONTEMPORARY METROPOLIS

In the annals of mathematics there is a famous argument about the invention of calculus – attributed first to Newton, then to Leibniz, and finally resting again with Newton. I prefer Leibniz's version – a mathematics not put to use to pursue

Figure 12.5
San Francisco's 20th Floor,
J. Stoner, 2002.

the elusiveness of limits, but rather an illustration of what cannot be known; not a useful science like City Planning but an aesthetic speculation.[11] It is easy to understand why Newton's concepts became more popular.

Calculus is the mathematics of events – the derivative gives us a rate of change, the integral the accumulation of quantities. Each is the inverse of the other, and in Newtonian terms each can be applied to conventional theories of urbanism.

But what is a calculus of urbanism according to Leibniz, if not space un-planned, space more attuned to the concept of the infinite than to the task of quantification? São Paulo is such an infinite city, both in the atomized reflections of Updike's poem and in the density of surveillance thresholds revealed in Caldiera's analysis.

This chapter supports the unravelling of the urban fabric, that very fabric that has compelled both planners and academicians to picture the city as something that *functions*. Leibniz is also generally credited with attaching the word 'function' to mathematics – from its more general meaning of execution or performance, to the particular association between a relational input and a singular result. The essential property of a function is that for each input there must be one unique output. Thus, for example,

$$\text{Root}\ (x) = \pm \sqrt{x}$$

does not define a function, because it can have two outputs. When 'images rain down into the high fantasy', the number of outputs for any given input is infinite; this is the antithesis of a Newtonian approach to urban design. The imaginative potential of the city becomes like a story by Borges, in which singularities engender multiple reflections, paths continually fork and never dead-end, and time can double back on itself. The reversal of architecture, then, contains the potential to increase the space of the city by substituting the making of solid form with the making of emptiness, and by replacing constructions with marks of erasure. Space is that aspect of the city that has no function.

CONCLUSION: THE VISIBLE CITY AND THE ECOLOGY OF THE IMAGINATION

> Space no longer exists; the street pavement, soaked by rain beneath the glare of electric lamps, becomes immensely deep and gapes to the very center of the earth.
>
> Umberto Boccioni, 'Futurist Painting' (cited in Harrison and Wood 2002: 150)

At the conclusion of his 'Visibility' lecture, Calvino (1985: 95) asks: 'Will the literature of the fantastic be possible in the twenty-first century, with the growing inflation of prefabricated images?' Calvino wrote his question more than 20 years ago, and the deluge of prefabricated images that engulf our daily life outstrips anything that he might have imagined. Yet, it is his very belief in the enduring qualities that continue to make literature matter that speaks to our search for a new approach to urban theory.

Literature is the ghostly conscience of a culture, even such a pragmatic one as our own. Thus we rewrite the city as a work of fiction, to which we can then apply Calvino's five lessons of lightness, quickness, exactitude, visibility and multiplicity. Calvino's most 'urban' work is *Invisible Cities* (1974), in which Venice is multiplied as in a hall of mirrors that at once distort and emphasize its qualities.

It is probably no accident that Calvino chose a watery city for this set of urban fantasies. Likewise, there is an element of fantasy in the city when it rains – a blurring of edges, a radiance of surfaces, a deepening of atmosphere, a reflection of images, a striation of colour. If one city can generate this many imaginary ones, it is possible to imagine, or *visualize*, a multiplicity of other cities for any modern metropolis – Detroit, Houston, Los Angeles, São Paulo, Lima, Naples, Warsaw, Kinshasa.

The reason that it is so much easier to apply fantasy to literature than to architecture is the very paradox of fantasy's ephemeral existence. The so-called 'visionary projects' in architecture are better left on paper; if built, they tend to collapse under the weight of their material (modernism illustrates this phenomenon well). While visionary theory assails our complacency, the built projects morph almost immediately into objects with a complacency of their own. Their very assertiveness defies the forces of nature. Etymologically, 'nature' refers to that which 'gives birth' – it is a source. In this period of postmodernity, it is the metropolis that is the source for architecture, as once were quarries and forests. The excavation of this new nature has not the purpose of obtaining the raw materials for building but, rather, of clearing space for living in. The city, not an intended simulation of anything, is by default a kind of replication of the original nature – a replication because at this historical moment we need it to be so.

I come now to an assertion with which I began this essay – that putting architecture in reverse will engender not projects, but empty space. A project is a plan. As a verb, 'to project' is 'to plan' but also 'to stick out', like a cornice, to cast an image onto a screen, like a film projector, 'to convey to others', as in an idea. It is to put forward, as into the future. Projection is the act of getting out in front of time, and the project is the result of that effort. The 'projects' of 1970s urban renewal are thus aptly named. They professed a certain clairvoyance, and were propelled by anthropological assumptions that treated these acts of building as science, rather than acknowledging science itself as an imaginative undertaking. The demolition of the Pruitt Iago towers in St Louis in 1972 is a landmark event that parallels the collapse of the modernist project itself.

In 1914, Antonio Sant'Elia wrote that architecture needed to redefine itself. He suggested that the city, and not the building, flux and not permanence, were its future

> architecture as the art of formal arrangement according to pre-established criteria is finished; . . . No formal or linear habit can grow from an architecture conceived this way, since the fundamental characteristics of Futurist architecture will be its impermanence and transience. THINGS WILL ENDURE LESS THAN US. EVERY GENERATION MUST BUILD ITS OWN CITY. This constant renovation of the architectonic environment will contribute to the Futurist victory already affirmed by WORDS-IN-FREEDOM, PLASTIC DYNAMISM, MUSIC WITHOUT QUADRATURE AND THE ART OF NOISES, and for which we fight ceaselessly against traditionalist cowardice.
>
> (cited in Conrads 1971: 38)

It is nearly 100 years since this Futurist Manifesto, and rather than having achieved and moved beyond its ambitions of a city in perpetual flux, we (at least in the United States) have resisted an architecture of impermanence, perhaps believing that solidity and the semblance of tradition can compensate for our relative newness on the global scene. We continue to claim nostalgia as innovation – 'new' urbanism is hardly new, and its cultural argument might be best left in another time and in other places.

In the wake of a century of obsessive planning, of the ambition to make order out of disorder, to establish projects, to outline territories, to prescribe adjacencies, to control time and the tides, I propose a period of suspension, of opposition, of willing mistakes and unwilling discoveries. Instead of the direct route, the detour, instead of additions, subtractions; instead of answers, questions; instead of theory, fiction. Didion (1979: 179) refers to a 'visionary time' following the Second World War. Perhaps we are now in another such time. But rather than a time of encapsulation, of casting adrift on the landscape these monuments to our nearly realized dreams, this can be an era of disinterment, of bringing to light and unwrapping images latent and buried in the logical urban enterprises of the past 50 years.

It is no exaggeration to say that architecture suffers from a lack of imagination. If we are to truly benefit from the potential of fantasy as an agent of urban transformations, we will do well to remember Guy Davenport's (1982: 14) assertion that 'the imagination is like a drunk man who loses his watch, and must get drunk again to find it'. We walk through the city in an inebriated state, intoxicated by the voids, the empty storefronts, the vacant lots, the acreages of floorspace ('Available for Lease': call 555-RENT). But we do not make the call; instead, we remove the sash from the windows and let the birds fly through.

These speculations are not linear. Unmaking the city is a positive act, and like Penelope, we must continue to unravel our work in order to bring Odysseus home. So here is Updike, at his hotel window in a gargantuan city of grey concrete, and it is the storm of rain that renders him deaf to Dante's thousand trumpets and open to an alternative city – one that casts its radiance upon the seemingly dismal view that he faces outside.

> Wet city, lush city, saturated city.
> Natural city, wild city, porous city.
> Visible city. Invisible city. City of holes.
> Empty city.
> Ephemeral city.

> Of course, this is fantasy – a place where it rains.

NOTES

1   The term 'grand narrative' is that used by Jean-François Lyotard (1984) to describe the kinds of totalizing theories, such as Marxism, that have implications beyond their original intentions.

2   In particular, the chapter 'Fortress L. A.' (Davis 1989).

3   Four of the images that accompany this essay I produced between 1991 (Detroit) and 2004 (São Paulo) as urban fantasies for which there is no corresponding intention to build.

4   In fact, this is already a priori part of the urban equation; cyber-cafés promote silence in the form of digital conversations.

5   'Fordism' is the term used by David Harvey to describe the economy of the modern period, as compared with 'flexible accumulation', the economy of postmodernism. See Harvey 1980.

6   This experience gave birth to a poem, 'Farming Detroit' in Stoner 2001.

7   Translation: 1st stanza: MIGHT IT EXIST, Otherwise than hallucination of scattered spray, MIGHT IT BEGIN AND MIGHT IT END, welling us as denied and bounded on show, at last, in some outpouring rarely spread, MIGHT IT BE COUNTED, evidence of a tot of the sum however little one, MIGHT IT ILLUMINE; 2nd stanza: **CHANCE,** *drops, the quill,* rhythmical suspending of defeat, *to bury itself, in the original spray, whence but lately whose frenzy sprang as far as a peak, blasted, by the identical neutrality of the gulf.* The different typographies throughout the poem establish a set of parallel texts, four of which are represented in this excerpt (Mallarmé 1982: 123).

8   There are many web sites devoted to specific aspects of the Peregrine Falcon recovery programme. One particularly good summary of the project, and some eloquent reflections on the presence of the raptors in the city, is available online at: www.terrain. org/articles/6/rowland.htm. The essay is by Lucy Rowland, 'From Death's Door to Life in the City'.

9   One of many web sites that offer real-time visual updates on the activities of urban peregrines is www.pge.com/peregrinenestcam.

10 Fredrick Jameson argues that 1973 marks the beginning of the postmodern period, marked by such events as the world oil crisis and the abandonment of the Bretton Woods gold standard. He defines this year as a time when 'the economic system and the cultural "structure of feeling" somehow crystallized' (Jameson 1991: xx) – in other words, the historical moment when culture itself became a business. Also in 1973, Congress passed 'The Endangered Species Act', which directly precipitated the beginning of the falcon recovery project. The collecting of birds for the captive breeding programme began in this year in Virginia, and in 1974 the first of the new generation of falcons were released into their urban surroundings.

11 Dirk J. Struik (1948: 112) in his survey, *A Concise History of Mathematics*, discusses Leibniz's calculus as the pursuit of the infinite and the abstract, in contrast to Newtonian calculus, with its more functional imperative.

REFERENCES

Bachelard, G. (1969) *The Poetics of Space*, Boston, MA: Beacon Press.

Banham, R. (1973) *Los Angeles: The Architecture of Four Ecologies*, Harmondsworth: Penguin.

Benjamin, W. (1986) 'Naples', in P. Demetz (ed.) *Reflections*, New York: Schocken Books.

—— (2006) *Berlin Childhood Around 1900*, trans. Howard Eiland, Cambridge, MA: Harvard University Press.

Berger, J. (1980) *About Looking*, New York: Pantheon Books.

Brown, L. (ed.) (1993) *The New Shorter Oxford English Dictionary*, Oxford: Clarendon Press.

Caldiera, T. (2000) *City of Walls*, Berkeley, CA: University of California Press.

Calvino, I. (1969) *Cosmicomics*, trans. W. Weaver, London: Cape.

—— (1974) *Invisible Cities*, trans. W. Weaver, Florida: Harcourt, Brace, Jovanovich.

—— (1985) *Mr. Palomar*, trans. W. Weaver, London: Secker & Warburg.

—— (1988) *Six Memos for the Next Millennium*, Cambridge, MA: Harvard University Press.

Conrads, U. (1971) *Programs and Manifestos on 20th Century Architecture*, Cambridge, MA: MIT Press.

Davenport, G. (1982) *The Geography of the Imagination*, New York: Pantheon Books.

Davis, M. (1989) *City of Quartz: Excavating the Future in Los Angles*, London: Verso.

Didion, J. (1979) *The White Album*, New York: Simon and Schuster.

Harrison, C. and Wood, P. (eds) (2002) *Art in Theory 1900–2000*, Oxford: Blackwell Publishing.

Harvey, D. (1980) *The Condition of Postmodernity: An Inquiry into the Origins of Cultural Change*, Oxford: Basil Blackwell.

Jameson, F. (1991) *Postmodernism, or The Cultural Logic of Late Capitalism,* Durham, NC: Duke University Press.

Lerup, L. (2001) *After the City*, Cambridge, MA: MIT Press.

Lyotard, J.-F. (1984) *The Postmodern Condition: A Report on Knowledge*, Manchester: Manchester University Press.

Mallarmé, S. (1945) *Oeuvres Completes*, Paris: Editions Gallimard.

—— (1982) *Selected Poetry and Prose*, ed. M. Caws. 'Dice Thrown Will Never Annul Chance', trans. Coffey, B., New York: New Directions.

Scholem, G. (1981) *Walter Benjamin: The Story of a Friendship*, New York: Schoken Books.

Stoner, J. (2001) *Poems for Architects*, San Francisco, CA: William Stout Publishers.

Struik, D. (1948) *A Concise History of Mathematics*, New York: Dover Publications.

Tafuri, M. (1988) *Architecture and Utopia: Design and Capitalist Development*, Cambridge, MA: MIT Press.

Updike, J. (1993) *Collected Poems 1953–1983*, New York: Knopf.

Index

Page numbers in *italics* denotes an illustration